Illustrated Guide t

Illustrated Guide to *HTTP*

PAUL S. HETHMON

MANNING

Greenwich
(74° w. long.)

For electronic browsing and ordering of this book, see http://www.browsebooks.com.

The publisher offers discounts on this book when ordered in quantity. For more information, please contact:

Special Sales Department
Manning Publications Co.
3 Lewis Street
Greenwich, CT 06830

Fax: (203) 661-9018
email: orders@manning.com

Library of Congress Cataloging-in-Publication Data
Hethmon, Paul S.
    Illustrated guide to HTTP / Paul S. Hethmon.
        p.   cm.
    Includes bibliographical refrences and index.
    ISBN 1-884777-37-6
        1. Hypertext systems. 2. HTTP (Computer network protocol)
    I. Title.
    QA76.76.H94H484   1997
    004.6'2—dc21
                                            97-1596
                                            CIP

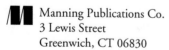
Manning Publications Co.
3 Lewis Street
Greenwich, CT 06830

Copyeditor: Maggie Mitchell
Typesetter: Dorothy Marsico
Cover designer: Leslie Haimes

Printed in the United States of America
1 2 3 4 5 6 7 8 9 10 – CR – 00 99 98 97

This book is for Marci and Zach

The more that you read,
the more things you will know.
The more that you learn,
the more places you'll go.

DR. SEUSS
I Can Read with My Eyes Shut!

contents

preface

In early Fall of 1995, my life was pretty full. I was working full time as a programmer/analyst, had one successful shareware application on the market, was writing a second one along with my brother, and had a wife and son at home to fill up the rest of my spare time. While reading a Usenet newsgroup one day, I noticed a posting titled "Can you write a web server?" My current shareware program was an ftp server and the new one was a mail server. I had planned to write a web server next, so the post definitely intrigued me. Upon reading the post, I found Manning Publications was looking for an author to write a book on programming a web server. "Well," I thought, "this is something I've always wanted to do—write a book." So I fired off an email to Len Dorfman and promptly forgot about it.

In November 1995, while checking my email I found a message from Len. I remember wondering what this message was about. Well as it turned out, Len was looking for someone to write the web server book and was asking me. With adrenaline pumping up my ego, I took my wife to lunch to ask what she thought of the idea and for her blessing for me to give it a try. If only she had known what she was getting herself into!

Over the course of the next twelve months, I found out what I was getting myself into. The process of writing a book is not unlike that of writing a software program. You start out with this grandiose idea of including everything but the kitchen sink. As time passes, you begin to realize the size of the hole you've dug. There were definitely times in the process that I felt someone was at the top of the hole shoveling dirt on top of me. Eventually, if you're venturesome, you keep plodding through the muck and you do find the light.

As in a software project, at the end you must finish and release. With this book, I felt the same way. I had been following the progression of the HTTP/1.1 standard for all of 1996, watching the changes as they advanced through the various drafts. Whenever a new draft came out, I'd grab another copy and rework the code to comply yet again. When draft 6 came out in July, the working group finally had a document that was mostly complete and stable. I rushed to finish the book and save some of my family's summer. Draft 7 was eventually released to correct minor typos in draft 6 and was just recently approved for Proposed Standard by the IESG (Internet Engineering Steering Group.) Even with the approval of the proposed standard, and the completion of my first draft, my job was not yet over. With reviews and rewriting, another three months would have passed and Christmas of 1996 was knocking at my door. So, finally, it was time to stop.

As with any of the programs I've written, I feel the book is not yet complete. There were so many features I wanted to include but could not if the book were ever to be published. Maybe I'll be lucky and this book will have a 2.0.

In the meantime, I hope you enjoy this book and find the information in it useful. Comments about the book are welcome and encouraged.

Paul Hethmon
phethmon@hethmon.com
Knoxville, Tennessee

acknowledgments

There are quite a few people who helped me in producing this book. Without their contributions, this book would not have made it:

From Manning Publications, Len Dorfman, Marjan Bace, Mary Piergies, and Ted Kennedy.

Leslie Haimes for the great frog.

Tony Winner for being willing to read a long manuscript and not killing me after finding out half of it was thrown out.

Maxine Houghton and her gang at the IBM Toronto Lab for providing a copy of Visual Age C++ for Windows.

Maggie Mitchell for the copy editing.

Aaron Lyon and Dottie Marsico for the book design and layout.

chapter 1

Introduction

1.1 Is this book for you?

It's a good question which every book should answer. You, as the reader, need to know if the author had you in mind as the book was written. So I'm going to start by listing those for whom I wrote this book:

- Webmasters
- HTTP (HyperText Transfer Protocol) Programmers
- CGI (Common Gateway Interface) Programmers
- Anyone interested in HTTP

That actually seems to be a pretty broad list, but the common ground to all is a need to understand the HTTP protocol to better fulfill their jobs. As a Webmaster, your job is to administer your server (or servers) in an effective way. Prior to HTTP/1.1, this was mostly making certain the server was running, had enough memory and disk space, and that pages were properly updated. With the advent of HTTP/1.1, your servers have grown more complex and given you many more options over the delivery of the information on them. Concepts such as content negotiation, digest authentication, and cache control are available. If your site previously allowed a user to pick different national languages by choosing from a list, you'll now be able to make this selection transparent to the user by utilizing content negotiation. With HTTP/1.0, your control was minimal over what pages from your site were cached. You included a `Pragma: no-cache` header in those responses and hoped for the best or resorted to unique URLs (Uniform Resource Locators), which were really mapped back to the same resource at the server. HTTP/1.1 introduces a carefully thought-out means for controlling cache behavior. You will be able to mark resources as never to be cached, how old they can become, and when a cache must revalidate the response with your server.

For HTTP programmers, the need is more obvious. If you are programming clients or servers which use the HTTP protocol, then understanding the protocol is definitely important. These people are not just the programmers at Netscape and Microsoft however. Many companies are implementing Web-based solutions for information delivery. It is much easier to adapt an existing application to server data through HTTP and then use standard browsers to view and control it than by using proprietary solutions. A look through any computer magazine will reveal how many applications are now Web enabled or have Web interfaces. These programmers are not building general purpose Web servers, but solutions to specific problems.

CGI programmers are closely aligned with HTTP programmers. CGI introduced a mode to implement dynamic content on the Web. In sending this content back to clients, the CGI program must understand the mechanics and capabilities of the protocol. CGI programs must be able to create and send to the client the proper headers describing the resource which is returned. Not only does this mean the standard `Content-Type` header, but now you might use `Content-Language`, `Range`, or `Vary` in a response. HTTP/1.1 provides more hooks to improve your programs and scripts.

The last group for whom this book will have an appeal are those who just have an avid interest in the subject. You probably are just like me. You buy books because of a thirst for knowledge or just because the example on some specific page had something you might use. I'm sure you'll find your own excuses to justify buying the book.

1.2 *Required background*

As the reader, you should be aware of what the book already expects you to know. First, you should be familiar with the Internet and the Web, as a user. This means being able to use a browser to go Web surfing. A rudimentary knowledge of previous versions of HTTP will help also. If you fit into the foregoing reader classifications, you probably have sufficient background. If HTTP is unknown to you, then it may take a couple of readings to fully grasp the material. It may also take reading more material before fully understanding it all.

For the programmers out there, you should be comfortable programming in C and C++. You don't have to be a C++ expert however. The C++ presented here is mostly an enhanced C style rather than true object-oriented programming. If you learned C first, then you should find it easy to understand. A good knowledge of sockets is not necessary to understand the protocol examples. You should be able to go through all of the chapters of this book without understanding sockets. One of the chapters is a primer on sockets and related construction of a socket class.

1.3 The material

Reflecting the audience, the material in this book is presented on two different levels. On the first level is the information relative to the protocol. This includes information about entity tags and range requests. This is the foundation which will help you understand the protocol. Everyone who reads this book will find this useful. On the second level are programming examples illustrating the concepts being explained. It is complete code, implementing the various parts of the protocol, not just snippets. The examples themselves are sometimes presented as snippets, but backing them up is a complete working HTTP server on the CD accompanying this book. Actually there are multiple servers on the CD, HTTP/0.9, HTTP/1.0, and HTTP/1.1 which run under both OS/2 Warp and Windows NT. The code, for the most part, is written in a non-operating system path and ninety-nine percent of it should adapt to other platforms without any problems.

You will also find many other concepts on the accompanying CD other than code examples, such as:

- The latest protocol specifications for HTTP/1.1.
- The complete RFC collection through the end of 1996.
- The Apache distribution.
- The libwww distribution from W3C (WWW Consortium).
- The Jigsaw distribution from W3C.
- A complete hypertext setup for viewing the information.

I hope the CD will provide as much information as the book itself in your application development and understanding of HTTP/1.1.

Before I go over what is covered in each chapter, I need to mention the basis for this book. It is based on Internet drafts. Internet drafts should not normally be considered as reference material or even cited as anything but work in progress. The Internet drafts for HTTP/1.1 and Digest Authentication have already been approved by the Internet Engineering Steering Group (IESG) as proposed standards. As the publishing deadline approached, the RFC editor had not yet issued them as formal Request For Comments (RFC). If the RFCs become available before the CD is due, then they will be included on the CD. At this point, the HTTP/1.1 specification is `draft-ietf-http-v11-spec-07.txt` and the Digest Authentication specification is `draft-ietf-http-digest-aa-05.txt`. By the time you are reading this, the official RFCs will have been published and will be available from the normal sources. The hypertext on the CD will guide you to find them.*

In Chapter 2, a brief overview of HTTP will be presented. This will guide you through a bit of the previous standards, the new standard and how HTTP operates in general. Chapter 3 will go into more syntax and semantics of the protocol. This is the general information about the protocol that is necessary to understand the more detailed parts. In Chapter 4, the syntax and semantics of the request message are presented, along with the request headers. Entity and general headers along with the cache control mechanism are presented in Chapter 5. Chapter 6 winds up with the response message and associated response headers. Chapter 7 covers TCP/IP socket programming through a C++ socket class which is used in the HTTP servers. Chapter 8 covers the construction of the HTTP/1.1 server. It is rather long, but the complete detail should help you understand the protocol better by understanding a complete server. This presentation is designed to group the different parts of the protocol into logical elements. Chapter 9, the last, covers CGI, or Common Gateway Interface support to complete our HTTP journey.

In appendix A, you will find a concise HTTP/1.1 syntax. This is an alphabetical listing of all of the syntax elements in both HTTP/1.1 and Digest Authentication. You will also find this in printable form on the CD. Appendix B reproduces Section 14 of the HTTP protocol standard covering the definitions of the HTTP message headers. It is a section of the document you will probably refer to frequently.

---

* RFC2068 and RFC2069 covering HTTP/1.1 have now been issued. Both are included on the CD.

1.4 Finishing

Before delving into Chapter 2, a couple of final words are offered on how to use this book to best advantage. This book is meant as a teaching aid in understanding the HTTP/1.1 protocol. In order to fully understand the protocol, you will need to read the protocol specification. This book serves to help teach the information in the specification but is not a replacement for it. I would urge you to print out a copy of the specification and have it close at hand while reading this book. The full specification is 153 pages in length, plus another 14 pages for Digest Authentication. This book is not too much longer. It leaves out some detail in favor of concentrating on the important and harder-to-understand portions of the protocol. If I don't make something clear to you, check out the specification. It is the final word.

chapter 2

HTTP overview

2.1 What is the World Wide Web?

Just what is the World Wide Web? During the last few years, just about everybody has defined what it is (and isn't). I'm not going to add another definition here, but if you are reading this book you should be familiar enough with it. Disregarding any definition, the World Wide Web has become one of the most important information technologies of the nineties.

2.1.1 The client/server model

From a programmer's viewpoint, the World Wide Web is the largest client/ server system implemented to date. It is made up of innumerable clients and servers, all exchanging information. In a typical client/server system, a proprietary client talks to a proprietary server to accomplish some task. The task might be a sales order system for a mail order firm, or a data mining system for corporate executives. The Web changes things a bit, making them more complicated and simple at the same time. The simple part comes from the open, well-defined protocols used between the clients and the servers. The complicated part comes from the loss of extensive programmer-defined protocols.

Let me explain the latter a little more thoroughly. If you were given the task of writing an application to handle order entry, you would typically define the types of transactions to occur between your client and server. A typical exchange might be to look up a description of an item in the catalog. The client would make a connection to the server, send a request which might be binary or plain text, and then would receive the reply which would typically be plain text. The reply might contain binary data also, such as a picture. Given a TCP/IP environment using sockets, the client would make a connection to a port on which the server is listening. Then it would send a packet of information to the server. In order to make interpreting the data easier, you might have defined a structure for request packets that consist of 4 bytes for a numerical request code. The server then knows to read 4 bytes from the socket and then interpret accordingly. When the server sends the response to the client, the client knows to expect a certain type of reply. (See Figure 2.1). In this case, you've defined a header of 4 bytes that contains the length of the description (in plain text), and the description immediately follows the header. If data follows the description, then the 4 bytes after it are the length of the binary data, the picture of the item. Once the binary data has been received, the server closes the connection and the transaction is finished.

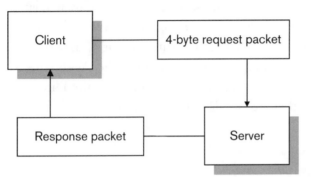

Figure 2.1   Client/server transaction

In this scenario, you as the programmer, had the utmost flexibility. You were able to define the exact messages and the format of the replies to them. Being able to do this makes your code very efficient. You don't have to interpret the transactions to any extent. You are able to minimize the amount of network traffic you generate and maximize the amount of data in each transaction. Continuing on with your application, you can quickly define and implement all of the transactions your client and server need to know for proper response.

But a couple of months down the road, the word comes down from the IS department that your nifty client/server application also needs to run under Windows 95 and OS/2 as well as the Mac client you originally wrote. So now you've got to go back and program two new clients and have the possibility of doing more in the future. It would have been nice to write a single client which would run on all of the possible operating systems. This is where HTTP comes into play. Instead of writing clients for every possible operating system, you can use a Web client such as Netscape Navigator, along with a Web server, to build your client/server system.

Routines are a bit different in the Internet world however. In your original client/server application you had the freedom to define your own messaging standards. Now, someone else is going to give you the blueprint to work from in the form of an RFC. As mentioned previously, RFC is short for Request For Comments. RFCs are the technical documents which describe the protocols in use on the Internet. HTTP is the protocol used to send and receive messages between Web clients and servers. HTML is the protocol used to create the Web pages sent as the data resource of the HTTP message. The two are closely related but distinct. The latest RFCs are on the CD-ROM accompanying this book. The principal US repository for RFCs is held at the Internic, the agency responsible for domain registrations, among other functions. The Web site is www.internic.net. From the main page, follow the prompts to the Directory and Database Services and from there to the RFC information.

2.2 General operation

HTTP is a request-response type of protocol. The client application sends a request to the server and then the server responds to the request. In HTTP/0.9 and HTTP/1.0, this was generally accomplished by making a new connection for each request. HTTP/1.1 introduces persistent connections as the default behavior. With persistent connections, the client and server maintain the connection, exchanging multiple requests and responses until the connection is explicitly closed by one. Even with persistent connections, HTTP remains a stateless protocol. No information is retained by the server between requests.

There are three general request-response chains in which HTTP operates. The first is when a user agent makes a request directly to the origin server as shown in Figure 2.2 herein. In this scenario, the user agent makes a connection directly to the origin server on the default port of 80 (unless otherwise specified) and sends its request. The server will be listening for incoming connections and start a new thread or process to serve the new request. Once the request has been processed, the server sends the response back over the connection.

The second request-response chain involves a proxy or cache agent as an intermediary. In this scenario, the user agent makes its request to the proxy

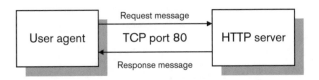

Figure 2.2 Basic client to server HTTP operation

instead of to the origin server (See Figure 2.3). The proxy then makes the request to the origin server on behalf of the client. The server replies to the proxy, and then the proxy relays this to the user agent, thus fulfilling the request. This type operation is mostly seen in firewall environments where the local LAN is isolated from the Internet. An alternate on this procedures is for the intermediate agent to also serve as a caching agent.

When making a request through the cache agent, the cache agent tries to serve the response from its internal cache of resources. The cache itself saves any response it receives, if the response is a cachable one. This shortens the request-response chain, improves response time, and reduces network load. Most proxy agents are also caching agents.

The final scenario is one involving an intermediate agent, acting as a tunnel. A tunnel blindly funnels requests and responses between two HTTP applications. As shown in Figure 2.4, it is, in essence, providing a path for the user agent to the server.

A tunnel is different from a proxy in how it operates. A tunnel is simply a mechanism via which the user agent sends requests and receives responses from an origin server. The tunnel itself does nothing to the requests, unlike a proxy

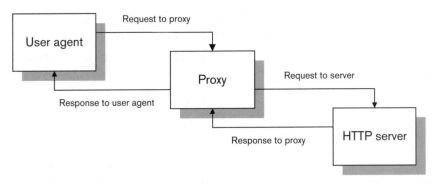

Figure 2.3 Client to proxy to server HTTP operation

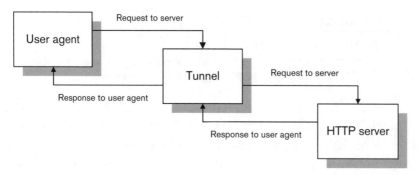

Figure 2.4   Client to server via tunnel HTTP operation

which may rewrite certain headers or require authentication from the user before providing services. A tunnel would be used most often to route HTTP traffic over a non-TCP/IP link.

Past the three basic request-response chains, anyone can put together any combination of intermediate agents. It is entirely reasonable for a user agent to send a request to a proxy, which sends it through a tunnel which reaches another proxy, and finally makes it to the origin server. Through all of this, the basic idea still maintains the request-response paradigm, although it may make many contortions along the way. Next, we will need to look in depth at the specific operation of HTTP.

2.3 A bit of history

Before we delve into HTTP/1.1, a bit of background is in order. In this section we'll examine the previous versions of HTTP: HTTP/0.9 and HTTP/1.0. HTTP/1.1 is a response to those established previous versions–their strengths and their shortcomings.

2.3.1 HTTP/0.9

The first implementation of HTTP is now known as HTTP/0.9. The entire description of that protocol encompasses only a few pages. In HTTP/0.9, a client program makes a connection to the server on TCP port 80. The client then sends its request in the following form:

```
GET document.html CRLF
```

The request starts with the word GET. No other methods are supported. A space character is then sent, followed by the document name. The document name may be fully qualified and is not allowed to have any spaces. To end the line, the client should send a carriage return line feed combination. The specification mentions that servers should be tolerant of clients by only transmitting the line feed.

One other option is allowed for the document name. The client may send a search request by appending a question mark, followed by a search term. Multiple search terms may be specified by putting a plus sign between each. This type request should only be generated when the document specified contains the ISINDEX HTML tag. This allows a request of:

```
GET document.html?help+me CRLF
```

For the reply, the server returns the contents of the document. There is no content information, MIME type, or any other information returned to the client. The protocol is, in fact, restricted to sending only HTML text documents. When the document has been sent, the server closes the connection to signify the end of the document. This is necessary since no length information is exchanged between the server and client. When sending the document, the server delimits each line by an optional carriage return, which is then followed by a mandatory line feed character.

As can be seen from this description, implementing the HTTP/0.9 protocol can be done in a few dozen lines of code. The problem, however, was the limitation it imposed. Only text documents could be served and there was no method for the client to submit information to the server.

2.3.2 HTTP/1.0

The HTTP/1.0 protocol was developed from 1992 to 1996. It has only appeared as an Informational RFC as recently as May 1996. Before that point,

HTTP/1.0 was based on what the major Web servers and clients did. Since RFC 1945 is only an informational RFC, it does not actually specify an official standard of the Internet. It does, however, describe the common usage of HTTP/1.0 and provides the reference for our server's later implementation via the enclosed CD.

HTTP/1.0 developed from the need to exchange more than simple text information. It became a way to build a distributed hypermedia information system adapted to many needs and purposes. From 1994 to 1997, the Web developed from a forum in which computer science departments could showcase their research into a center where everyone has a Web page. In fact half of the television commercials today include a URL. In order for this to happen, HTTP expanded tremendously from its original specification.

The first major change from the HTTP/0.9 specification was the use of MIME-like headers in request messages and in response messages. On the client side, the request message grew from the one line request to a structured, stable multi-line request:

```
Full-Request =Request-Line
              *( General-Header |
                 Request-Header |
                 Entity-Header   )
              CRLF
              [ Entity-Body ]
Request-Line = Method SP Request-URI SP HTTP-Version CRLF
```

The added headers resulted from the need to transmit more information in the request. For clients, this information included sending preferences for the type of information desired. This was expressed in terms of MIME media types: terms such as `text/html` and `image/gif` were initiated so clients and servers could send information each could understand and use. The additional headers also let clients implement conditional retrievals using the `If-Modified-Since` header. This header allows the client to request that the resource be returned only if it has changed since the given date. With this, clients could cache frequently requested pages and update them only when necessary, thus saving valuable time and bandwidth.

On the server side, the server was finally allowed to send back content information, along with the resource. In HTTP/0.9, only the resource was sent. With the expanded response syntax, the server could now tell the client exactly what type information was in the resource and, finally, substantially send more than HTML documents:

```
Full-Response = Status-Line
                *( General-Header  |
                   Response-Header |
                   Entity-Header )
                CRLF
                [ Entity-Body ]
Status-Line =   HTTP-Version SP Status-Code SP Reason-Phrase CRLF
```

The addition of the `Content-Type` header allowed the server to include the media type of the resource. Along with the original HTML documents, images and audio files became popular and commonplace as forms of information to present on a Web site.

The next HTTP change was the definition of new request methods. Along with the original `GET` request, `HEAD` and `POST` were now allowed. The `HEAD` request allows a client application to request a resource and receive all of the information about the resource without actually receiving the resource. This had uses for Web robots and spiders, which traverse links to gather update information and detect broken links. The `POST` method is what brought real interactivity to the Web. Now clients had a way to send substantial information to a server for processing. The `GET` method had been used at first as a way to transmit information to a server, but was limited by the amount of information a server would accept as part of the `request-URI`.* Now with `POST`, virtually unlimited entity bodies could be sent in a request message. With this, came the use of the Web for inputting information: order forms, surveys, and requests could be made from a Web page.

Servers also gathered the ability to respond with a status code to the client's request. The infamous `404 Not Found` status code could now be sent whenever the resource was not present. Beyond this, the server could also respond with `200` to indicate a general success response, `302` to indicate a resource had moved temporarily to a different location, `401` to indicate authorization was required, or `500` to indicate a general server error while trying to fulfill the request.

---

* Uniform Resource Identifiers (URIs) are covered in Chapter 3.

The `401 Unauthorized` status code leads us into the final point to make about HTTP/1.0. It introduced the idea of restricted access to resources. A server could require a client to supply a username and password before returning certain resources. The idea of basic authentication allowed someone to build a Web site with private information. Information could be restricted to a certain person or group of people. This also allowed a Web site to track a person throughout his visit. This ability permits a site to create a shopping cart for a user to track the items he wishes to purchase through multiple pages. At the end of the visit, the server can supply the complete list of items the user has selected. Given the stateless nature of HTTP, this allows commerce to flourish much easier on the Web.

From these enhancements to the protocol, HTTP developed from a simple information retrieval system into a general purpose transaction system capable of building quite complex systems with standard applications across multiple platforms. With this success came problems. Users demanded faster loading of pages, which led to clients making multiple connections to a single server. The higher number of connections led to bandwidth and server overload at times. Problems also appeared as more vanity servers appeared on the Internet. Servers which host multiple virtual domains on a single machine required a unique IP address for each virtual domain to identify each to the software. This has caused the finite supply of IP addresses to dwindle just a bit faster. Problems also arose as caching agents were introduced. Servers did not have a good way to specify what could and could not be safely cached, which led many sites to use cache-busting techniques, which prohibit a cache agent from being able to cache a particular response. Throughout 1995 and 1996, the IETF/HTTP Working Group worked to develop HTTP/1.1 to build upon HTTP/1.0, improve HTTP's general capabilities, and fix some of the problems which had appeared.

2.4 HTTP/1.1

In operation, HTTP/1.1 closely resembles HTTP/1.0. It still consists of the request-response paradigm and is highly compatible with HTTP/1.0

applications. There are seven areas we'll discuss here about how HTTP/1.1 differs from HTTP/1.0:

- New request methods
- Persistent connections
- Chunked encoding
- Byte range operations
- Content negotiation
- Digest Authentication
- Caching

2.4.1 New request methods

The HTTP 1.1 specification has defined two new methods which are highly beneficial to the end user: PUT and DELETE. The PUT method allows a user agent to request a server to accept a resource and store it as the request-URI given by the client. This method allows a user agent to update or create a new resource on a server. In use, an HTML editor might implement this as a way for the user to maintain pages on a Web site. The user could create the pages and have them automatically updated by the editor. Notice that this behavior is different from the previously available POST method. Using POST, the user agent was requesting the resource identified by the request-URI to accept the entity sent by the client. In essence, it was viewed as subordinate to the request-URI. The PUT method is asking the server to accept the entity as the request-URI. Another use of this method might include implementing an HTTP based revision control system.

The DELETE method is self-explanatory: the user agent is requesting that the request-URI be removed from the server. Along with PUT, there is now a standard method to implement Web based editing. The protocol specification specifically allows the server to defer the actual deletion of a resource when it receives a request. It should move the resource to a nonaccessible location however. This relaxation allows a server to save deleted resources in a safe place for review before final deletion and should probably be implemented in this way by any server. Both the DELETE and PUT methods allow a user agent to create, replace, and delete resources on a server. Because of this, access to both methods should be controlled in some manner, either using IP address based restrictions or via one of the authentication methods within HTTP.

The OPTIONS method is used to query a server about the capabilities of a specific resource or about the server in general. A user agent can make an OPTIONS request against a specific resource to find out which methods the server supports when accessing the resource. The response returned by the server should include any communications related information about the resource. Typical information in the response would include an Allow header listing the supported methods when requesting the resource. A user agent may also make a general OPTIONS request of the server and receive the same information as it applies to the server as a whole.

The final method added, TRACE, is used for debugging purposes at the application level. A client program can use the method to have its original request echoed back to it. Using this information, the client can debug problems which might occur to an origin server when several intermediate agents handle its request. In use, an HTTP traceroute can be accomplished by letting the request advance one server at a time, checking the response back from each.

2.4.2 Persistent connections

As mentioned a bit earlier, in the quest for user satisfaction, Web browsers began making multiple connections to origin servers in order to speed up response times. Unfortunately, this led to some major congestion since a few clients could quickly bog down a slow link. The practice also suffered from the inherit mechanisms of making TCP connections where setup time can usurp a good portion of the total connection cycle. Starting with HTTP/1.1, the protocol implements, as a default behavior, the practice of persistent connections. This means that once a client and server open a connection, the connection remains open until one or the other specifically requests that it be closed. While open, the client can send multiple, but separate, requests and the server can respond to them in order. Clients are also free to send multiple requests without waiting for the responses, basically pipelining the requests. In practice, a client might do this when requesting all of the graphic images from a particular page. It can also make the requests for the images, one after the other, and then finally listen for the responses from the server. Implemented well, response time to the users will be high, without the inefficiencies of individual requests.

2.4.3 Chunked encoding

One problem arises for servers when persistent connections become the default behavior: they must now return a proper Content-Length header with each response. Previously, servers could signify the end of the entity body by simply closing the connection. With persistent connections, the server can no longer do this and must be able to determine the length of any entity it sends to the client. For most resources, this is not a problem. The length of HTML, and image files can be determined through the operating system. Where trouble arises is in dynamically generated responses.

Fortunately, HTTP/1.1 also provides a solution: *chunked encoding*. Using chunked encoding, a server or CGI process can send back an entity body of unknown initial length by sending it back in chunks of known length. We'll discuss the details in a later chapter, but Figure 2.5 shows the basic format.

As shown, the server sends the size of the upcoming chunk in bytes and then the actual chunk of data. This is repeated until all the data is sent. Once all of the data is sent, a final size of 0 is sent, indicating the end of the data. Following this, the server may optionally send footers, or header fields which are allowed to be sent after the entity body. With this method, it becomes easy for a server to send dynamically generated data and easy for the client to decode it.

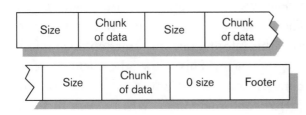

Figure 2.5 Chunked encoding format

2.4.4 Byte range operations

Another optimization and convenience introduced is *byte range operations*. I'm sure almost everyone has experienced trying to download the latest beta software from a favorite vendor, only to have the connection fail with 100 bytes to go (out of 5 MB, of course). At that point, download is attempted again, hoping for the best. Now, the user agent can just ask for the last 100 bytes of the resource instead of asking for the entire resource again. This can improve both the mood and response time. When requesting a byte range, a client makes a request as normal, but includes a `Range` header specifying the byte range the resource is to return. The client may also specify multiple byte ranges within a single request if it so desires. In this case, the server returns the resource as a `multipart/byteranges` media type.

The use of byte ranges is not limited to recovery of failed transfers. Certain clients may wish to limit the number of bytes downloaded prior to committing a full request. A client with limited memory, disk space, or bandwidth can request the first so-many bytes of a resource to let the user decide whether to finish the download. Servers are not required to implement byte range operations, but it is a recommended part of the protocol.

2.4.5 Content negotiation

There are times when a server may hold several different representations of a single resource in order to serve clients better. The alternate representations may be national language versions of a page or a resource which is available, both in its regular media type and as a gziped version. In order to provide to the client the best representation, content negotiation may be performed. This can take the form of server-driven, agent-driven, or transparent negotiation.

The first form, *server-driven negotiation,* is performed on the origin server, based on the client's request. The server will inspect the various `Accept-*` headers a client may send and, using this information plus other optional information, send the best response to the client. This allows the client to send `Accept`, `Accept-Charset`, `Accept-Language`, or any combination of the `Accept-*` headers, stating their preference for responses. When servers perform this negotiation, they must then send a `Vary` header to the client stating over which parameters the server chose the particular resource. The `Vary` header is required to be returned in order to provide caches with enough information to properly determine which future requests may be satisfied by the response.

The second form of content negotiation is *agent-driven*. In this approach, the server provides to the user agent the information needed to pick the best representation of the resource. This may come in the form of the optional `Alternates` header or in the entity body to the initial response. The `Alternates` header is mentioned in the appendices to the HTTP protocols, but the exact definition will be provided in a later specification thereto. Using either approach allows the server to provide a list of choices to the user agent. The user agent may then automatically, or with user input, pick the best representation.

The final form is called *transparent negotiation*. In transparent negotiation, an intermediate cache provides server-driven negotiation, based on the agent-driven information from the server. In more concrete terms, the cache has the agent-driven negotiation information from the server for a particular resource with multiple representations. Assuming the cache understands all of the ways in which the representations vary, it may pick the best response when a client request is received. This allows an off-loading of server duties onto cache agents and improves response time to clients while providing accurate responses.

2.4.6 Digest Authentication

Digest Authentication is included in HTTP/1.1 as a replacement for Basic Authentication. Basic Authentication suffers from the problem of passing the user's password in clear text across the network. With Digest Authentication, the password is kept as a shared secret between the client and server. The server and client compute a *digest* value, using the MD5* (Message Digest 5) algorithm over a concatenation of the secret password and a few other values. This digest is then sent across the network. Since only the client and server know the secret password, the client can compute the digest value, send it to the server, and then the server can verify it against the information it holds. Since no one else knows

---

* MD5 is detailed in RFC1321.

the secret password, authenticity is more secure. This algorithm is similar to the POP3 protocol's APOP method of authentication.

Digest Authentication is still only a reasonably secure method, however. It still requires an outside mode of exchanging the password between clients and servers. Digest Authentication, therefore, is meant solely as a replacement for Basic Authentication.

2.4.7 Caching

The caching model in HTTP/1.1 allows the server a great deal of control over the caching of responses. First, the specification makes it clear what is cachable and what is not. Generally speaking, only GET or HEAD responses are cachable; responses to any other method must be explicitly marked as cachable by the server. The protocol uses the Cache-Control header to transmit caching instructions from servers and clients to caches.

For servers, the cache control directives can be segregated into five groups: what is cachable, what is not cachable, how old it can be, don't serve anything past its age, and don't transform. In the first group are directives which allow an origin server to explicitly mark something as cachable when it normally would not be. This can be used to allow caching of authenticated responses or responses to POST requests. An example of a cachable POST request might be the results of a search engine on a Web site. Under many circumstances, the results from a search would remain valid for several hours or even a few days. If the response is cachable and serves one other client request, the server has off-loaded some work onto cache agents.

The what is not cachable group of directives include the no-cache and no-store directives. Basically, these directives instruct the cache agents to never save a response which includes the directive. The no-cache applies to responses only, while the no-store applies to both the request and response messages. The no-store directive can be thought of as the stronger. It instructs caches to remove the request/response from volatile storage (i.e., memory) as soon as possible and to never store it in nonvolatile storage (i.e., hard disk).

A server who wishes to control how long a response may be cached will use the max-age directive. This directive sets a time limit from when it is served to when the response is considered stale. A client may still request a cache return of a response, even though it has become stale. In these situations, the server can include a directive from the don't serve anything past its age group. These directives (`must-revalidate` and `proxy-revalidate`) instruct a cache to revalidate a response with the origin server to make certain it is still valid. If the response is not valid, the server will normally supply a fresh response; if the server cannot be contacted to revalidate the response, then the cache will return an error to the requesting client.

The final category of directives is the don't transform group. The directive here is called `no-transform`. Its function is to prevent an intermediate agent from transforming a response in any way. The typical example would be a server sending out medical images. Given the nature of medical images, the content authors wish to maintain the images in their original formats, perhaps TIFF. An intermediate agent may normally wish to transform all images into JPEG format because of the space savings on disk and in bandwidth. This would result in a loss of information which is unacceptable in the given context, hence the `no-transform` directive.

The client agents also gain some control in HTTP/1.1 over the responses that caches serve to them. The directives can be broken down into three basic groups: not cachable, how old can it be, and don't make a new request. The not cachable group uses the `no-cache` and `no-store` directives as do the servers. Here, the meaning is slightly different. When a client requests `no-cache` or `no-store`, it is instructing the cache agent to not send any responses it may have stored, but instead to make a new request to the origin server. It also instructs the cache agent to not cache the response from the server.

In the how old can it be group, the cache control directives permit an agent to control the age of a response which a server returns to it. It can specify this by the age of the response (how long has it been since the origin server generated it), by specifying how stale it can be (how long past its age is permissible), or by specifying how much longer the response must be fresh (how long until it becomes stale). Using these directives, or combinations of them, the client can control whether the response comes from the cache or from the origin server. If a client wishes to receive a response which is no more than five minutes old and no more than two minutes stale, it may specify a `max-age=300` and `max-stale=120` in its request message (values are expressed in seconds). If the client wishes to force the cache to revalidate a response, it can specify `max-age=0`. This forces the cache to revalidate the response with the origin server.

The last directive, `only-if-cached`, forms the don't make a new request group. This directive can be used in a request to have the cache only return a response if it already exists in the cache. If the response does not exist, then the client agent will receive a `504 Gateway Timeout` error.

2.5 *Finishing*

This chapter has provided a broad overview of what constitutes HTTP, and in particular, HTTP/1.1. In the next chapter, we will cover syntax and semantics specific to HTTP/1.1

chapter 3

Basic HTTP—syntax and semantics

In order to understand HTTP, you first need an understanding of the terminology used in the protocol specification. As with most Internet protocols, there exists a plethora of terms and definitions unique to HTTP. In this chapter, we'll discuss the basics. Many of these terms are presented verbatim from the protocol. Given the need for precision here, it seems best to present a restatement from the protocol and then expand upon it if necessary, hence this is the approach taken.

We'll start by going over some terminology. Words which have a particular meaning within the protocol may not be the first meaning you would assign to the word. Next, we'll go over some of the basic grammar constructs used in the protocol. This will cover items which are not protocol-specific, but are necessary in order to build up to the protocol's specific terms. Finally, we'll cover some basic concepts of HTTP, including factors such as byte ranges and entity tags. This chapter should give you a basis for better understanding of the succeeding Chapters 4, 5, and 6.

3.1 *Terminology*

The HTTP protocol defines many terms precisely. We'll restate those definitions here, enclosed in quotes, and discuss them further as needed. The first three terms are not technical terms, but instead are those which describe the various requirements of the protocol. Certain parts of the protocol are required to be implemented in an application in order for the application to be compliant, while other requirements are only recommended or optional. The protocol uses specific words to denote the different meanings:

Must   "This word *must* or the adjective *required*, means that the item is an absolute requirement of the specification."

To qualify as a compliant, an HTTP/1.1 application must satisfy all parts of the protocol which are described with *must* or *required*. For a general purpose client or server, compliance can be considered mandatory. All parts of the protocol would be implemented. For a limited-use client or server, perhaps compliance should be embedded into an application, but then only a limited set of requirements might be implemented. The application would thus not be compliant but instead would use a subset of HTTP/1.1 to accomplish its task.

Should   The word *should* "or the adjective *recommended*, means that there may exist valid reasons, in particular circumstances, to ignore this item, but the full implications should be understood, and the case carefully weighed before choosing an alternative course."

To be unconditionally compliant with HTTP/1.1, an application must implement all of the *should* requirements. If it does not, then it can only be conditionally compliant. Generally speaking, an all purpose HTTP client or server will implement the requirements of this category. The wording, however, gives flexibility to those programmers implementing special purpose applications of the HTTP protocol.

An example of a *should* requirement which might not be implemented is accepting unbounded URI lengths in requests from clients. The protocol recommends that an application be able to handle arbitrary and unbounded length URI strings. In practice, if one were to implement a source code version control system using HTTP, then an upper bound could be placed on the URI length, given limitations within the server's filesystem on the maximum path length. If the local filesystem only supports path lengths to 512 characters, then the HTTP server could reasonably expect to not see URIs above this length.

May   The word *may* "or the adjective *optional* means that this item is truly optional. One vendor may choose to include the item because a particular marketplace requires it, or because it enhances the product–for example, another vendor may omit the same item."

A good example of an optional behavior is the handling of the Host field in a HTTP/1.1 style multihomed server. If a server is not multihomed, then the value of the Host field will not matter in determining with which resource to respond. Only the URI sent will be significant. A multihomed server, however, will need to determine resources based on the URI and the Host field.

Therefore, the following terms are technical in nature with precise meanings within the protocol.

Age "The age of a response involves the time since it was sent by, or successfully validated with, the origin server."

Cache Cache is defined as "a program's local store of response messages and the subsystem that controls its message storage, retrieval, and deletion. A cache stores cachable responses in order to reduce the response time and network bandwidth consumption on future, equivalent requests. Any client or server may include a cache, although a cache cannot be used by a server that is routinely acting as a tunnel."

Cachable "A response is cachable if a cache is allowed to store a copy of the response message for use in answering subsequent requests. The rules for determining the cachability of HTTP responses are defined in Section 13 (of the protocol.) Even if a resource is cachable, there may be additional constraints on whether a cache can use the cached copy for a particular request."

Client A client consists of "a program that establishes connections for the purpose of sending requests."

Connection A connection is "a transport layer virtual circuit established between two programs for the purpose of communication."

Content negotiation Content negotiation encompasses "the mechanism for selecting the appropriate representation when servicing a request, as described in Section 12 (of the protocol.) The representation of entities in any response can be negotiated (including error responses)."

Entity An entity is "the information transferred as the payload of a request or response. An entity consists of metainformation in the form of entity-header fields and content in the form of an entity-body, as described in Section 7" (of the protocol).

Explicit expiration time Explicit expiration time denotes "the time at which the origin server intends that an entity should no longer be returned by a cache without further validation."

First-hand   "A response is first-hand if it comes directly and without unnecessary delay from the origin server, perhaps via one or more proxies. A response is also first-hand if its validity has just been checked directly with the origin server."

Fresh   "A response is fresh if its age has not yet exceeded its freshness lifetime."

Freshness lifetime   Freshness lifetime involves "the length of time between the generation of a response and its expiration time."

Gateway   A gateway is "a server that acts as an intermediary for some other server. Unlike a proxy, a gateway receives requests as if it were the origin server for the requested resource; the requesting client may not be aware that it is communicating with a gateway."

Heuristic expiration time   Heuristic expiration time is "an expiration time assigned by a cache when no explicit expiration time is available."

Message   A message is "the basic unit of HTTP communication, consisting of a structured sequence of octets matching the syntax defined in Section 4 of the protocol and transmitted via the connection."

Origin server   An origin server is "the server on which a given resource resides or is to be created."

Proxy   Proxy is "an intermediary program which acts as both a server and a client for the purpose of making requests on behalf of other clients. Requests are serviced internally, or by passing them on, with possible translation, to other servers. A proxy must routinely implement both the client and server requirements of this specification."

Representation   Representation embodies "an entity included with a response that is subject to content negotiation, as described in Section 12 (of the protocol). There may exist multiple representations associated with a particular response status."

Request   Request implies "an HTTP request message, as defined in Section 5" of the protocol.

Resource   A resource is "a network data object or service that can be identified by a URI, as defined in Section 3.2 (of the protocol). Resources may be available in multiple representations (e.g. multiple languages, data formats, size, resolutions) or vary in other ways."

Response   Response embodies "an HTTP response message, as defined in Section 6" of the protocol.

Semantically transparent   "A cache behaves in a *semantically transparent* manner, with respect to a particular response, when its use affects neither the requesting client nor the origin server, except to improve performance. When a cache is semantically transparent, the client receives exactly the same response (except for hop-by-hop headers) that it would have received had its request been handled directly by the origin server."

Server   A server constitutes "an application program that accepts connections in order to service requests by sending back responses. Any given program may be capable of being both a client and a server; our use of these terms refers only to the role being performed by the program for a particular connection, rather than to the program's capabilities in general. Likewise, any server may act as an origin server, proxy, gateway, or tunnel, switching behavior based on the nature of each request."

Stale   "A response is stale if its age has passed its freshness lifetime."

Tunnel   A tunnel is "an intermediary program which is acting as a blind relay between two connections. Once active, a tunnel is not considered a party to the HTTP communication, although the tunnel may have been initiated by an HTTP request. The tunnel ceases to exist when both ends of the relayed connections are closed."

User agent "The client which initiates a request. These are often browsers, editors, spiders (Web-traversing robots), or other end-user tools."

Validator A validator is "a protocol element (i.e., an entity tag or a `Last-Modified` time) that is used to determine whether a cache entry is an equivalent copy of an entity."

Variant "A resource may have one, or more than one, representation(s) associated with it at any given instant. Each of these representations is termed a *variant*. Use of the term variant does not necessarily imply that the resource is subject to content negotiation."

3.2 Protocol syntax

As in many RFCs, the HTTP/1.1 protocol uses an augmented Backus-Naur Form (BNF) first found in RFC 822. The exact usage of this format has varied from protocol to protocol, so it is worth specifying exactly what is meant within the HTTP document.

First we have the basic definitions:

name = *definition* The name of a rule is simply the name itself (without any enclosing "<" and ">") and is separated from its definition by the equal "=" character. white space is only significant in that indentation of continuation lines is used to indicate a rule definition that spans more than one line. Certain basic rules are in uppercase, such as `SP`, `LWS`, `HT`, `CRLF`, `DIGIT`, `ALPHA`, etc. Angle brackets are used within definitions whenever their presence will facilitate discerning the use of rule names.

"literal" Quotation marks surround literal text. Unless stated otherwise, the text is case insensitive.

rule1 | *rule2*   Elements separated by a bar "|" are alternatives, i.e., yes | no will accept yes or no.

(rule1 rule2)   Elements enclosed in parentheses are treated as a single element. Thus, (elem (foo | bar) elem) allows the token sequences elem foo elem and elem bar elem.

rule   The character "" preceding an element indicates repetition. The full form is <n>*<m>element indicating at least <n> and at most <m> occurrences of element. Default values are 0 and infinity so that *(element) allows any number, including 0; 1*element requires at least one; and 1*2element allows one or two.

[rule]   Square brackets enclose optional elements; [foo bar] is equivalent to *1(foo bar).

N rule   Specific repetition: <n>(element) is equivalent to <n>*<n>(element); that is, exactly <n> occurrences of (element). Thus 2DIGIT is a two-digit number, and 3ALPHA is a string of three alphabetic characters.

#rule   A construct "#" is defined, similar to "*", for defining lists of elements. The full form is <n>#<m>element indicating at least <n> and at most <m> elements, each separated by one or more commas (",") and optional linear white space (LWS). This makes the usual form of lists very easy; a rule such as (*LWS element *(*LWS "," *LWS element)) can be shown as 1#element. Wherever this construct is used, null elements are allowed, but do not contribute to the count of elements present, that is, (element), , (element) is permitted, but counts as only two elements. Therefore, where at least one element is required, at least one non-null element must be present. Default values are 0 and infinity so that #element allows any number, including zero; 1#element requires at least one; and 1#2element allows one or two.

comment   A semicolon, set off some distance to the right of rule text, starts a comment that continues to the end of line. This is a simple way of including useful notes in parallel with the specifications.

*implied *LWS* The grammar described by this specification is word-based. Except where noted otherwise, linear white space (LWS) can be included between any two adjacent words (token or quoted-string), and between adjacent tokens and delimiters (tspecials), without changing the interpretation of a field. At least one delimiter (tspecials) must exist between any two tokens, since they would otherwise be interpreted as a single token.

3.3 *The basic grammar*

Throughout the HTTP protocol, the grammar presented makes use of several basic constructs. These define functions such as what a carriage return or space character is exactly. The basic constructs are predicated on the US-ASCII coded character set as defined by ANSI X3.4-1986, as follows:

```
OCTET         = <any 8-bit sequence of data>
CHAR          = <any US-ASCII character (octets 0 - 127>)
UPALPHA       = <any US-ASCII uppercase letter "A".."Z">
LOALPHA       = <any US-ASCII lowercase letter "a".."z">
ALPHA         = UPALPHA | LOALPHA
DIGIT         = <any US-ASCII digit "0".."9">
CTL           = <any US-ASCII control character
                (octets 0 - 31) and DEL (127)>
CR            = <US-ASCII CR, carriage return (13)>
LF            = <US-ASCII LF, linefeed (10)>
SP            = <US-ASCII SP, space (32)>
HT            = <US-ASCII HT, horizontal-tab (9)>
"             = <US-ASCII double-quote mark (34)>
CRLF          = CR LF
LWS           = [CRLF] 1*( SP | HT )
TEXT          = <any OCTET except CTLs,but including LWS>
HEX           = "A" | "B" | "C" | "D" | "E" | "F" | "a" |
                "b" | "c" | "d" | "e" | "f" | DIGIT
token         = 1*<any CHAR except CTLs or tspecials>
tspecials     = "(" | ")" | "<" | ">" | "@" | "," | ";" |
                ":" | "\" | <"> | "/" | "[" | "]" | "?" | "=" |
                "{" | "}" | SP | HT
comment       = "(" *( ctext | comment ) ")"
ctext         = <any TEXT excluding "(" and ")">
quoted-string = ( <"> *(qdtext) <"> )
```

```
qdtext       = <any TEXT except <">>
quoted-pair  = "\" CHAR
```

3.4 Basic HTTP concepts

Last to be discussed are basic HTTP concepts. These ideas are used in the protocol although they do not stand on their own as distinct requests or responses.
Instead they are used by the actual protocol messages to convey certain meanings. An example of this would be giving the HTTP version number such as
HTTP/1.1. An application does not use this standalone, but instead includes it
as part of either a request or response line to convey the HTTP version as used
by the application.

3.4.1 HTTP version

Each HTTP request and response includes a version number to indicate the protocol version supported by the sender. This version number is not necessarily the
version number of the particular request or response but is instead the version
number supported by the sender. This allows a HTTP/1.1 client to send a
request labeled HTTP/1.1 to a server without knowing whether or not the server
supports HTTP/1.1 features. The request in this example may only include
HTTP/1.0 features. The server, however, can interpret the request as coming
from an HTTP/1.1 compliant application and return a response which uses the
capabilities of HTTP/1.1.

   Similarly, upon receiving an HTTP/1.0 request from a client, an HTTP/1.1
server may return the HTTP/1.1 version within the response, so long as the
response itself is compliant with the HTTP/1.0 specification. This allows the
server to inform the client of the 1.1 capabilities of the server. In effect, the
HTTP version is an upper limit on the capabilities of the sender, not an indication of the content of the message. An application which does not wish to receive
HTTP/1.1 messages should never send an HTTP version of 1.1. It should
restrict itself to HTTP/1.0, even if it understands some parts of HTTP/1.1.

For proxy applications, a special word of caution here: since the HTTP version indicates the version of the *sender* (which is the proxy), the proxy may be forced to downgrade a request or response when it does not understand the level indicated. An HTTP/1.1 compliant proxy, upon receiving an HTTP/1.2 request, must downgrade the version number of the request to HTTP/1.1. The danger here to the proxy application is that it may need to modify header fields when downgrading the request. Some of the modifications may not be permitted by the protocol. As an alternate, the proxy can respond with an error message or switch to tunnel behavior to handle the request.

Grammatically, the HTTP version is defined to be:

```
HTTP-Version = "HTTP" "/" 1*DIGIT "." 1*DIGIT
```

The first number in the version is considered the major version number. This number is incremented whenever the format of messages within the protocol change. This would be for a change such as moving from the current RFC 822 style headers to a binary header format. The second number in the version is the minor version number. This number is incremented for extensions to the protocol which extend the capabilities without altering the message format. An example of this would be when the additional header fields in the 1.1 specification are not present in the 1.0 specification. The general format of the headers is still the same, although additional capabilities have been defined.

You should also note that because of this definition, the major and minor version numbers are treated independently. A version number of HTTP/1.5 is lower than HTTP/1.12. Likewise, a version number of HTTP/1.12 is lower than a version number of HTTP/2.0. Applications must treat the major and minor numbers separately when determining the overall version.

3.4.2 Uniform Resource Identifiers

Uniform Resource Identifiers (URI) are used in HTTP to identify a particular resource available via the HTTP protocol. Many terms are used interchangeably in this respect: Uniform Resource Locators, Uniform Resource Names, Universal Document Identifiers, and simply WWW or Web addresses. Within the HTTP protocol, they define how a HTTP client requests a resource and how a HTTP server interprets the request. This use does not extend to how a URI is used within an HTML document, only to what the HTTP application does with it, once it is removed from the document.

The current (as of this writing) definitions of URI syntax and semantics are in RFC 1738 and RFC 1808. The syntax presented in the HTTP protocol is actually a superset of what is presented in RFC 1738. HTTP allows national characters beyond RFC 1738, hence an HTTP application should be careful to implement the syntax presented in HTTP, not just what is presented in RFC 1738 and RFC 1808. You should also be aware of work being done to update the URI standards and should check the RFC and Internet Draft archives for the latest standards and proposals.

The syntax for HTTP URIs is given by:

```
URI          = ( absoluteURI | relativeURI ) [ "#" fragment ]
absoluteURI  = scheme ":" *( uchar | reserved )
relativeURI  = net_path | abs_path | rel_path
net_path     = "//" net_loc [ abs_path ]
abs_path     = "/" rel_path
rel_path     = [ path ] [ ";" params ] [ "?" query ]
path         = fsegment *( "/" segment )
fsegment     = 1*pchar
segment      = *pchar
params       = param *( ";" param )
param        = *( pchar | "/" )
scheme       = 1*( ALPHA | DIGIT | "+" | "-" | "." )
net_loc      = *( pchar | ";" | "?" )
query        = *( uchar | reserved )
fragment     = *( uchar | reserved )
pchar        = uchar | ":" | "@" | "&" | "=" | "+"
uchar        = unreserved | escape
unreserved   = ALPHA | DIGIT | safe | extra | national
escape       = "%" HEX HEX
reserved     = ";" | "/" | "?" | ":" | "@" | "&" | "=" | "+"
extra        = "!" | "*" | "'" | "(" | ")" | ","
safe         = "$" | "-" | "_" | "."
unsafe       = CTL | SP | <"> | "#" | "%" | "<" | ">"
national     = <any OCTET excluding ALPHA, DIGIT,
                 reserved, extra, safe, and unsafe>
http_URL     = "http:" "//" host [ ":" port ] [ abs_path ]
host         = <A legal Internet host domain name
```

```
                or IP address (in dotted-decimal form),
                as defined by Section 2.1 of RFC 1123>
port         = *DIGIT
```

As indicated by the grammar, HTTP does not place limits on the length of a URI. However, applications should be aware that many (especially older) applications may restrict the length of a URI which is accepted. A limit of 255 octets is common. Server applications must be able to handle URIs of any resource they serve. If a resource is identified by a URI of 2,000 octets, then the server must be able to accept it in a request from a client. Similarly, if a server accepts GET based forms, then it should be able to handle arbitrary length URIs which such forms might generate.

Whenever an HTTP application needs to know whether or not two URIs are equal, then the application must do a comparison. Comparisons of URIs are done with six rules:

- Comparisons are case sensitive and done octet-by-octet except as noted.
- A port which is empty, or not given, is equivalent to the default port for that URI.
- Comparisons of hostnames are case insensitive.
- Comparisons of scheme names are case insensitive.
- An empty absolute path is equivalent to an absolute path of "/".
- Characters are equivalent to their "%" HEX HEX encoding except for reserved and unsafe sets.

This leads to the following URIs being equivalent:

```
http://example.com:80/~jones/welcome.html
HTTP://EXAMPLE.COM/~jones/welcome.html
HTTP://example.com/%7ejones/welcome.html
http://Example.com/%7Ejones/welcome.html
```

The next URI is not equivalent to the previous examples:

```
http://Example.com/%7EJones/welcome.html
```

3.4.3 Formats for date and time

HTTP applications have traditionally used three different formats to represent date and time values. Two of the formats are based on RFCs while the third format is from the C language library call `asctime()`. The `asctime()` format can be defined as:

```
asctime-date = wkday SP date3 SP time SP 4DIGIT
wkday        = "Mon" | "Tue" | "Wed" | "Thu" | "Fri" |
               "Sat" | "Sun"
date3        = month SP ( 2DIGIT | SP 1DIGIT )
month        = "Jan" | "Feb" | "Mar" | "Apr" | "May" | "Jun" |
               "Jul" | "Aug" | "Sep" | "Oct" | "Nov" | "Dec"
time         = 2DIGIT ":" 2DIGIT ":" 2DIGIT
```

This gives us a date value of:

```
Mon Nov  4 21:52:34 1996
```

This format has been deprecated for use within HTTP/1.0 and HTTP/1.1 applications. The biggest drawback to this format is the lack of a time zone. Applications which receive dates in this format should assume the time value is expressed in GMT (UTC).

The other deprecated format in use within HTTP is based on RFC 850. It is defined to be:

```
rfc850-date = weekday "," SP date2 SP time SP "GMT"
weekday     = "Monday" | "Tuesday" | "Wednesday" |
              "Thursday" | "Friday" | "Saturday" | "Sunday"
date2       = 2DIGIT "-" month "-" 2DIGIT
```

This format includes the GMT indicator for time zone, but lacks a necessary 4-digit year value:

```
Monday, 04-Nov-96 21:52:34 GMT
```

The final format is the one required by the HTTP/1.1 protocol:

```
rfc1123-date = wkday "," SP date1 SP time SP "GMT"
date1        = 2DIGIT SP month SP 4DIGIT
```

This format is derived from RFC 822 as updated by RFC 1123 and gives us all of the desired characteristics:

```
Mon, 04 Nov 1996 21:52:34 GMT
```

All HTTP/1.1 date values must be expressed in Greenwich Mean Time (GMT, also known as UTC). In addition, the RFC 1123 format allows a four-digit year which prevents ambiguous dates for the next ten thousand years.

As per the protocol standard, all HTTP/1.1 applications are required to only generate the RFC 1123 date for messages. This does not preclude them from using an alternate date format for log files or to present same to the user. HTTP/1.1 applications must also be able to accept all three formats. In practice, this is not as difficult as it sounds. At most, two characters of a date string must be examined to determine the format in question. The short code example in the next section illustrates how to do this.

3.4.4 Code: date handling

This function is designed to parse any of the three possible date formats and return a `time_t` style value, this value being the number of seconds which have elapsed since the epoch value of January 1, 1970. This gives us a format which is easy to manipulate with the standard C library functions for the requisite date and time values:

```
time_t ConvertDate(char *szDate)
{
    char szMonth[64];   // Allow extra for bad formats.
    struct tm tmData;

    if (strlen(szDate) > 34)   // Catch bad/unknown formatting.
      {
        return( (time_t) 0 );
      }
```

As shown here, we'll make, at most, four checks before returning a default value of 0. The first check is for the length of the date string passed into the function. Given the possibilities of the three date formats, there should be no date string with more than 34 characters in it. If we find one, we immediately return a value of 0 since there is no hope of parsing it:

```
if (szDate[3] == ',') // RFC 822, updated by RFC 1123
  {
    sscanf(szDate, "%*s %d %s %d %d:%d:%d %*s",
           &(tmData.tm_mday), szMonth, &(tmData.tm_year),
           &(tmData.tm_hour), &(tmData.tm_min),
           &(tmData.tm_sec));
    tmData.tm_year -= 1900;
  }
```

The second If statement looks for the preferred format. By inspecting the specification, the fourth character position must contain the comma character in this format. No other format shares this characteristic, so we can key on it and parse the given string if we find it:

```
else if (szDate[3] == ' ') // ANSI C's asctime() format
  {
    sscanf(szDate, "%*s %s %d %d:%d:%d %d",
           szMonth, &(tmData.tm_mday), &(tmData.tm_hour),
           &(tmData.tm_min), &(tmData.tm_sec),
           &(tmData.tm_year));
    tmData.tm_year -= 1900;
  }
```

The next format for which we check is the asctime() format. In this format (and no other), the fourth character must be a space character. Given a space, we parse according to the syntax:

```
else if (isascii(szDate[3])) // RFC 850, obsoleted by RFC 1036
  {
    sscanf(szDate, "%*s %d-%3s-%d %d:%d:%d %*s",
           &(tmData.tm_mday), szMonth, &(tmData.tm_year),
           &(tmData.tm_hour), &(tmData.tm_min),
           &(tmData.tm_sec));
  }
```

Finally, we make another check for the RFC 850 format. The fourth character in this format will always be an ASCII character, specifically part of the weekday. For robustness, we test for this condition instead of defaulting to it. The final else clause returns a time of zero again:

```
else  // Unknown time format
  {
    return ((time_t)0);
  }
```

The remainder of the function then converts the `struct tm` data into the `time_t` value. The entire function is presented on the accompanying CD.

Delta seconds   One last note should be made about date and time values within HTTP/1.1. Some message headers permit values to be expressed in delta seconds, which is the number of seconds that have elapsed since a message was received. The syntax for this is simply:

```
delta-seconds = 1*DIGIT
```

3.4.5 Character sets

The term *character set* is used in HTTP in the same manner as in MIME. It is used to denote a method of converting a sequence of octets into a sequence of characters according to a table mapping. Quoting RFC 1521, Section 2, page 6:

> The term *character set* is used in this document to refer to a method used with one or more tables to convert encoded text to a series of octets. This definition is intended to allow various kinds of text encodings, from simple single-table mappings such as ASCII to complex table switching methods such as those that use ISO 2022's techniques. However, a MIME character set name must fully specify the mapping to be performed.

When used in this manner, the term character set entails more closing, fulfilling *character encoding*. The character set tables define how an application should interpret a sequence of octets. This allows an HTTP application to send an entity body encoded in a character set other than US-ASCII. You should also note when a character set, other than US-ASCII, is used for the entity body, then the HTTP protocol allows the use of the equivalent characters for carriage return and line feed in that character set. So, for any character set an HTTP application accepts, it must be able to determine line breaks, based on the characters of that set.

You should note that the use of character sets is restricted to the entity body of an HTTP message. Only US-ASCII may be used within message headers. The definition and use of character sets within HTTP is solely to enable applications to reliably transfer non US-ASCII text.

When using character sets, applications should use only those character sets registered with the IANA Character Set registry. The Internet Assigned Numbers Authority (IANA) serves as a central clearinghouse for assigning unique parameters to Internet protocols. In this role, the Character Set registry maintains a list of approved names for individual character sets. HTTP applications must respect any character sets in this registry, and represent them precisely as indicated in the registry.

In the HTTP protocol, character sets are defined to be:

```
charset = token
```

Character set tokens are case insensitive.

3.4.6 Content codings

In order to reduce the number of bytes transferred between HTTP applications, a content encoding transformation of the entity body may be performed. This allows an application to serve resources in a compressed format, while preserving its underlying media type. As an example of this usage, this mechanism would be an HTTP server which distributes video files. Typical video files are rather large, so the server stores the files in compressed format and transfers them to the client in this format. By using a content coding, the server can indicate the compressed form of the file, while still sending the original media type of the file.

Content codings for HTTP are case insensitive and defined by:

```
content-coding = token
```

For HTTP/1.1, three different content codings are defined: *GZIP*, *compress*, and *deflate*. GZIP is defined in RFC 1952, deflate in RFC 1950 and RFC 1951. Compress is the common Unix format. New content codings are allowed, and the protocol recommends that all new codings be registered and the algorithms freely available for implementation.

3.4.7 Transfer codings

From the name, you might think transfer codings are similar to content codings, but in practice they are orthogonal to one another. A transfer coding is known as a transformation which has been applied to the entity body of a message. It is a property of the message and not of the entity body. In simpler terms, it means the entity body is being transferred in an encoded fashion.

For HTTP/1.1, the only transfer coding defined is *chunked encoding*. With this encoding the entity body is transferred as a series of *chunks* which encode their own length. Normally, an HTTP application must send a `Content-Length` message header to tell the receiving application the number of bytes in the entity body. For dynamically produced entity bodies, this value may not be known ahead of time since determining the length may be an expensive operation in terms of resources or time. In cases such as these, the sending application can apply the chunked encoding to a dynamic resource as it is produced. The receiving application must then decode the chunked encoding to put together the actual entity body:

The syntax for chunked encoding is given by:

```
Chunked-Body    = *chunk
                  "0"CRLF
                  footer
                  CRLF
chunk           = chunk-size [ chunk-ext ] CRLF
                  chunk-data CRLF
hex-no-zero     = <HEX excluding "0">
chunk-size      = hex-no-zero *HEX
chunk-ext       = *( ";" chunk-ext-name [ "=" chunk-ext-value ] )
chunk-ext-name  = token
chunk-ext-val   = token | quoted-string
chunk-data      = chunk-size(OCTET)
footer          = *entity-header
```

There are a couple of factors you should notice in this definition. First, unlike most of HTTP/1.1, for chunked encoding, the number of octets in a chunk is represented in hexadecimal form. There must not be any leading zeros as part of the hexadecimal number either. A chunk size of zero is reserved to mark the end of the chunked encoding transfer. Another point to notice is that the chunk size does not include the 2 bytes of the carriage return line feed at the end of the chunk.

A footer is permitted as part of the chunked encoding transfer. This is to allow dynamically generated entity headers to be included with the response. On a dynamically generated resource, the value of the entity headers may not be known before the entity is generated and sent. This allows the server to append the final entity headers after the fact.

All HTTP/1.1 applications must understand how to receive and decode chunked encoding. If a transfer coding which an application does not understand is received, it should always return a 501 error code to the sender and not accept the encoding. The protocol further recommends closing the connection after sending the 501 response. Applications sending chunked encoding must never send it to an HTTP/1.0 application. While transfer coding is meant mostly for dynamically generated responses, the protocol does not forbid a client application from using it to send an entity body to a server. Therefore, routine server applications should not overlook the requirement of being able to accept chunked encoding. The code snippet in the next section shows an implementation of receiving such chunked encoding.

3.4.8 Code: chunked encoding

The HTTP/1.1 protocol presents an algorithm for receiving an entity body transferred using the chunked encoding method. Here, we'll present working C code. The code example uses two C++ classes which are also presented in the accompanying CD. The socket class is also presented in Chapter 7.

```
// --------------------------------------------------------
//
// GetChunked
//
// Receive the entity using the chunked method.
//

int GetChunked(Socket *sClient, ofstream &ofOut, Headers *hInfo)
{
  BOOL bNotDone = TRUE;
  char *szPtr;
```

```
int iBytes, i, j, l, iFactor;

while (bNotDone == TRUE)
  {
    sClient->RecvTeol(NO_EOL); // Grab a line. Should
                               // have chunk size.
```

The loop starts by grabbing a line of data from the socket. The `RecvTeol()` method retrieves the data up unto the terminating line feed delimiter. The `NO_EOL` flag passed in causes the method to not return the end-of-line marker:

```
if (strcmp(sClient->szOutBuf, "0") == 0)
  {
    bNotDone = FALSE;   // The end of the chunks.
    continue;
  }
```

Since the ending marker is simply a zero, a simple string comparison suffices to determine the end of the chunks. Finding the end causes the loop flag to `FALSE` and the outer `while` loop ends:

```
szPtr = strchr(sClient->szOutBuf, ';');
if (szPtr != NULL) *szPtr = NULL;  // Mark end of chunk-size.
```

Here we learn whether or not a chunk extension was sent. The code here does not recognize any extensions, but does look for the semicolon which would mark the start of a chunk extension. If found, we simply place a new terminating `NULL` in the string overwriting the semicolon:

```
l = strlen(sClient->szOutBuf); // Find last hex digit.
l--;
iBytes = 0;
iFactor = 1;
// Convert to decimal bytes.
while (l >= 0)
  {
    iBytes += iFactor * Hex2Dec(sClient->szOutBuf[l]);
    l--;
    iFactor *= 16;
  }
i = 0;
```

This section converts the hexadecimal number to a decimal number for internal manipulation. The `Hex2Dec()` function (presented as follows) converts a single hex digit to the equivalent decimal digit:

```
    // Now receive the specified number of bytes.
    while (i < iBytes)
       {
         j = sClient->Recv(iBytes - i);       // Some data.
         i += j;                              // Total the bytes.
         ofOut.write(sClient->szOutBuf, j); // Save to disk.
       }
    sClient->RecvTeol(NO_EOL);   // Discard end of chunk marker.
  }
```

The loop here uses another method in the `Socket` class to receive the correct number of bytes from the sender. As the bytes are received, they are written in raw form to disk using `ofstream`:

```
  // Now consume anything in the footer.
  hInfo->RcvHeaders(sClient);
```

The final operation is to check for any additional headers the client may have sent. The class method used understands the various headers and fills in the class data members as new information is received:

```
  return 0;
}


// ----------------------------------------------------
//
// Hex2Dec
//
// Convert a hex character to a decimal character.
//

int Hex2Dec(char c)
{
  switch (c)
     {
        case 'A':
        case 'a':
          return 10;
        case 'B':
```

```
        case 'b':
          return 11;
        case 'C':
        case 'c':
          return 12;
        case 'D':
        case 'd':
          return 13;
        case 'E':
        case 'e':
          return 14;
        case 'F':
        case 'f':
          return 15;
        default:
          return (c - 48);
    }
}
// ---------------------------------------------------------
```

While the BNF grammar looks a bit imposing, the actual implementation of chunked encoding is straightforward. Modifying this code to straight C would only require a bit more work.

3.4.9 Media types

In order to specify the type of data within an entity body, HTTP uses Internet Media Types such as are used in MIME. Internet Media Types are registered with the IANA, the same organization which handles character set registration. Anyone may register a new media type using the procedure outlined in RFC 1590. Some examples of registered media types include:

- `text/plain`
- `text/tab-separated-values`
- `application/zip`
- `application/wordperfect 5.1`
- `application/pdf`
- `image/gif`
- `video/mpeg`

The protocol encourages applications to only use registered types. At the time of this writing, the official list of media types can be retrieved via anonymous FTP from the IANA archives at:

```
ftp://ftp.isi.edu/in-notes/iana/assignments/media-types
```

Media types are defined by:

```
media-type  = type "/" subtype *( ";" parameter )
type        = token
subtype     = token
parameter   = attribute "=" value
attribute   = token
value       = token | quoted-string
```

The type, subtype, and attribute tokens are not case sensitive. The value of the parameter may or may not be case sensitive depending on its definition. HTTP applications must take care not to insert white space characters between the type and subtype names or between attributes and their values. HTTP/1.1 applications should also be aware that older HTTP applications might not correctly recognize parameter values for media types:

Canonical forms for media types   All Internet media types are registered in terms of a canonical form. This canonical form defines the format of the entity body itself. In the case of text media types, this form may include entities with varying forms of end-of-line delimiters: carriage return line feed, carriage return, or line feed. Although a bit of a pain to support in code, the HTTP protocol allows an application to use any of these conventions when sending text media types. If the character set used in the entity body does not use the same octets to represent carriage return and line feed as ISO-8859-1, then the protocol allows the use of the octet sequences defined by the character set. So to be truly international, an application needs to be aware of the differences between character sets in this regard.

The relaxation of rules here for the entity body does not apply to any other part of the protocol. An application must still generate and send the carriage return line feed combination between headers and elsewhere as required in the protocol. Also, the specification does not allow the switching of end-of-line sequences within an entity body. If the entity body uses a carriage return, then it must use a carriage return throughout the entire entity body.

Multipart types   As in the MIME standard, HTTP/1.1 allows the use of multi-part types such as media types which encapsulate more than one entity within a single message body. The multipart type allows sending multiple types of data or discrete elements of an entity in a single response. For HTTP/1.1, this is used by server applications to send multiple byte range responses to a client. If a client requests bytes 1 through 10 and 35 through 65 of a resource, then the server must use a multipart type to send both byte ranges within the same routine response message.

HTTP applications can send applicable headers within a body part. When sending headers within a body part, and when separating the body parts, the application must always use a carriage return line feed to delineate the lines.

3.4.10 Product tokens

HTTP applications are allowed to send a product token, an identifying string, as part of HTTP messages. These tokens are specifically to identify a product by name and version. Their use for advertising is forbidden by the protocol. Given the fact only applications are likely to ever see them, their use for advertising is minimal, at best, anyway. The syntax is:

```
product         = token [ "/" product-version]
product-version = token
```

3.4.11 Quality values

Quality values are used in HTTP content negotiation to indicate relative importance of similar parameters. This allows an application to request multiple types and indicate which types it would prefer. An example would be:

```
Accept: text/html, text/plain; q=0.6, text/richtext; q=0.8
```

This specifies that the requesting application prefers `text/html`, but will accept `text/richtext` and then `text/plain`. The quality values are represented as three-digit floating point numbers with higher numbers preferred. The range allowed is from 0.000 to 1.000. The syntax is:

```
qvalue = ( "0" [ "." 0*3DIGIT ] ) | ( "1" [ "." 0*3("0") ] )
```

3.4.12 Language tags

A language tag is similar in concept to a character set value, but represents a different quantity. While a character set defines an encoding from octets to glyphs, a language tag merely represents a natural language. This language may be spoken, written, or used in some form to convey information. Computer languages are excluded from this definition. Language tags are used in the `Accept-Language` and `Content-Language` tags to negotiate and tag the language used in the resource.

This allows a server to keep the same document in several different languages and return the one preferred by the client, based on the value in the `Accept-Language` header. When the server does return the specified document, it indicates the language of the document using the `Content-Language` response header.

As in Media Types, the IANA maintains a registry of language tags per RFC1766. The syntax is:

```
language-tag = primary-tag *( "-" subtag )
primary-tag  = 1*8ALPHA
subtag       = 1*8ALPHA
```

3.4.13 Entity tags

Entity tags arose from the need to make unambiguous comparisons between two or more entities from the same requested resource. A typical application of this would be to verify whether a page has changed between two visits. The use of entity tags allows for the precise comparison between the two requests. Furthermore, there is also the concept of a weak entity tag which implies the semantic content of the resource has not changed, even though it is not exactly the same. This can be used when something such as the background image is changed, but the words on the page are the same.

The actual value of the entity tag is considered an opaque quoted string. The actual bytes which make up the quoted string are only of significance to the generating application. The application comparing the values must do a simple string comparison only. Depending on the use of the entity tag, either a weak or strong comparison is made. The protocol specifies which are used in which instances. The syntax for entity tags is given as:

```
entity-tag = [ weak ] opaque-tag
weak       = "W/"
opaque-tag = quoted-string
```

Applications which generate entity tags must take care to never generate the same tag for two entities which are accessed via the same resource. In simpler terms, an application may choose to use something such as the last modification time of a file as an entity tag. This usage is permissible only so long as there is no chance for that entity to be updated more than once within a single time step. If the file system keeps last modification times to a one-second precision and the entity can be modified more than once within a given second, then a simple timestamp value is not sufficient for an entity tag.

3.4.14 Range units

As mentioned in the explanation of chunked encoding, an HTTP/1.1 application can request that only a certain range (or ranges) of an entity be returned in a response. This allows an application to limit the size of a requested resource, or to only retrieve a missing part of a resource. HTTP/1.1 allows arbitrary range units to be used in this manner, although only byte ranges are defined as follows by the protocol:

```
range-unit       = bytes-unit | other-range-unit
bytes-unit       = "bytes"
other-range-unit = token
```

3.5 Finishing

This chapter has covered most of the basic mechanics of HTTP. In the next chapter we will look in detail at the request messages sent by clients.

chapter 4

The request

The first thing to look at for HTTP/1.1 is the request. The request line is the message sent by the client to the server to request a resource or an action to take place. First, let us take a look at the overall construction of the request message.

4.1 The Request Message

The term `Request Message` is used to indicate the full message sent by a client to a server to request a resource. This includes the `Request-Line` and possibly a set of header lines. The overall syntax is defined as:

```
Request            = Request-Line
                     *( General-Header
                      | Request-Header
                      | Entity-Header )
                     CRLF
                     [ Entity-Body ]
Request-Line       = Method SP Request-URI SP HTTP-Version CRLF
```

Given a Web server located on `hops.ag.utk.edu`, and the resource `os2/index.html`, the `Request-Line` would be:

```
GET /os2/index.html HTTP/1.1
Host: hops.ag.utk.edu
User-Agent: IBM-WebExplorer-DLL/v1.1b
Referer: http://www.hethmon.com/index.html
```

The other general form a client might forward is when an entity body is sent with the request:

```
POST /cgi/search.cmd HTTP/1.1
Host: hops.ag.utk.edu
User-Agent: IBM-WebExplorer-DLL/v1.1b
Content-Length: 22
Content-Type: text/plain

term=ibm&type=b&num=20
```

In this example, a POST method is used to send an entity body with the request. This is formed similarly to the previous example but has the addition of an entity body after a blank line. It is important to note that the client must send two CRLFs in a row before the beginning of the entity body. The first CRLF marks the end of the User-Agent line. The second one follows with no intervening characters–in essence a blank line. This way, the server has a clear and concise delineation between the header fields and the entity body. The actual form of the data in the entity body is defined by the application level and not within the HTTP protocol. In this example we've shown a typical request involving plain text for a routine form submission.

All request lines begin with a Method. This is a keyword such as GET or POST which indicate the type action the request is asking the server to execute. Following the Method, the client sends the Request-URI, indicating the resource upon which the Method acts. Finally, the line ends with the client's HTTP version number. Remember this version number indicates the HTTP capabilities of the client, not necessarily the version of the actual request. The client may send only HTTP/1.0 compliant requests and still indicate a HTTP/1.1 version here. The client must be prepared to accept HTTP/1.1 responses in this situation. In practical terms, the client would only send the highest version number it wishes to accommodate.

We'll start looking at these different pieces next, starting with the different methods available to HTTP/1.1 applications.

4.2 Method definitions

In this section, we'll take a look at the different methods available for HTTP/1.1 requests. With HTTP/1.1, there are seven basic methods: OPTIONS, GET, HEAD, POST, PUT, DELETE, and TRACE.

4.2.1 The OPTIONS method

The OPTIONS method is used to query a server about the capabilities available from the server, or from a particular resource on the server. When querying about general capabilities, the client will send:

```
OPTIONS * HTTP/1.1
```

The server, in turn, will reply with the general capabilities available. This will likely include an `Allow` header listing the methods supported by the server. Any general or response header fields which are appropriate should be returned. What must not be returned are entity headers. There must not be an entity body in a response to an `OPTIONS` request, unless it is an error response. Since there is no entity body, entity headers are not appropriate.

If the request from the client uses a URI instead of the "`*`", then the response should only include information relevant to that resource. A server is expected to resolve the URI and determine which methods are supported. This may mean returning an `Allow` header with only `GET` and `HEAD`, and perhaps an `Accept-Ranges` header indicating byte range retrieval that is allowed for the resource:

```
Request:    OPTIONS * HTTP/1.1

Response:   200 Ok
            Allow: OPTIONS, GET, HEAD, POST, PUT
            Accept-Ranges: bytes
            Accept-Encoding: gzip

Request:    OPTIONS /cgi-bin/order HTTP/1.1

Response:   200 Ok
            Allow: POST
            Accept-Encoding:
```

It should be pointed out that in the last example, the `Accept-Encoding` line is correct. The standard allows an empty value indicating that the server does not accept any form of content encoding.

4.2.2 The GET method

GET serves as the work horse method for HTTP. It is the only method defined in the original HTTP/0.9 standard. When a client sends a request using the GET method, it is requesting that the server return the entity body of the resource identified in the `Request-URI`. As mentioned before, this may be a simple resource such as a Web page, an image, or an audio file. In those cases, the server will return the entity body as part of the response to the client.

The request may be more complicated when the client uses the query symbol within the `Request-URI`. This is the use of the question mark symbol (?)

after the resource in order to pass information to the resource indicated. In simple terms, this means passing parameters to a CGI resource and having the CGI resource use the parameters to determine the exact resource to be returned to the client. This can be used to implement a search engine of available documents, as an index into a database, or as a definitive way to pass coordinates for an imagemap.

Either form of a GET request may be modified by the inclusion of an If-Modified-Since request header in the request. If this header is present, then the GET is performed as a conditional operation. Only if the resource has been modified since the date given in the header is TRUE, is the resource returned to the client. This means, if your resource has a last-modified date of September 29, 1996, at 5:12 P.M. and the client sends a last modified date of September 15, 1996, at 1:00 A.M., then the server should return the resource to the client.

For our examples here, assume the resource named index.html has a last-modified date of September 29, 1996, at 5:12 P.M. For each example, we'll outline the response the server should make:

Request: GET /index.html HTTP/1.1

Response: The resource index.html.

Request: GET /index.html HTTP/1.1
           If-Modified-Since: Wed, 25 Sep 1996 09:45:23 GMT

Response: The resource index.html.

Request: GET /index.html HTTP/1.1
           If-Modified-Since: Tue, 1 Oct 1996 14:09:34 GMT

Response: A 304 not modified response. No resource is sent.

Request: GET /cgi/search?http+book HTTP/1.1

Response: The output from the resource search given the two terms http and book.

4.2.3 The HEAD method

As noted previously, the HEAD method has the same semantics as the GET method. The difference between the two methods is in the responses returned by the server. For HEAD, the server never returns an entity body in a response. This allows clients to verify links and check for modifications to resources without the expense of transferring the entity body. A client may not perform a conditional HEAD akin to a conditional GET. If a server receives an If-Modified-Since header as part of a HEAD request, it should ignore it and return the normal header information as if it were not present.

For the examples, we use the same resource as in the GET section.

Request: `HEAD /index.html HTTP/1.1`

Response: The response headers for `index.html`.

Request: `HEAD /index.html HTTP/1.1`
              `If-Modified-Since: Wed, 25 Sep 1996 09:45:23 GMT`

Response: The response headers for `index.html`.

4.2.4 The POST method

POST is used by a client to transfer an entity body to the server. The entity body is thought of as being subordinate to, and accepted by, the resource in the Request-URI. This allows for data submission via HTTP to accomplish various goals, such as database updating or order entry. This method was developed as a way to transmit larger sizes of data from clients to servers over the GET plus query term method.

There is one other big difference between GET and POST. This is the idea of *idempotence.* In simple terms, it means that performing a GET request multiple times should always result in the same response. If a client requests a GET for a specific Web page, then the same Web page will always be returned. For POST, this does not hold true. Submitting a POST request multiple times may very well result in multiple copies of forms being submitted for processing to a data handling process. In more practical terms, if you were to POST an order form for a pound of chocolate ten times, then you would likely receive ten pounds of chocolate plus a bill for it. Most HTTP clients have a setting to warn the user about this possibility.

When a client uses the POST method, it must include a Content-Length header as part of the request. This must be included as a way for the server to determine the end of the entity body. Since the socket connection must remain open for the server to send a response, the client cannot simply close the connection to mark the end of the data, as is done for FTP transfers. Check the following examples:

Request:
```
POST /cgi-bin/submit HTTP/1.0
Content-Length: 3819

[3819 bytes of data]
```

Response: The output from the process submit.

Request:
```
POST /cgi-bin/order HTTP/1.0
Content-Length: 6082

[6082 bytes of data]
```

Response: The output from the process order.

4.2.5 The PUT method

The PUT method is analogous to a sending a file via FTP. The client requests the server to accept the enclosed entity body, and store it as the Request-URI in the request line. This is different from the POST method, since the POST method implies the entity is to be passed or given to the Request-URI for processing. With the PUT method, clients now have a way to implement updating a Web site through HTTP itself.

When a server accepts a PUT request, it must respect any Content-* headers sent with the request. This provision is required to ensure that if a Content-Encoding header is given, the server must be capable of decoding the entity body before updating the associated URI. If the server cannot honor a content header, then it must issue an error response and discard the request. See the following examples.

Request:
```
PUT /users/phethmon/welcome.html HTTP/1.1
Content-Type: text/html
Content-Length: 3109

[ 3109 bytes of entity ]
```

Response:
```
204 No Content
Server: 3wd/1.1
```

Request:
```
PUT /catalog/sect1/pg34.html HTTP/1.1
Content-Type: text/html
```

```
        Content-Length: 4526
        Content-Encoding: gzip

        [ 4526 bytes of entity ]
```

Response: 501 Not Implemented
         Server: 3wd/1.1

4.2.6 The DELETE method

The DELETE method allows a client to request a URI to be removed from the server. This method is explicitly allowed to be overridden on the server. A successful response code only indicates the server expects to carry out the operation. In practice, a server might remove the resource from the server tree and place it in temporary storage, until reviewed by the server operator for permanent deletion. Given the ability for widespread mayhem with this method, any implementation should enforce some sort of mandatory security over using it.

Typical Web servers require authentication only when a resource indicates it. For the DELETE method, a better way would be to always require authentication, and deny it when none is specified.

Request: DELETE /catalog/sales/oct96.html HTTP/1.1

Response: 204 No Content

Request: DELETE /company/about.html HTTP/1.1

Response: 202 Accepted Pending Approval

4.2.7 The TRACE method

TRACE is used by client applications to do loopback requests. When a server receives a TRACE request, it should respond with a message containing all of the headers sent in the TRACE request. This allows a client to trace the progress of a request through multiple proxies and firewalls for error detection. A client may also attach a Max-Forwards request header to this type of request to limit the number of proxies and gateways passing the request. If Max-Forwards reaches zero before reaching the destination server, the proxy or gateway to decrement the value to zero should return a response.

Request:
```
TRACE / HTTP/1.1
Host: www.utk.edu
Max-Forwards: 10
User-Agent: JoeBrowser/10.0
```

Response:
```
200 OK
Content-Type: message/http
Content-Length: 84

TRACE / HTTP/1.1
Max-Forwards: 10
User-Agent: JoeBrowser/10.0
Host: www.utk.edu
```

4.3 The request header fields

Along with the request line sent by the client, several request, entity, and general header fields are normally sent to make the full request message. The information contained in these header fields provides information about the client as well as the entity body, if one is present. The header fields, used only for requests, or generally only for requests, are presented in this section.

4.3.1 Accept

The `Accept` header field is used by the client to signal which media types it prefers. This field may have multiple values, each with a relative quality value. Servers which can serve different versions of a document based on the client's preference should look at this field. If the server cannot furnish an acceptable resource, it should return a `406` code.

Syntax:
```
Accept= "Accept" ":" #(media-range [accept-params] )

media-range=( "*/*"
            | (type "/" "*" )
            | ( type "/" subtype )
            ) *( ";" parameter )

accept-params= ";" "q" "=" qvalue
            *( accept-extension )

accept-extension= ";" token [ "=" ( token | quoted-string ) ]
```

Example: `Accept: text/plain; q=0.8, text/html`

In this example, the client is requesting a `text/html` version of the document first, but if none is available, then a `text/plain` may be substituted.

4.3.2 Accept-Charset

This header is used by the client to request that a resource be delivered in a certain character set. When used, it is one of the headers over which server-driven negotiation takes place. When a server cannot furnish a resource in a requested character set, it should return a `406` response. The standard does allow sending an unacceptable response, basically allowing the server to ignore the header if it cannot satisfy the request. Depending on the circumstances, this may be preferred to not sending a response. As in the `Accept` header, quality values may be routinely used:

Syntax: Accept-Charset ="Accept-Charset" ":"
                        1#(charset [";" "q" "=" qvalue])

Example: Accept-Charset: ISO-2022-JP-2, ISO-2022-JP; q=0.8

4.3.3 Accept-Encoding

The client uses `Accept-Encoding` to signal to the server whether it will accept a `Content-Encoding` on responses from the server. The absence of this header signifies to the server that the client will accept any encoding defined in the standard. At the moment, this includes GZIP, compress, and deflate. If the header is present, but contains no values, then no encodings are acceptable to the client. Client applications should always take care to use this header if they are unable to accept encoded responses.

Syntax: Accept-Encoding = "Accept-Encoding" ":" #(content-coding)

Example: Accept-Encoding: gzip

4.3.4 Accept-Language

The client may use this request field to indicate which natural languages are acceptable for responses. This field is used in the same way the other `Accept-*`

fields are used by the server. The server should look at this field for the client preferences and attempt to satisfy them if possible. Language tags are matched exactly and as a function of the prefix. This prefix rule says that if a client requests en-gb for English–Great Britain, then matching on en- is allowed. This does not mean all languages follow the same rules for prefixes. Said another way, it is possible for prefixes to match, but if the client does not understand the other languages, it is a function of the language family.

Syntax:
```
Accept-Language = "Accept-Language" ":"
                  1#( language-range
                  [ ";" "q" "=" qvalue ] )

language-range  = ( ( 1*8ALPHA *( "-" 1*8ALPHA ) ) | "*" )
```
Example:
```
Accept-Language: da, en;q=0.5
```

4.3.5 Authorization

The Authorization header field is used by the client to send authorization information from the client to the server. This information is used to verify whether a client can make the request. The most common use for this header is to protect pages from viewing by a restricted audience. Another common use is to use the authorization information to track a user as it visits a Web site. Since HTTP is a stateless protocol, that is information from one request/response that is not used in the next request/response. This allows sites to track users through a site by requiring the authorization information for each resource requested. The syntax for the Authorization header is:

```
Authorization = "Authorization" ":" credentials
```

For HTTP/1.1, there are two authentication methods: *Digest Access Authentication* (which will be covered in Chapter 6) and *Basic Authentication*. With Basic Authentication, the client sends a username/password combination to the server for verification. The username and password are not encrypted during transfer. They are encoded though using Base64 encoding as defined in RFC 1521. For Basic Authentication we have the following definition:

```
credentials       = basic-credentials
basic-credentials = "Basic" SP basic-cookie
```

```
basic-cookie      = <base64 encoding of userid-password,
                    except not limited to 76 char/line>
userid-password   = [ token ] ":" *TEXT
```

This defines the credentials to be a concatenation of the userID, a colon, and the password. Once concatenated, the result is encoded using the Base64 algorithm. As an example thereof, consider the userID of phethmon and a password of sambo:

First concatenate: phethmon:sambo

Now encode: cGhldGhtb246c2FtYm8=

```
Authorization: Basic cGhldGhtb246c2FtYm8=
```

Finally, this gives us an example of:

```
GET /private/prices.html HTTP/1.1
Authorization: Basic cGhldGhtb246c2FtYm8=
```

4.3.6 Code: Base64

Base64 is not a difficult algorithm to program. It is designed to encode arbitrary octet sequences in a way that passes through SMTP mail agents where only 7-bit characters are guaranteed. To encode, a 24-bit sequence is transformed into a 4-character encoded sequence. To arrive at the 4 characters, the 24-bit group is broken into four 6-bit groups. Each of these 6-bit sequences is interpreted as an index into the Base64 alphabet. If fewer than 24 bits are available when the end of the data is reached, special encoding is done using the "=" character. If only 8 bits are available, then two characters are generated and the data is padded with two "=" characters. If 16 bits are available, then three characters are generated and the encoded output is padded with a single "=" character.

Let's take a look at the process of encoding a 24-bit sequence. Given the sequence:

```
00110011 00110011 00110011
```

We look at it as:

```
001100 110011 001100 110011
```

This gives us our four 6-bit sequences. Now we must view each as the lower 6 bits of an 8-bit byte:

00001100 00110011 00001100 00110011

These byte values are then used to index into the Base64 alphabet:

ABCDEFGHIJKLMNOPQRSTUVWXYZabcdefghijklmnopqrstuvwxyz0123456789+/=

The *A* character is considered to be at index 0 and the "/" character at index 63. The "=" character is the special character at index 64. Here is our complete function to encode an arbitrary string in Base64:

```
// ------------------------------------------------------------
//
// 0xfc = 11111100   Bit sequences needed for masks
// 0x03 = 00000011
// 0xf0 = 11110000
// 0x0f = 00001111
// 0xc0 = 11000000
// 0x3f = 00111111
// 0x30 = 00110000
// 0x3c = 00111100
//
// ------------------------------------------------------------
// The Base64 alphabet

const
char szB64[] =

"ABCDEFGHIJKLMNOPQRSTUVWXYZabcdefghijklmnopqrstuvwxyz0123456789+/=";

// ------------------------------------------------------------
//
// ToB64()
//
// This function takes a character string as input and
// transforms it to Base64 encoding. The return value
// is dynamically allocated and must be freed by the caller.
//

char * ToB64(char *szStr)
{
  char *szEnc;
```

```
    int iLen,
        i,
        j;

iLen = strlen(szStr);
   szEnc = new char [(int)((float)iLen * 1.5)]; // Space for the
                                                // encoded string.

   j = 0;
   for (i = 0; i < (iLen - (iLen % 3)); i+=3)    // Encode 3 bytes at a
      {                                          // time.
         szEnc[j]   = szB64[ (szStr[i] & 0xfc) >> 2 ];
         szEnc[j+1] = szB64[ ((szStr[i] & 0x03) << 4)    | ((szStr[i+1] &
                       0xf0) >> 4) ];
         szEnc[j+2] = szB64[ ((szStr[i+1] & 0x0f) << 2) | ((szStr[i+2] &
                       0xc0) >> 6) ];
         szEnc[j+3] = szB64[ (szStr[i+2] & 0x3f) ];
         j += 4;
      }

i = iLen - (iLen % 3);   // Where we left off before.
   switch (iLen % 3)
      {
        case 2:  // One character padding needed.
           {
              szEnc[j] = szB64[ (szStr[i] & 0xfc) >> 2 ];
              szEnc[j+1] = szB64[ ((szStr[i] & 0x03) << 4) | ((szStr[i+1]
                         & 0xf0) >> 4) ];
              szEnc[j+2] = szB64[ (szStr[i+1] & 0x0f) << 2 ];
              szEnc[j+3] = szB64[64];   // Pad
              break;
           }
        case 1:  // Two character padding needed.
           {
              szEnc[j] = szB64[ (szStr[i] & 0xfc) >> 2 ];
              szEnc[j+1] = szB64[ (szStr[i] & 0x03) << 4 ];
              szEnc[j+2] = szB64[64];   // Pad
              szEnc[j+3] = szB64[64];   // Pad
              break;
           }
      }
   szEnc[j+4] = NULL;
   return (szEnc);
}

// ----------------------------------------------------------------
```

4.3.7 From

This header field can be used by a client to send an Internet email address of the user controlling the client. For typical browser usage, this field is recommended to be completely user configurable. The client should allow the user to send, not send, or change the email address at anytime. For applications such as Web robots and spiders, a From header should be included as a contact point in case the automated agent is causing problems for a Web site.

Syntax: From   = "From" ":" mailbox
             mailbox = [RFC 822 definition]

Example: From: phethmon@hethmon.com

4.3.8 Host

Host is a new header in HTTP/1.1 used to help differentiate between virtual hosts on the same machine. When a request for the default root "/" comes into a server providing virtual hosts, the Host field can be used. This field is required for all HTTP/1.1 requests. If a HTTP/1.1 request does not have a Host field, the server must refuse it with a 400 response code.

Syntax: Host = "Host" ":" host [":" port]

Example: Host: apacweb.ag.utk.edu

4.3.9 If-Modified-Since

If-Modified-Since is used with the GET method to make a conditional request. The field of the header contains a date/time stamp. When the client requests a resource and includes this header, three possibilities exist:

- If the resource is valid and has not been modified, then a 304 response is regularly returned.
- If the resource is valid and has changed, then a 200 response with the entity is returned.
- If the resource is invalid or the request results in a response other than a 200, then the error response code is returned as if the header were not included.

The use of this header allows for efficient checking of a resource to see if a cached response can be used instead. If the response has not changed, then a minimum number of bytes is sent for the response. But if the resource has changed, a second request is not needed in order to retrieve it.

Syntax: `If-Modified-Since = "If-Modified-Since" ":" HTTP-date`

Example: `If-Modified-Since: Fri, 04 Oct 1996 18:13:34 GMT`
               `If-Modified-Since: Thu, 31 Oct 1996 23:59:59 GMT`

4.3.10 If-Match

`If-Match` is a new header for HTTP/1.1, and is used to make a request conditional. The `If-Match` field may be used for any method. The value is an entity tag, which the server will match against the current entity tag for the resource in the request URI. If there is a match, then the server should carry out the requested operation. A typical use of this would be to make certain a `DELETE` operation is only performed on the correct resource. When the match fails, the server should return a `412 Precondition Failed` response code. Only strong comparisons are allowed for `If-Match`. A client may send the special case value of "*" when they wish to match any current entity.

Syntax: `If-Match = "If-Match" ":" ( "*" | 1#entity-tag )`

Example: `If-Match: "abcde"`

4.3.11 If-None-Match

`If-None-Match` is a header which serves as another conditional, but in the negative sense. The client only wants the operation carried out if there is not a match of entity tags. The weak entity tag comparison function may be used if the method is GET or HEAD. Other methods require the strong comparison function. As per the `If-Match` header, there also exists the special value "*" which matches any entity tag of the resource. If there is a match, then the server should respond with a 304 code for GET or HEAD, and 412 for other methods.

Syntax: `If-None-Match = "If-None-Match" ":" ( "*" | 1#entity-tag )`

Example: `If-None-Match: W/"abcde", "xyz"`

4.3.12 If-Range

If-Range provides a way for a client to do a conditional GET with a Range request. Normally, when a client would do a GET with a byte range request, it would use either If-Unmodified-Since or If-Match to make sure it got a byte range for the matching entity. If the match failed, then the client would have to make another request for the full resource. Using the If-Range header, the client can send the request, and if the match fails on the entity tag or date in the header, then the server will automatically send the complete entity. This saves the extra request by the client:

Syntax: If-Range = "If-Range" ":" (entity-tag | HTTP-date)

Example: If-Range: Sat, 20 Jul 1996 18:53:21 GMT

4.3.13 If-Unmodified-Since

This field is another conditional modifier field. Its meaning is to only perform the requested operation if the resource has not been modified since the given date. On failure, the server should return a 412 Precondition Failed response:

Syntax: If-Unmodified-Since = "If-Unmodified-Since" ":" HTTP-date

Example: If-Unmodified-Since: Sat, 20 Jul 1996 19:01:54 GMT

4.3.14 Max-Forwards

This request field is only used with the TRACE method. The client may specify the maximum number of forwards it wishes the request to go through before being returned. Servers will ignore this field, since the TRACE request will cause them to send a response to the client. Intermediate agents, such as proxies and caches, decrement the number given as it passes through. If an intermediate agent decrements the value to zero, then the forwarding is considered at its limit. At this point, the intermediate agent must return the proper response to the TRACE request:

Syntax: Max-Forwards = "Max-Forwards" ":" 1*DIGIT

Example: Max-Forwards: 5

4.3.15 Proxy-Authorization

After receiving a `Proxy-Authenticate` response from a proxy, the client may use this header to validate themselves. This header uses the same mechanics as the `Authorization` header, but is used specifically to authenticate the transaction with a proxy server:

Syntax: `Proxy-Authorization = "Proxy-Authorization" ":" credentials`

Example: `Authorization: Basic cGhldGhtb246c2FtYm8=`

4.3.16 Range

Byte range retrievals are a new feature of HTTP/1.1, designed to improve performance. There are many times when a client will only receive part of a resource before unexpected conditions cause the connection to drop. The `Range` header allows a client to request only the byte range of the resource it does not have, instead of requesting the entire resource again. In normal operation, the `Range` header will be used with an `If` header to make the retrieval conditional upon matching the resource. The client may also send the `If-Range` header to receive the entire resource, if it does not match what it currently has. A client may send multiple byte ranges in a single request, but should only do so if it can handle receiving the `multipart/byteranges` media type. The `Range` header may also be used by a client to request a maximum size of a resource when bandwidth or storage limitations preclude retrieving unlimited size resources:

Syntax:
```
Range                   = "Range" ":" ranges-specifier
ranges-specifier        = byte-ranges-specifier
byte-ranges-specifier   = bytes-unit "=" byte-range-set
byte-range-set          = 1#( byte-range-spec |
                            suffix-byte-range-spec )
byte-range-spec         = first-byte-pos "-" [last-byte-pos]
first-byte-pos          = 1*DIGIT
last-byte-pos           = 1*DIGIT
suffix-byte-range-spec  = "-" suffix-length
suffix-length           = 1*DIGIT
```

Example:
```
Range: bytes=0-308
Range: bytes=-450
Range: bytes=200-340,700-
```

When specifying a range, the numbers given refer to the byte offset of the resource. This means the first offset of an entity is 0, not 1. Likewise, if the entity is 1,000 bytes, then the last byte offset is 999. In the second foregoing example, the range given is referred to as a suffix byte range. This is a request for the last 450 bytes of the resource. An implementation note here is that it is possible to give overlapping ranges within a single range request.

4.3.17 Referer

`Referer` is an optional request header field used to indicate to the server the source of the current `Request-URI`. The field is optional to allow for privacy of the browser user. The value of the field can either be an absolute or relative URI. If the field is only a partial URI, then the server must interpret it relative to the `Request-URI`. The client must not include a fragment with the URI:

Syntax: `Referer = "Referer" ":"( absoluteURI | relativeURI )`

Example: `Referer: http://www.software.ibm.com/os/warp/index.html`
`Referer: /public/index/a_f.html`

4.3.18 User-Agent

This field is used as the signature field of the browser. The information given here can be used by the server for auditing, statistics, or tailoring responses around browser limitations:

Syntax: `User-Agent = "User-Agent" ":" 1*( product | comment )`

Example: `User-Agent: Mozilla/2.02E (OS/2; I)`
`User-Agent: fido/0.9 Harvest/1.4.pl2`

4.4 Implementation

For the rest of this chapter, we'll take a look at some examples and implementation details for request messages. What we will cover will be typical of all request messages and how a server interprets the messages. We'll also look at some code for certain parts when the implementation may not be quite clear. Do remember that the complete code to implement a HTTP/1.1 server is included on the CD. The code presented herein is excerpted from there.

4.4.1 GET and HEAD

Our first example will be on the most common methods in HTTP: GET and HEAD. The GET method is the workhorse of HTTP. Each resource a client wishes to obtain must be done via a GET request. For this example, we'll use a server setup on the host www.example.com. A quick note here, in case you are not aware of it, is that the domain example.com is a reserved domain for just what we are doing here, namely presenting examples. It won't actually resolve to a real Internet host.

On our server, we'll create a document tree (see Figure 4.1) with a main welcome document called welcome.html and then present two branches: public and private.

The first request to examine is the default resource for the Web site. This corresponds to the resource identified as http://www.example.com/. With this type request, the client application is requesting that the default resource be returned to it. When the client constructs this request on behalf of the user, it must include several headers per HTTP/1.1:

```
GET / HTTP/1.1
Host: www.example.com
User-Agent: Mozilla/2.02E (OS/2; I)
Accept: text/*
Accept-Encoding: gzip
From: phethmon@hethmon.com
```

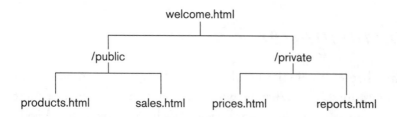

Figure 4.1   www.example.com document tree

Strictly speaking, the only part of the request message required here is the initial request line and the Host header field. The other fields are optional although likely to be sent by a typical client. The Accept field indicates the client will accept any resource in the text type range. This might include text/html or text/plain. The Accept-Encoding header is optional, but is likely to always be sent since its absence indicates the client is willing to accept any form of content encoding of the entity body. In our example, the client is indicating it will only accept encoding in the GZIP format. The final header, From, is again optional.

In this basic type request, the header lines sent by the client are mostly dictated by the capabilities of the client. If the client cannot accept any content encoding, then the Accept-Encoding header should be sent without a value to indicate this. Similarly, if the client wishes to restrict the character sets it accepts, then a properly formatted Accept-Charset header should be sent.

When the server receives the request, it must parse out the different headers to fully understand the client's request. The example server provided on the CD uses multiple threads to service requests from clients. This would be typical for most non UNIX-based implementations and also for newer UNIX ones (where the operating system supports threads). The example server uses a socket class to accept new connections and then spawns a thread to service the request:

```
for ( ; ; )                             // Forever
  {
    sClient = sSock.Accept();  // Listen for incoming connections

if (sClient != NULL)
      {
        // We established a connection, start a thread to handle it
        iRc = _beginthread(W3Conn, 0, STACKSIZE, (void *)sClient);
        if ( iRc == -1 )
          {
            // Failure to start thread. Close the connection.
            sClient->Close();
            delete sClient;
          }
      }
  }
```

In this code fragment, sSock is an instance of the Socket class. The class method Accept() performs the typical functions required to accept an incoming connection, and then creates a new class instance, sClient, to perform all network-related operations. Once the connection has been established, a new thread is created to service the request. At this point the server has not yet received the actual request from the client. The function W3Conn() does this.

```
iRc = sClient->RecvTeol(NO_EOL);   // Get the message

// Parse the components of the request
sscanf(sClient->szOutBuf, "%s %s %s", szRequest, szUri, szVer);

if (stricmp(szVer, "http/1.0") == 0)
   {
     DoHttp10(sClient, szRequest, szUri);
   }
else if (stricmp(szVer, "http/1.1") == 0)
   {
     iRc = DoHttp11(sClient, szRequest, szUri);
     while (iRc == TRUE)   // Do persistent connections.
        {
          sClient->RecvTeol(NO_EOL);
          sscanf(sClient->szOutBuf, "%s %s %s", szRequest,
               szUri, szVer);
          iRc = DoHttp11(sClient, szRequest, szUri);
        }
   }
else   // Treat this request as a HTTP/0.9 request.
   {
     DoHttp09(sClient, szRequest, szUri);
   }
```

Using the Socket class, the first line of code receives the first line of the request message from the client. The server simply parses the request line into the three components and switches, based on the HTTP version number. For HTTP/1.0 or HTTP/0.9 requests, the server simply services the request and ends the connection. For HTTP/1.1 requests, the server services the request and will continue to do so until the client drops the connection or ends the connection explicitly. This allows for the implementation of persistent connections.

At this point, the server has only received the request line and determined that the client is sending an HTTP/1.1 compliant request for a resource. The server must then determine which resource the client is requesting, and whether any of the headers present in the request message modify the way in which the server would return the resource. In order to do this, the server must receive all of the headers and parse them into their components and meaning. This means receiving each line of the request from the client and saving the values.

Our server here uses a `Headers` class to handle the dirty work of receiving and parsing the header lines. The class declaration is partially shown as follows:

```
class Headers
{
  public:

  Headers();
  ~Headers();
  int RcvHeaders(Socket *sClient);
  int CheckHeaders();
  int FindRanges(int iSize);

  char *szMethod,
       *szUri,
       *szVer,
```

What is missing from this code are the remaining data fields for storing the header values. We'll leave it on the CD and present a fragment of the `RcvHeaders()` method instead:

```
do
  {
    iRc = sClient->RecvTeol(NO_EOL);   // Get the message.
    if (iRc < 0) break;
    if (sClient->szOutBuf[0] == NULL) break;

    szTmp = sClient->szOutBuf;
    if (! isspace(szTmp[0]) )     // Replace the header if not
                                  // continuation.
      {
        i = 0;
        while ((*szTmp != ':') && (*szTmp)) // Until the
                                            // delimiter
          {
            szHdr[i] = *szTmp; // Copy.
            i++;               // Advance.
            szTmp++;
```

```
          }
       szHdr[i] = NULL;   // Properly end string.
       strlwr(szHdr);     // Lowercase only.
     }
   szTmp++;               // Go past the ':' or ' '.
   while ((*szTmp == ' ') && (*szTmp))
     {
       szTmp++;  // Eliminate leading spaces.
     }
   switch(szHdr[0])
     {
       case 'a':
         {
           if (strcmp(szHdr, "accept") == 0)
             {
               if (szAccept)
                 {
                   szBuf = new char[strlen(szAccept)
                       + strlen(szTmp) + 2];
                   sprintf(szBuf, "%s,%s", szAccept, szTmp);
                   delete [] szAccept;
                   szAccept = szBuf;
                 }
               else
             {
                   szAccept = strdup(szTmp);
             }
     }
```

The server first grabs a line of the request message from the client. It must then check to see if the line is a new header or a continuation header. It does this by checking to see whether or not the first character is a space. This may actually be a space character or a horizontal tab character. If it is not a continuation line, then the header field name must be parsed out of the line. Our algorithm here is to copy the name into a separate buffer until we reach the colon delimiter. Once copied, the buffer holding the header name is properly terminated, changed to lowercase, and saved for a moment. Next, the temporary pointer, szTmp, is advanced to the beginning of the header field value, including bypassing any leading spaces.

Now, the header class has the header name in one buffer and a pointer to the field value in the other buffer. In order to determine the field, a simple algorithm is used. The first step is to use a switch statement keyed on the first letter of the field name. This breaks down the header fields into smaller chunks for processing. By using a `switch-case` construction here, for efficiency the code itself can be well optimized by the compiler. Once the broad category has been determined, a string comparison is made to match the header name exactly. Since we've already changed the header name to lowercase, an exact comparison can be made instead of a case-insensitive comparison. Given the sheer number of headers available in HTTP/1.1, it makes sense to narrow the search as quickly as possible. With a smaller number of possibilities, a merely simple `if-else-if` tree could be used.

As shown in the code for the `Accept` header, it is possible for the header to have multiple values and even to appear multiple times. If a value has already been stored for the header, as evidenced by the `szAccept` variable having a value, then the new value is appended to the current one. Otherwise the value is simply stored. For some headers, the protocol only allows a single value. In those cases, the last value received is the one saved by the header class.

The server now has all of the information from the client in order to process the request. For this particular request, the server must determine the default resource to be returned to the client since no specific resource was requested. The exact resource returned will vary, depending on the server application. For a Web server, this is usually specified as being the `welcome.html` or `index.html` file within a certain directory of the server machine.

Once the server determines which resource to send back, it can check this resource against the headers sent by the client. In our example, the media type of the resource is checked against the `Accept` header type given: `text/*`. Since our server is sending back a HTML document, the media types match. Remember the server has a choice to respond with an error message if the media types do not match, or to return a resource with a different media type. The protocol recommends a server *should* return an error message when it cannot return the proper media type.

The server should now return the resource to the client via the already open connection. When sending the response back, the server constructs an appropriate response message containing the resource. In Chapter 6, we will take a close look at how the response message is constructed. For now, it is sufficient to say the resource is returned as the entity body.

If the request method had been HEAD instead of GET, then the server would have performed the identical steps up until the last. For HEAD requests, the server application must never send an entity body. The response is constructed exactly the same as if for a response to a GET request. This allows a client to query about a specific resource without actually retrieving the resource. This can be useful for verifying links.

4.4.2 POST

The POST method is used as a way for a client application to submit data to a resource on a server application. This is the method used for form data on Web pages in most instances. GET may also be used, but is more limited. Using the POST method, the client sends an entity body to the server for processing. The Request-URI in this case points to the resource on the server which will accept the entity body. Depending on the server implementation, this may be a Perl or REXX script, an executable program, or a dynamic link library. The possibilities here are only limited by the server's implementation. Once the resource acts upon the entity body, a response is generated and returned to the client.

Once again, using our example.com domain, a client has constructed a request, based on a form filled out by the user (see Figure 4.2).

When the client submits the form, it creates a request message such as:

```
POST /cgi-bin/survey HTTP/1.1
Host: www.example.com
From: phethmon@hethmon.com
Content-Type: text/plain
Content-Length: 23

week=ToMuch&access=Psycho
```

For this request message, the client has indicated which resource is to handle the POST data in the request line. This information comes from the Web form. The information which is different from a GET request is the addition of Content-Type and Content-Length headers. Since the request contains an entity body, the client must indicate the media type of the entity and the size. The size is especially important since the server must know when the entity body

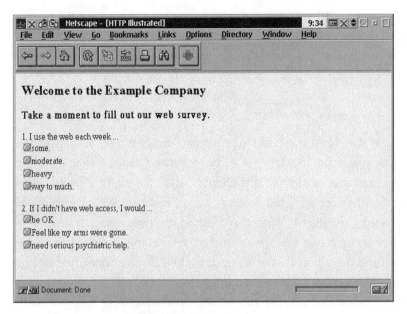

Figure 4.2   Screen shot of filled out form

ends in order to start processing the request. The entity body itself comes after a single blank line after the headers. In more specific terms, the client sends the normal carriage return line feed to mark the end of the `Content-Length` header and then immediately sends another carriage return line feed to mark the start of the entity body. After the 23 bytes of the entity body, the client again sends a carriage return line feed to mark the end of the entity body.

On the server side, as before, the server receives the initial request and then parses the headers. Once the headers are parsed, the server must then receive the entity body based on the `Content-Length` value of 23 bytes. Once the entity body has been received, the protocol actually leaves the picture.

The HTTP/1.1 protocol does not specify standards for what happens after a server accepts an entity body via a `POST` request. The server must decide what to do and how to generate a response to the request. For a Web server, this is usually done via executing a CGI script or compiled program. Most servers then leave it up to the executed process to generate a response and an entity body to return to the client. Given the example here, the executed resource might simply store the posted data into a database and return a generic response to the client, thanking it for its input. In this case, the response would be an entity body containing the thank you message, along with the proper related response headers describing the response.

4.4.3 PUT

A client using the PUT request method will construct headers very similar to the POST method. The difference actually, is in the interpretation, rather than the construction. As mentioned earlier in this chapter, the PUT method indicates to the server to accept the enclosed entity body and store it, using the request-URI given by the client. With this method, no processing of data takes place. Either a new resource is created or an old resource is replaced. For our example, we'll assume the client wishes to update the resource identified by the URI http://www.example.com/private/prices.html. This resource is considered to be in a private area of the server, accessible only to those with rights. In light of the PUT method and its ability to replace a resource, we would also want to control access to the PUT method. Our client might therefore send a request message such as:

```
PUT /private/prices.html HTTP/1.1
Host: www.example.com
From: phethmon@hethmon.com
Content-Type: text/html
Content-Length: 1830
If-Match: "x83wzir9"
Authorization: Basic cGhldGhtb246c2FtYm8=

[1830 byte entity body]
```

When the server receives this request, it interprets it as meaning to store the enclosed entity body as the resource /private/prices.html, replacing the current entity body. Before the server can do this however, it must check two things: The first, is the Authorization header. The server must verify that the given user and password are satisfactory, and allow the requested operation. If the user is verified, then the server must further qualify the request by matching the entity tag given in the If-Match header. Once these conditions are met, the server may then carry out the requested operation and return the appropriate response to the client.

4.4.4 DELETE

Constructing a DELETE request message is simple for the client. After identifying the resource to be removed, the client uses this as the request-URI, adds the necessary header fields and sends the request to the server. For our example domain, assume that the client wishes to remove the /public/sales.html resource. The client further wishes to make certain that the resource has not been updated since November 23, 1996, at 5:01 P.M., before deleting it. Given these circumstances, we can construct a request message such as:

```
DELETE /public/sales.html HTTP/1.1
Host: www.example.com
From: phethmon@hethmon.com
If-Unmodified-Since: Sat, 23 Nov 1996 17:01:00 GMT
Authorization: Basic cGhldGhtb246c2FtYm8=
```

Once the server receives and parses the request message, it makes its authorization check on the credentials given in the request. If the credentials are valid, it then checks the date given in the If-Unmodified-Since header against the date of the resource. The semantics here say to only carry out this request if the date of the resource is earlier than the date given. If this is true, then the server removes the resource and returns the appropriate response to the client.

In this example, we again show the client sending authorization credentials to be verified by the server. As with the PUT method, servers should be cautious about accepting the DELETE method. As a policy, all requests using either method should require some type of authorization instead of defaulting to the typical model of only requiring authorization when required by the resource.

4.4.5 OPTIONS

The OPTIONS header can be used by the client to find out the capabilities of the server. A client may wish to find out what methods the server supports for www.example.com. To do this, the client sends a request message using the OPTIONS method:

```
OPTIONS * HTTP/1.1
Host: www.example.com
From: phethmon@hethmon.com
```

The server, upon receiving the OPTIONS request, must first determine if the request applies to the server as a whole, or to a specific resource on the server. In the example here, the request URI has been set to the "*" case, indicating general resources of the server. For the response to this method, the server uses the internally configured data it has. The server may allow the administrator to deny all DELETE requests. Thus, even though the server may have supported the method, it should not return it since the support has been disabled.

4.4.6 TRACE

An example of the TRACE method would be when a client application is having difficulties contacting a particular server. If this occurs, the client may wish to send a TRACE request to find out the route the request is taking. It might be that the route between the client and server includes multiple proxies or gateways. For our example, the client needs to perform a TRACE on the connection from it to www.example.com:

```
TRACE / HTTP/1.1
Host: www.example.com
Max-Forwards: 5
```

The server simply returns the entire request message as the entity body of the response to the client. The media type of this message body is considered to be message/http. If the application is, instead, a proxy or gateway, then the request must be passed on, after decrementing the Max-Forwards value by one. If, as a proxy or gateway, a value of zero for Max-Forwards has been received, then a reply to the client should be returned.

4.5 Finishing

We have now covered the basics of HTTP, along with request messages. In the next chapter, we will take a look at entity and general headers plus the practical concept of cache control.

chapter 5

Entity and general headers, and Cache-Control

During the exchange of information between clients and servers, there exists a certain amount of information which falls into the entity and general category. Informational headers relative to the entity body are referred to as *entity headers*. Headers which supply ancillary information not directly related to requests, responses, or the entity body, are referred to as *general headers*.

5.1 The entity headers

Entity headers are used to describe the attributes of the entity body being sent by the client or server applications. This includes information such as the size of the entity, encoding which may have been applied to it for transfer, or the media type of the entity. Clients and servers should use these headers, as appropriate, to convey information to the recipient.

5.1.1 Allow

`Allow` is an entity header field used to transmit to the client the different methods supported by the resource as identified by the request URI. This field is mandatory if the server returns a `405 Method Not Allowed` response. A client may still attempt methods not listed in the `Allow` header, although the client should respect it:

Syntax: `Allow = "Allow" ":" 1#method`

Example: `Allow: GET, HEAD`

5.1.2 Content-Base

The `Content-Base` field is used to specify the base URI for resolving any relative URLs within the entity body. This field takes precedent over `Content-Location`, if present, and the original URI of the request, when resolving relative URLs.

Syntax: `Content-Base = "Content-Base" ":" absoluteURI`

Example: `Content-Base: apacweb.ag.utk.edu/etpcug/`

5.1.3 Content-Encoding

The `Content-Encoding` entity field specifies codings which have been applied to the entity body before transmission. This is used to allow the server to compress an entity body before transmission to reduce the size of the transmission. The server must respect any `Accept-Encoding` header sent by the client, when applying a content encoding.

Syntax: `Content-Encoding = "Content-Encoding" ":" 1#content-coding`

Example: `Content-Encoding: compress`

5.1.4 Content-Language

`Content-Language` specifies the natural language or languages of the entity being returned. If the server performs negotiation of the resource that is to be returned to the client, based on an `Accept-Language` header, then it should return this header and value to indicate the result of the server-based negotiation. The header may also be returned with any entity body, not just those in which negotiation has taken place.

Syntax: `Content-Language = "Content-Language" ":" 1#language-tag`

Example: `Content-Language: en`

5.1.5 Content-Length

The `Content-Length` field is one of the more important of the fields available. This field is used to specify the byte length of the entity body being sent. With persistent connections, both the client and server must specify the length of any entity sent. When the length of an entity body is unknown, chunked encoding may be used in place of this header.

Syntax: `Content-Length = "Content-Length" ":" 1*DIGIT`

Example: `Content-Length: 1964`

5.1.6 Content-Location

The `Content-Location` entity field can be used to supply the location of the entity being returned. This is useful when a particular resource has multiple entities associated with it (i.e., national language versions) and each of them may be accessed individually:

Syntax: `Content-Location = "Content-Location" ":" ( absoluteURI |`
`                            relativeURI )`

Example: `Content-Location: /home/lang/en/`

5.1.7 Content-MD5

The `Content-MD5` field may be used by the server to provide an end-to-end integrity check of the entity body. It is not a means of securing a transaction, but a means of detecting accidental modifications during transmission. The MD5 algorithm used is the same as presented in RFC 1864. If present, it is computed only on the entity body. It is not computed over any `Transfer-Encoding` which may have been applied to the entity body, but is merely computed over any `Content-Encoding`:

Syntax: `Content-MD5 = "Content-MD5" ":" md5-digest`
`            md5-digest  = <base64 of 128 bit MD5 digest as per RFC 1864>`

Example: `Content-MD5: MDEyMzQ1Njc4OTAxMjM0NQ==`

5.1.8 Content-Range

When a client requests a byte range response of a resource, the server must use the `Content-Range` entity field to specify which byte ranges are being returned, and the total length of the entity. If only a single byte range is being returned, the server must also include a `Content-Length` header showing the number of bytes actually sent. If multiple byte ranges are being sent, then the `multipart/byte ranges` media type is used. We'll discuss this further in Chapter 7.

Syntax: `Content-Range          = "Content-Range" ":"`
`                            content-range-spec`

```
content-range-spec      = byte-content-range-spec
byte-content-range-spec = bytes-unit SP first-byte-pos "-"
                          last-byte-pos "/" entity-length
entity-length           = 1*DIGIT
```

Example: Content-Range: bytes 459-2408/4707

5.1.9 Content-Type

The Content-Type field indicates the media type of the entity being returned:

Syntax: Content-Type = "Content-Type" ":" media-type

Example: Content-Type: image/gif

5.1.10 ETag

This entity field gives the entity tag for the entity in the message:

Syntax: ETag = "ETag" ":" entity-tag

Example: ETag: "472497203910"

5.1.11 Last-Modified

The server should return the Last-Modified field with all responses containing an entity. This time value should be the time the server believes the resource was last modified. For files, it may simply be the timestamp, while database information may consist of the last time a field was updated:

Syntax: Last-Modified = "Last-Modified" ":" HTTP-date

Example: Last-Modified: Sat, 20 Jul 1996 19:05:28 GMT

5.2 The general headers

General headers apply to the connection, rather than to the entity body of a request or response.

5.2.1 Connection

The Connection field allows either the client or server to specify options to apply to the current session. For HTTP/1.1, this field is used to communicate the sender's desire to close the current connection, once the response is sent. The only value defined for HTTP/1.1 is close:

Syntax: Connection   = "Connection" ":" 1#(connection-token)
               connection-token = token

Example: Connection: close

5.2.2 Date

The Date is generated by the server in every response to time-stamp when a message originated. It must use the RFC 1123 style time format. The date specifically does not refer to the time the entity body was generated:

Syntax: Date = "Date" ":" HTTP-date

Example: Date: Sat, 20 Jul 1996 15:35:00 GMT

5.2.3 Pragma

Pragma is a general header field that is defined in HTTP/1.1 solely for backward compatibility with HTTP/1.0 practice. The most common use of Pragma is to specify no-cache behavior and as such, is the same as using Cache-Control: no-cache. The HTTP protocol will not be defining any new directives for Pragma:

Syntax: Pragma   = "Pragma" ":" 1#pragma-directive
               pragma-directive = "no-cache" | extension-pragma
               extension-pragma = token ["=" (token | quoted-string)]

Example: Pragma: no-cache

5.2.4 Transfer-Encoding

The Transfer-Encoding field signals what transformations have been made to the message body for transport. Common application of this field is for the chunked method of transfer coding which allows a client or server to send an entity without knowing its length in advance.

Syntax: `Transfer-Encoding  =   "Transfer-Encoding" ":"`
                                 `1#transfer-encoding`

Example: `Transfer-Encoding: chunked`

5.2.5 Upgrade

This field is used to negotiate a change in protocols between the client and server. As future versions of HTTP evolve, a client may send the `Upgrade` field when it does not know what version of HTTP the server supports. If the server supports a higher level, then the server may send the response of `101 Switching Protocol` and indicate to which protocol it is switching. The change only applies to the protocol layer on the existing transport layer connection:

Syntax: `Upgrade = "Upgrade" ":" 1#product`

Example: `Upgrade: HTTP/2.0`

5.2.6 Via

This header must be inserted by gateways and proxies to indicate the protocols and recipients which handled the request between the client and server. It can be used for tracking down loops and identifying protocol capabilities of the intermediate handlers among others:

Syntax: `Via              = "Via" ":" 1#( received-protocol`
                                 `received-by [ comment ] )`
            `received-by      = [ protocol-name "/" ] protocol-version`
            `protocol-name    = token`
            `protocol-version = token`
            `received-by      = ( host [ ":" port ] ) | pseudonym`
            `pseudonym        = token`

Example: `Via: 1.0 proxy.ag.utk.edu`

5.3 Cache-Control

`Cache-Control` is one part of HTTP/1.1 which evolved heavily from previous versions. The caching aspects of the protocol have been designed to allow for efficient caching with quite a bit of control by both origin servers and clients alike. The general goal of caching is to reduce network traffic by reducing or eliminating the need for a client application to make a request to an origin server. In simpler terms, if a client or cache agent has a copy of a resource already stored, we want to be able to reuse the resource if at all possible.

When using a cache, whether in the user agent or in a stand-alone cache agent, the goal of the protocol is to always provide a semantically transparent operation. This means the user agent should always receive the same representation of a resource via a cache as if the resource were obtained directly from the origin server. There are conditions which may exist when this condition is not met. When this happens, the protocol provides for explicit warnings to the user.

A typical scenario involving a cache would be when a company provides a proxy cache agent for internal users to access the Internet. This might have been set up for bandwidth or firewall considerations. In this usage, the client browsers must send all requests through the proxy agent. The proxy agent then makes the request on behalf of the original user and caches as many responses as it can. The first step which occurs, as shown as **1** in Figure 5.1, is for user agent A to make a request to the proxy cache. The proxy cache then makes request **2** to the origin server for the resource. In step **3**, the origin server returns the response to the proxy cache which, in turn, returns it to user agent A in step **4**.

Now, at some later point, user agent B makes the same request to the proxy cache. But this time, instead of making a request to the origin server, the proxy cache checks its internal cache, finds the resource which matches, and returns it to User agent B in step **2** (see Figure 5.2).

When a cache is operating in this manner, it is said to be a public or shared cache. Any client which connects to it may receive any resource the cache agent has cached. In other terms, cached resources are not associated with a specific

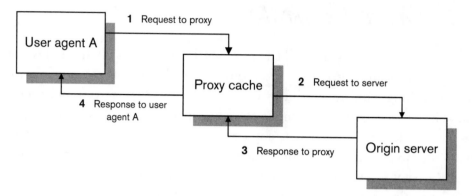

Figure 5.1   Proxy/cache operation

user. The HTTP/1.1 protocol allows a server to specifically deny caching a specific resource in a public cache, but would allow it in what is termed a private cache. A private cache is a cache dedicated to a specific user. Resources which may be allowed in a private (but not public) cache might include those requiring a user authorization to retrieve. If specific user authorization is required, such as a bank requiring a username and password before reviewing a checking statement, then it is likely this information is private in nature. If the protocol allowed it to be cached in a public cache, then sensitive information could be accessible to nonauthorized users.

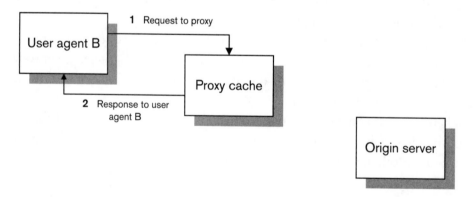

Figure 5.2   Proxy/cache operation

5.3.1 What is cachable?

Broadly speaking, anything not specifically forbidden to be cached is cachable. Responses which are specifically forbidden as cachable include responses to:

- POST requests
- PUT requests
- DELETE requests
- OPTIONS requests
- TRACE requests
- Requests which include an Authorization header

What this leaves as cachable are responses to GET and HEAD requests. Given the nature of HTTP usage, this accounts for the bulk of user requests. The GET and HEAD responses are required to have a status code of either 200, 203, 206, 300, 301, or 410. If a cache does not support byte ranges, then it may not cache the 206 responses, since these are partial responses by definition.

As with anything, there are exceptions to the broad rules presented above. Let us first take a look at the headers used in cache-control, and the specific cache-control directives which can modify behavior of a cache.

5.3.2 Age

The Age header is a response header used to transmit the sender's estimation of the age of a response. This can be either the original response from the origin server, or the time since an original response was revalidated with the origin server. HTTP/1.1 caches are required to send an Age header in every response sent. If a cache receives an age value which is larger than it can represent numerically, it must instead send a value of 2,147,483,648. This is a value of 2^{31} and is recommended for all caches to be able to handle numbers up to this size. Values for Age are always expressed in delta seconds, in the process using only nonnegative decimal integers:

```
Age       = "Age" ":" age-value
age-value = delta-seconds
```

Note   The meaning of the wording in this section of the draft specification was the subject of a bit of controversy in the HTTP Working Group. Some members felt the Age header should only be sent if the response had been resident in the cache, not when the cache is acting as a proxy. Implementors should refer to the latest HTTP specification for current guidelines.

5.3.3 Cache-Control

This header controls most of what happens with HTTP/1.1 caching. Directives which are sent via a Cache-Control header must be carried out by any caches which receive them. Caches and other intermediate HTTP agents must also pass through any cache directives since they may also apply to other agents along the request/response chain:

Syntax:
```
Cache-Control    = "Cache-Control" ":" 1#cache-directive
cache-directive = cache-request-directive
                 | cache-response-directive

cache-request-directive =
              "no-cache" [ "=" <"> 1#field-name <"> ]
            | "no-store"
            | "max-age" "=" delta-seconds
            | "max-stale" [ "=" delta-seconds ]
            | "min-fresh" "=" delta-seconds
            | "only-if-cached"
            | cache-extension

cache-response-directive =
              "public"
            | "private" [ "=" <"> 1#field-name <"> ]
            | "no-cache" [ "=" <"> 1#field-name <"> ]
            | "no-store"
            | "no-transform"
            | "must-revalidate"
            | "proxy-revalidate"
            | "max-age" "=" delta-seconds
            | cache-extension

cache-extension = token [ "=" ( token | quoted-string ) ]
```

The cache directives no-cache and private allow the sender to optionally specify the header fields to which the cache directive applies. If header fields are specified, then the directive only applies to those fields which are listed. If no header fields are listed, then the directive applies to the entire message.

5.3.4 Expires

The Expires field is used to give a date at which the response should be considered stale. For finer control, the server should use the newer Cache-Control directives. To indicate a response which will not expire, the server should use a date one year from the current date. To indicate a response which is expired, the server should use the same date as in the Date header:

Syntax: `Expires = "Expires" ":" HTTP-date`

Example: `Expires: Sat, 20 Jul 1997 15:35:00 GMT`

5.3.5 Warning

The Warning response field is used to convey additional information about a response beyond that indicated in the general response code. Within the HTTP/1.1 protocol, this is used to relay additional information about the response when semantic transparency may have been violated. This can occur when a cache agent returns a stale (out of date) response to a client, or after a transformation has been applied to the entity body (changing an image format from GIF to JPEG). Multiple Warning headers are allowed in a response message, and intermediate agents must not remove any they receive unless permitted by the specific warning code after the resource has been revalidated. This can happen when a warning value of 10 (Response is stale) is attached to a response. If the cache holding this response is later able to validate the response as fresh, then it may remove the 10 warning value. When an intermediate agent adds an additional Warning header, it should do so after any previous Warning headers. User agents should look at earlier Warning headers first, when multiple headers are encountered:

```
Syntax:   Warning       = "Warning" ":" 1#warning-value
          warning-value = warn-code SP warn-agent SP warn-text
          warn-code     = 2DIGIT
          warn-agent    = ( host [ ":" port ] ) | pseudonym
          warn-text     = quoted-string
```

The current warning codes are:

- *10: Response is stale*   This *must* be included whenever the returned response is stale. A cache may add this warning to any response, but may never remove it until the response is known to be fresh.

- *11: Revalidation failed*   This *must* be included if a cache returns a stale response because an attempt to revalidate the response failed, due to an inability to reach the server. A cache may add this warning to any response, but may never remove it until the response is successfully revalidated.

- *12: Disconnected operation*   This *should* be included if the cache is intentionally disconnected from the rest of the network for a period of time.

- *13: Heuristic expiration*   This *must* be included if the cache heuristically chose a freshness lifetime greater than 24 hours and the response's age is greater than 24 hours.

- *14: Transformation applied*   This *must* be added by an intermediate cache or proxy if it applies any transformation changing the content-coding (as specified in the `Content-Encoding` header) or media-type (as specified in the `Content-Type` header) of the response, unless this `Warning` code already appears in the response. It *must not* be deleted from a response even after revalidation.

- *99: Miscellaneous warning*   The warning text may include arbitrary information to be presented to a human user, or logged. A system receiving this warning *must not* take any automated action.

5.3.6 Cache operation

When in operation, a cache tries to satisfy as many requests as it can with as few requests to origin servers. In serving the requests it receives, it must satisfy semantic transparency, if possible, and return warnings or errors when it cannot. We will look at how a cache must operate by looking at the different directives it encounters enroute.

Cache-Control: no-cache   When a cache agent receives the `no-cache` directive, it may not cache the response under any circumstances.

Cache-Control: no-store   The `no-store` directive may either be sent with a request or a response message. If it is sent with a request message by a client, then neither the request nor the response to it may be cached anywhere along the request/response chain. If sent in a response, then the response may not be cached. This directive does not apply to user agents who cache responses as part of a history mechanism, nor does it apply to users specifically saving the response to permanent storage (i.e., save to file).

Cache-Control: max-age   When used in a request message, `max-age` allows the user agent to specify how old a response it will accept in terms of age of the response. A cache agent can compare this value to the age value associated with a normal response.

When sent by an origin server, the `max-age` value specifies the expiration time for the response.

Cache-Control: max-stale   The `max-stale` directive allows a user agent to make a request specifying that it will accept an out of date response up to a certain value. If the user agent gives 300 for a value, then a cache may return a response which is up to 300 seconds past its expiration time. A cache agent sending such a reply must attach a `Warning` header to the response with a code of `10` (`Response is stale`).

Cache-Control: min-fresh   If a client wishes to receive a response which will remain fresh for a given amount of time after it receives it, then it may use the `min-fresh` directive to specify the amount of time. For the cache, this means adding the `min-fresh` time to the current age and verifying that the response would still be fresh at that point.

Cache-Control: only-if-cached   In certain situations, a client may only wish to retrieve a resource if the resource is currently stored in the cache agent. This may occur because of disconnected operation or limited bandwidth constraints. In this situation, the client may send the `only-if-cached` directive. If the cache has a copy of the resource that meets any other requirements of the request, it then returns it. If, however, it does not, it returns a `504 Gateway Timeout` response to the client.

Cache-Control: public   The public response directive instructs the cache that the response is cachable even though normally it would not be. Under normal conditions, a cache agent may only cache responses with a status code of 200, 203, 206, 300, 301, or 410 and then only responses to GET and HEAD methods. If this directive is present in a response to another method, then the response may be cached.

If the request required authorization using the Authorization header, then it would only be cachable in a shared cache, that is, if the public directive were present.

Cache-Control: private   The origin server sends a private directive when the response is only cachable by the requesting user. The cache agent may cache this only for the requesting user. Private caches may cache these responses as they normally would.

Cache-Control: no-transform   A server may use the no-transform directive to forbid transformations of the resource to the entity body. This can prevent a cache or proxy agent, when serving clients, from translating a TIFF image into a JPEG image in order to save disk space within the cache or bandwidth. Some applications require the client to receive an exact duplicate of the original entity. Intermediate agents may not change the following headers when no-transform is specified: Content-Encoding, Content-Length, Content-Range, and Content-Type.

Cache-Control: must-revalidate   The must-revalidate response directive allows a server to require revalidation of a resource once it is considered stale. When present, a cache may use the resource to serve subsequent requests for the resource until the resource becomes stale. Once the resource is considered stale, the cache must revalidate the resource with the origin server for each request. If it cannot reach the server to revalidate the response, it must return a 504 (Gateway Timeout) response to the requesting agent.

Cache-Control: proxy-revalidate   The proxy-revalidate directive is the same as the must-revalidate directive, except that it does not apply to the private caches.

5.3.7 Expiration of responses

Much of how cache-control works is based on the idea of expiration times. When a resource has reached its expiration time, it is said to be *stale*. The expiration time of a resource may be calculated in different ways. The first, and best method, is for the origin server to explicitly set an expiration time. The server has two ways to accomplish this. The first way is to provide an `Expires` header. This method has the advantage of also being defined in HTTP/1.0. When presented with an expiration time this way, a cache has an explicit date at which to mark the saved resource as stale. The second way the server may use is the `max-age` directive. This directive lets the server specify how long a response remains fresh in regard to the *freshness* of the response. A server may include both an `Expires` header and a `max-age` directive in the same response. HTTP/1.1 compliant caches must disregard the `Expires` header in these cases. This allows the server to specify one expiration time for HTTP/1.0 caches (which may be shorter) and a longer one for HTTP/1.1 caches (which may be longer or modified by further cache-control directives).

If a server does not specify an expiration time using either `Expires` or `max-age`, then the cache may apply a heuristic to the response in order to assign one. One way a cache may do this is to look at the `Last-Modified` and `Date` header values. If the response includes both, then the cache may calculate the expiration time as some fraction of the time between those two dates. As an example, assume a response has an absolute time of 72 hours between the `Last-Modified` and `Date` values. The cache then takes a percentage of this value to use as a `max-age` value, say 5% or 3.1 hours. The cache could also base the percentage on a sliding scale where time differences of greater than 1 week are assigned at 10% of the difference on the assumption the resource is less likely to change if it has been the same for a longer period. In cases where the response does not include a `Last-Modified` header, the cache may still assign an expiration time, although it should be especially conservative about it. If the heuristically assigned expiration time is greater than 24 hours, the cache must include a `Warning` header with a code of 13 when it sends the response to a client.

Once the HTTP/1.1 cache calculates the expiration time, this value is referred to as the *freshness lifetime*. The freshness lifetime is the number of seconds a response remains fresh within the cache.

An HTTP/1.1 server should always try to assign an explicit expiration time to cachable responses. For file based servers where administration of individual expiration times is difficult, a server could offer to assign an expiration time based on the heuristics described herein. The server could further offer the administrator a choice of percentages based on the age of the file. Another option would be to assign expiration times, based on the media type of the resource. Images used on a page, especially logos and bullets, are unlikely to change for long periods of time, and could have correspondingly long expiration times.

5.3.8 Fresh and stale responses

Once the cache knows an expiration time for a particular response, it must then decide when the resource is *fresh,* and when it is *stale.* A fresh response is one which may still be sent to a client. It has not passed its expiration date. A stale response is one which has passed its expiration date and may not normally be sent to a client, unless warnings are attached and semantic transparency is explicitly relaxed. A cache must first determine the age of a response in order to determine the freshness or staleness of it.

The age of a response is considered to be the time which has elapsed since the response was generated at the origin server. It includes time spent in transit and time spent as resident in caches. It may be calculated by figuring the difference between the current time and the time in the `Date` header or by the `Age` header if only HTTP/1.1 caches are in the response path. The HTTP/1.1 specification presents the following algorithm to calculate the age of a response:

```
/*
 * age_value
 *      is the value of Age: header received by the cache with
 *              this response.
 * date_value
 *      is the value of the origin server's Date: header
 * request_time
 *      is the (local) time when the cache made the request
 *              that resulted in this cached response
 * response_time
 *      is the (local) time when the cache received the
 *              response
 * now
```

```
*      is the current (local) time
*/
apparent_age = max(0, response_time - date_value);
corrected_received_age = max(apparent_age, age_value);
response_delay = response_time - request_time;
corrected_initial_age = corrected_received_age + response_delay;
resident_time = now - response_time;
current_age    = corrected_initial_age + resident_time;
```

This algorithm is a conservative one and will, on average, overestimate the age of a response. This is intentional within the protocol, to be certain no one receives a stale response by accident.

Now that the cache knows both the freshness lifetime and the age of the response, it can determine whether the response is fresh or stale. If the freshness lifetime is greater than the age of the response, then the response is fresh, and it does not require validation before the cache can use it as a response to a client. If the response is stale, then the cache must validate the response before sending it to a client.

5.3.9 *Validating a response*

When a response is stale, a cache must validate it with the origin server, or an upstream cache, before using it for further responses to its clients. HTTP/1.1 provides a way for caches to use validators within a request to a server to check on whether or not the response is still valid. In general, a cache would do this by issuing a conditional get which includes a validator for the response. Then if the resource had not changed, the server can respond with a 304 Not Modified response and save the expense of retransmitting the entity body. If the resource had changed, then the server simply sends the new entity body in a standard response. Either way, the minimum of network traffic has taken place.

HTTP/1.1 provides two different validators: Last-Modified dates and entity tags. Both types may be considered either as *weak* or *strong* validators, depending on usage and indications by the origin server. The strong validator is a validator which changes whenever the entity with which it is associated changes in any way, no matter how minor. The weak validator is a validator which changes only when the entity changes in a semantically significant way. This might be used by a server when only the background color of a page has changed. Even though it is not exactly the same, the information conveyed by the resource is still the same.

When comparing validators, HTTP/1.1 defines two operations:

- *Strong comparison*   Both validators must be identical and both must be strong

- *Weak comparison*   Both validators must be identical, but one or both may be weak

Entity tags are always considered strong, unless explicitly tagged as weak. Last modified dates are always considered weak unless certain conditions are met as outlined by the protocol specification:

- The validator is being compared by an origin server to the actual current validator for the entity and,

- That origin server reliably knows that the associated entity did not change twice during the second covered by the presented validator.

  or

- The validator is about to be used by a client in an `If-Modified-Since` or `If-Unmodified-Since` header, because the client has a cache entry for the associated entity, and

- That cache entry includes a `Date` value, which gives the time when the origin server sent the original response, and

- The presented `Last-Modified` time is at least 60 seconds before the listed `Date` value.

  or

- The validator is being compared by an intermediate cache to the validator stored in its cache entry for the entity, and

- That cache entry includes a `Date` value, which gives the time when the origin server sent the original response, and

- The presented `Last-Modified` time is at least 60 seconds before the listed `Date` value.

5.3.10 Examples

Caching is a complex subject in HTTP/1.1. It answers the needs of those who need to conserve resources such as bandwidth, and the needs of those who need control over when, where, and how their responses are cached. The protocol specification is the final word on this and does contain many points not brought up in this section of this book. If you are going to administer or implement a HTTP/1.1 cache, you will need to read the protocol and know what it says. Let us now go over some examples to more precisely illustrate the use of the cache-control mechanisms.

Example 1   In example 1, the cache agent has a copy of the resource stored. The origin server has not placed any extra restrictions on the cachability of the resource. At the moment, the cache has calculated the age of the resource as well as the expiration time, and has concluded that the resource is still fresh:

```
age-value           = 100
freshness-lifetime  = 300
```

Now let us look at some specific requests for the resource given under these conditions: We will consider /resource to be the correct URI for the resource. Non-essential headers are omitted:

Request 1:   `GET /resource HTTP/1.1`

Response1: `The cache uses the stored copy.`

Request 2:   `GET /resource HTTP/1.1`
`Cache-Control: min-fresh=250`

Response 2: `The cache must validate the resource.`

Request 3:   `GET /resource HTTP/1.1`
`Cache-Control: no-cache`

Response 3: `The cache must reload the resource from the origin server.`

Request 4: GET /resource HTTP/1.1
Cache-Control: max-age=0

Response 4: The cache must validate with the origin server.

Request 5: GET /resource HTTP/1.1
Cache-Control: max-age=500

Response 5: The cache uses the stored copy.

Example 2 In this example, the cache once again has a copy of the resource in storage. This time the age and freshness are:

```
age-value          = 500
freshness-lifetime = 400
```

Our requests from the client are:

Request 1: GET /resource HTTP/1.1

Response 1: The cache validates the resource.

Request 2: GET /resource HTTP/1.1
Cache-Control: no-store

Response 2: The cache must reload the resource from the origin server and not store the response. The specification is silent on the disposition of the currently cached copy. Conservative caches would flush the resource from the cache.

Request 3: GET /resource HTTP/1.1
Cache-Control: max-stale=200

Response 3: The cache returns the resource after attaching a Warning 10 to it.

Request 4: GET /resource HTTP/1.1
Cache-Control: only-if-cached

Response 4: The cache returns the resource after attaching a Warning 10 to it.

Request 5: GET /resource HTTP/1.1
Cache-Control: max-age=600, max-stale=300

Response 5: The cache returns the resource after attaching a Warning 10 to it.

5.4 *Finishing*

In this chapter, we have covered the basics of entity and general headers, such being the headers which may occur in either request or response messages. Also covered has been the concept of cache-control, which is all new in HTTP/1.1. In the next chapter we will look further into the response messages sent by the HTTP server.

chapter 6

The response

6.1 *The response message*

The response message is the complete message returned by a server to a client. It encompasses a status line, one or more header lines, and an optional entity body. In sum, it is the response to the client's request for a resource retrieval or data transmission. The syntax for the response message is:

```
Response = Status-Line
           *( general-header  |
              response-header |
              entity-header    )
           CRLF
           [ message-body ]
Status-Line = HTTP-Version SP Status-Code SP Reason-Phrase CRLF
```

A typical response for a HTTP server would be:

```
HTTP/1.1 200 OK
Date: Wed, 27 Nov 1996 16:33:28 GMT
Server: 3wd/1.1
Content-Type: text/html
Content-Length: 200
Last-Modified: Thu, 31 Oct 1996 12:00:00 GMT
ETag: "3w8fgw9iu08"

[200 bytes of entity body]
```

In this response, the server has indicated a status code of 200, meaning the request was accepted and honored. It also includes the mandatory Date field showing the time the response was generated, and the Server header which shows the server software and version. The last four headers consist of entity headers describing characteristics of the enclosed entity body. Following the ETag header, is the blank line required between the headers and the entity body. It is formed therefore, as in request messages, by two consecutive carriage return line feed combinations.

The first part of the response message we want to examine more closely is the status code. HTTP/1.1 status codes are dividing into five general categories:

- *100 to 199: Informational* Providing information about a request but not the final status.

- *200 to 299: Success* Indicating the client's request was accepted and has been performed.

- *300 to 399: Redirection* The client must perform additional actions to complete the request.

- *400 to 499: Error* The client request contains an error, either syntax or denied by the server.

- *500 to 599: Error* The server encountered an error servicing the request.

The individual status codes defined by HTTP/1.1 include:

```
Status-Code    = "100" ; Continue
               | "101" ; Switching Protocols
               | "200" ; OK
               | "201" ; Created
               | "202" ; Accepted
               | "203" ; Non-Authoritative Information
               | "204" ; No Content
               | "205" ; Reset Content
               | "206" ; Partial Content
               | "300" ; Multiple Choices
               | "301" ; Moved Permanently
               | "302" ; Moved Temporarily
               | "303" ; See Other
               | "304" ; Not Modified
               | "305" ; Use Proxy
               | "400" ; Bad Request
               | "401" ; Unauthorized
               | "402" ; Payment Required
               | "403" ; Forbidden
               | "404" ; Not Found
               | "405" ; Method Not Allowed
               | "406" ; Not Acceptable
               | "407" ; Proxy Authentication Required
               | "408" ; Request Time-out
               | "409" ; Conflict
               | "410" ; Gone
               | "411" ; Length Required
               | "412" ; Precondition Failed
               | "413" ; Request Entity Too Large
               | "414" ; Request-URI Too Large
               | "415" ; Unsupported Media Type
               | "500" ; Internal Server Error
               | "501" ; Not Implemented
```

```
|  "502" ; Bad Gateway
|  "503" ; Service Unavailable
|  "504" ; Gateway Time-out
|  "505" ; HTTP Version not supported
|  extension-code

extension-code = 3DIGIT

Reason-Phrase  = *<TEXT, excluding CR, LF>
```

The foregoing phrases as well as those shown in Table 6.1 are only suggestions as given in the protocol specification. Servers may modify them to local conditions (such as providing messages in French), without affecting the meaning of the status code. As noted in the syntax, HTTP/1.1 provides for more status codes to be added under the `extension-code` heading. When a client encounters a status code they do not understand, they should fall back to interpreting the status code under the five main categories. This means if a code of `517` is received by a client, they should interpret it as a server error of unknown type. If this does happen and an entity body is sent with the response, then the client should show the entity body to the user since it probably contains a more understandable explanation for the failure. Table 6.1 below includes each status code and a short explanation of each. For a more complete explanation, refer to HTTP/1.1 protocol specification included on the enclosed CD.

Table 6.1 Status codes

Status code	Explanation
100 Continue	This reply is intended as an interim reply to a client. Likely uses are by proxies or servers when a final reply may take a measurable amount of time.
101 Switching Protocols	This code is not currently used in HTTP/1.1, but is intended as a way for compliant applications to switch to a more advantageous or efficient protocol as indicated by the Upgrade header.
200 OK	General success code.
201 Created	This code can be used a response to a PUT request to indicate a new resource has been created and is available.
202 Accepted	Indicates the server has accepted the request but is deferring processing for later. This response does not guarantee the request will be ultimately fulfilled.

Table 6.1   Status codes (continued)

Status code	Explanation
203 Non-Authoritative Information	Indicates the information in the entity headers is not the definitive set from the origin server.
204 No Content	Indicates the request succeeded but did not result in a new entity body being returned. The client should maintain the current view.
205 Reset Content	This code is meant to be used as a way to do repetitive data entry via HTTP. Upon receiving this code, the client should reset the view to the default originally supplied by the server.
206 Partial Content	Success code for range retrievals.
300 Multiple Choices	Indicates the requested resource is available in different representations along with information to enable the client to select the best representation.
301 Moved Permanently	Indicates the resource has moved to a new location. The client should use the new URI as returned.
302 Moved Temporarily	Indicates the resource has moved temporarily. The client should continue to use the present URI.
303 See Other	Indicates the user agent should retrieve the desired response via a GET request to the returned URI. This allows POST requests to redirect to another resource.
304 Not Modified	Indicates the conditional GET on a resource has found the resource has not changed.
305 User Proxy	Indicates the user agent must request the resource through a proxy.
400 Bad Request	Indicates bad syntax in the request.
401 Unauthorized	The resource requires authentication before access can be granted.
402 Payment Required	Reserved for future use.
403 Forbidden	The server understood the request but will not fulfill it.
404 Not Found	The indicated resource was not located on the server.
405 Method Not Allowed	The method used by the client is not allowed on the resource.
406 Not Acceptable	The response which would normally be returned by the server does not fulfill the clients indicated Accept-* headers.
407 Proxy Authentication Required	The user must authenticate themselves with the proxy agent.
408 Request Timeout	The server timed out waiting for the full client request.
409 Conflict	A conflict in the current state of the resource prevented the request from being fulfilled.
410 Gone	Indicates the resource is not available now and will not be in the future.
411 Length Required	The client must supply a valid Content-Length.
412 Precondition Failed	Indicates one of the conditional headers was false.

Table 6.1 **Status codes (continued)**

Status code	Explanation
413 Request Entity Too Large	The request entity is larger than the server will accept.
414 Request-URI Too Long	The request-URI is longer than the server will accept.
415 Unsupported Media Type	The media type of the entity is not acceptable to the server.
500 Internal Server Error	General server error encountered.
501 Not Implemented	The requested method is not supported by the server.
502 Bad Gateway	An invalid upstream response was received while trying to fulfill the client's request.
503 Service Unavailable	The server cannot fulfill the request at the moment. This is an indication of temporary conditions such as overloading or server maintenance.
504 Gateway Timeout	Acting as a proxy, the server did not receive a timely response.
505 HTTP Version Not Supported	The server does not or is unwilling to support the HTTP version of the request.

6.2 *The response header fields*

The response header fields are used by the server to convey additional information about the response, beyond what can be implied by the status line. This information can include authentication challenges, server names and versions, or additional location information. The information, though, is just of concern to the particular response it accompanies. HTTP/1.1 defines the following response header fields:

```
response-header = Age
                | Location
                | Proxy-Authenticate
                | Public
                | Retry-After
                | Server
                | Vary
                | Warning
                | WWW-Authenticate
```

In this section, we will discuss each one individually, with the exception of the `Age` header which was covered in the last chapter. This section also delves into both the `Accept-Ranges`, which is a response header but is omitted from the `response-header` definition in the draft specification, and the `Authentication-info` header from the Digest Authentication draft.

6.2.1 Accept-Ranges

This response field can be used by the server to indicate whether or not it accepts range requests. A client may send range requests without the server's sending this field. Whenever a server receives an `OPTIONS` request, it should include this field in the responses. This could be as a negative or positive response. If the response is positive, the value sent will be `bytes`, if negative, `none`. The HTTP/1.1 protocol has been designed so that a server does not have to support byte range retrieval in order to implement it. However, for efficiency of network transmissions, servers should implement byte ranges:

Syntax:
```
Accept-Ranges      = "Accept-Ranges" ":" acceptable-ranges
acceptable-ranges = 1#range-unit | "none"
```
Example: `Accept-Ranges: bytes`

6.2.2 Authentication-info

The `Authentication-info` header can be used by a server after a successful `Digest Authentication` authorization. In it, the server can provide information for the user agent about the current response and the next request. For the current response, the server can provide an MD5 digest over the entity body to provide a check that the entity has not been altered in transit. For the next request, the server can supply a new nonce value for the user agent to use. Clients are strongly encouraged to use this nonce value if it is present:

Syntax:
```
Authentication-info = "Authentication-info" ":"

                      1#( digest | nextnonce )
nextnonce           = "nextnonce" "=" nonce-value
digest              = "digest" "=" entity-digest
```
Example: `Authentication-info: nextnonce="389348dkediz"`

6.2.3 *Location*

The server can use the `Location` field to redirect the client to a different location for completion of a request if the response is a 3xx. If the response code is 201, then it directs the client to the newly created resource:

Syntax: `Location = "Location" ":" absoluteURI`

Example: `Location: http://apacweb.ag.utk.edu/os2/new.html`

6.2.4 *Proxy-Authenticate*

This header field is used by proxies when the client must authenticate with the proxy before access is granted. This is similar to the `WWW-Authenticate` field used by servers:

Syntax: `Proxy-Authenticate = "Proxy-Authenticate" ":" challenge`

Example: `Proxy-Authenticate: basic realm="proxy1"`

6.2.5 *Proxy-Authenticate-info*

This header is used similarly to the `Authenticate-info` header except only by a proxy agent. The proxy may only send the `nextnonce` field however:

Syntax: `Proxy-Authenticate-info = "Proxy-Authenticate-info" ":"`
`                                nextnonce`

Example: `Proxy-Authenticate-info: "dierq420744"`

6.2.6 *Public*

This response header can be used by the server in a response to list the methods the server supports. The methods listed apply to the server as a whole and not to the request URI given by the client. It is merely an indication of the general capabilities of the server.

Syntax: `Public = "Public" ":" 1#method`

Example: `Public: GET, HEAD, POST, PUT, TRACE`

6.2.7 Retry-After

When a server responds with a `503 Service Unavailable` response, it may wish to inform the client when to retry the request and expect success. Thus the `Retry-After` field may be sent with the response to let the client know the retry time, which may be specified absolutely or relative to the current time:

Syntax: Response = "Response" ":" (HTTP-date | delta-seconds)

Example: Retry-After: 300

6.2.8 Server

This field is used to identify the server software and version servicing the request:

Syntax: Server = "Server" ":" 1*(product | comment)

Example: Server: 3wd/1.1

6.2.9 Vary

The `Vary` response header is used to inform the client over which parameters the server performed server-driven negotiation of the resource. The server must include an appropriate `Vary` response with any response which is cachable. A value of "*" means the server performed the server-driven negotiation on some unspecified parameters such as the IP address of the client:

Syntax: Vary = "Vary" ":" ("*" | 1#field-name)

Example: Vary: Accept-Language

6.2.10 Warning

The `Warning` header is used when additional information about a response needs to be transmitted to the client. This is typically used by a cache when semantic transparency may be compromised:

Syntax:
```
Warning        = "Warning" ":" 1#warning-value
warning-value  = warn-code SP warn-agent SP warn-text
warn-code      = 2DIGIT
warn-agent     = ( host [ ":" port ] ) | pseudoym
warn-text      = quoted-string
```

Example: `Warning: 10 proxy.ag.utk.edu "Response is stale"`

6.2.11 WWW-Authenticate

This response field must be present if a server sends a `401 Unauthorized` response to a client. It will contain the information necessary for the client to validate itself by sending an `Authorization` header:

Syntax:
```
WWW-Authenticate = "WWW-Authenticate" ":" 1#challenge
challenge        = auth-scheme 1*SP realm *( "," auth-param )
realm            = "realm" "=" realm-value
realm-value      = quoted-string
auth-scheme      = token
auth-param       = token "=" quoted-string
```

Example: `WWW-Authenticate: basic realm="cowdudes"`

6.2.12 Code: Digest Access Authentication

In Chapter 4, we covered Basic Authentication. HTTP/1.1, which includes Digest Access Authentication as a replacement for Basic. When a server supports Digest Access Authentication, it uses the following syntax to challenge the client:

```
WWW-Authenticate    = "WWW-Authenticate" ":" "Digest"
                        digest-challenge

digest-challenge    = 1#( realm | [ domain ] | nonce |
                      [ digest-opaque ] |[ stale ] | [ algorithm ] )

realm               = "realm" "=" realm-value
realm-value         = quoted-string
domain              = "domain" "=" <"> 1#URI <">
nonce               = "nonce" "=" nonce-value
nonce-value         = quoted-string
opaque              = "opaque" "=" quoted-string
stale               = "stale" "=" ( "true" | "false" )
algorithm           = "algorithm" "=" ( "MD5" | token )
```

A close inspection will show a `digest-opaque` parameter which does not have a corresponding definition. There is, however, an opaque parameter which is meant to be the same. This inconsistency exists in the last protocol draft, but may have been corrected in the RFC.

As an example, consider the request for `http://www.example.com/ private/prices.html`, which is a Digest-protected document. Upon receiving the initial request for the document, the server will reply with:

```
WWW-Authenticate: Digest realm="sales@www.example.com",
                  nonce="dcd98b7102dd2f0e8b11d0f600bfb0c093",
                  opaque="9d9dkdkew93453kdihgnpqd94300xx9"
```

With this example, the server has indicated the realm for which the user must supply authentication, along with the nonce value and opaque value. The nonce value is incorporated by the client into the digest, according to the following syntax:

```
response-digest  =
      <"> < KD ( H(A1), unquoted nonce-value ":" H(A2) > <">

A1                    = unquoted username-value ":" unquoted realm-value
                                                 ":" password

password              = < user's password >
A2                    = Method ":" digest-uri-value
```

For our example, the username is `john.salesman` and the password is 5+5=10. To calculate the correct response digest value, the user agent must first calculate `A1`:

```
A1 = john.salesman:sales@www.example.com:5+5=10
```

The `H(A1)` value is the MD5 algorithm (as presented in RFC 1321) and as applied over `A1`:

```
H(A1) = d6c21e4ad73713764d32800decafd357
```

The user agent next calculates the `H(A2)` value:

```
A2 = GET:/private/prices.html
H(A2) = 254bd53db6966fa1387fa1973bb5e53c
```

Finally, `response-digest` is calculated as:

```
response-digest = KD(secret, data) = H(concat(secret, ":", data))
response-digest = KD(H(A1), unquoted nonce-value ":" H(A2)
```

```
response-digest = KD(d6c21e4ad73713764d32800decafd357,
  dcd98b7102dd2f0e8b11d0f600bfb0c093:254bd53db6966fa1387fa1973bb5e53c)
```

(The next line shown over 3 lines for readability only, the digest is computed on a single string with no line breaks or spaces.)

```
response-digest = H(d6c21e4ad73713764d32800decafd357:
                    dcd98b7102dd2f0e8b11d0f600bfb0c093:
                    254bd53db6966fa1387fa1973bb5e53c)
response-digest = d87051c6f8ca76e671ba2d52f12ef976
```

Finally, the user agent constructs the following `Authorization` header:

```
Authorization = username="john.salesman",
                realm="sales@www.example.com"
                nonce="dcd98b7102dd2f0e8b11d0f600bfb0c093",
                uri="/private/prices.html",
                response="d87051c6f8ca76e671ba2d52f12ef976",
                opaque="9d9dkdkew93453kdihgnpqd94300xx9"
```

The server accepts this information and performs the MD5 algorithm in the same way. All information, except the password, is sent over the HTTP protocol. If the calculated digest value matches, then the server grants access to the client.

6.3 Digest Access Authentication

As of this writing, the Digest Access Authentication draft is a separate draft from the main HTTP/1.1 draft. It is possible the RFC editor might choose to incorporate it into the main HTTP/1.1 draft instead of leaving it as a separate RFC. Either way, Digest Access Authentication (Digest) is a part of the proposed HTTP/1.1 standard, and the working group consensus seems to be to make it a requirement to implement it if authentication is implemented within an HTTP application (whether client or server).

As mentioned earlier herein, Digest is meant as a replacement for Basic Authentication. Basic Authentication suffers from sending the user's password as clear text across the connection. Digest provides a mechanism for verifying a user without sending the password as clear text, although both client and server must still have a means of distributing the password. In Digest, the server responds in the WWW-Authenticate header with several pieces of information for the client. The client takes this information and, together with the secret password, performs an MD5 algorithm over it. The MD5 algorithm encrypts the secret password with other per connection information in such a way that a user's authenticity may only be verified by the server.

MD5 is short for Message Digest 5 and is described in RFC 1321. Basically, MD5 performs a checksum over a string of data. It is this checksum which clients and servers calculate and use to verify authenticity. RFC 1321 is included on the CD, along with the code implementing it for the Digest method. The MD5 algorithm is used in the Content-MD5 header field and also in the APOP authentication method for the POP3 protocol.

The syntax for the server challenge is:

```
WWW-Authenticate     = "WWW-Authenticate" ":" "Digest"
                           digest-challenge

digest-challenge     = 1#( realm | [ domain ] | nonce |
                         [ digest-opaque ] |[ stale ] | [ algorithm ] )

realm                = "realm" "=" realm-value
realm-value          = quoted-string
domain               = "domain" "=" <"> 1#URI <">
nonce                = "nonce" "=" nonce-value
nonce-value          = quoted-string
opaque               = "opaque" "=" quoted-string
stale                = "stale" "=" ( "true" | "false" )
algorithm            = "algorithm" "=" ( "MD5" | token )
```

In this definition are several pieces of information which the client needs in order to perform the Digest method. The first piece is the realm value. This is the area of the server in which the user must supply a username and password. The second is the nonce value. This value is an opaque string to the client, but it is important for the server to pick a good value. A good value for a nonce would include connection-specific information such as the client IP address, a time-stamp value, and a secret key. These values can be concatenated together and the MD5 digest applied to them to produce the nonce value.

The `opaque` value can be used by the server for any purpose. One intended (or at least possible) purpose is to keep track of state information about a particular user during its connections to the server. The opaque value could be a key into a database to keep a record of various items a user might order when visiting an electronic store. The `stale` value can be used to indicate that the username and realm were correct for the previous authorization request, but the nonce value was not. In this way, the user agent may transparently retry the authorization using the new nonce value as well as the current username and password supplied by the client. The `algorithm` value allows an alternate algorithm to be used with Digest. No other algorithms are thus defined by the specification.

If the server calculates a nonce value in this manner, when the client returns the nonce value in the authorization header, the server can recalculate the nonce value and verify it against the one received. Since the nonce value incorporates the client IP address and a timestamp, it makes it harder for an eavesdropping application to pick up on the connection and try to use the nonce values to gain unauthorized access to documents.

After the authentication challenge, the client performs the digest function over the information, per the previous code example. For the nonprogrammers, the digest is performed over a combination of the username, password, realm value, nonce value, request method, and request URI. This digest is then returned as part of the `Authorization` header as shown by the syntax:

```
Authorization       = "Authorization" ":" "Digest" digest-response

digest-response     = 1#( username | realm | nonce | digest-uri |
                          response | [ digest ] | [ algorithm ] |
                          opaque )

username            = "username" "=" username-value
username-value      = quoted-string
digest-uri          = "uri" "=" digest-uri-value
digest-uri-value    = request-uri          ; As specified by HTTP/1.1
response            = "response" "=" response-digest
digest              = "digest" "=" entity-digest

response-digest     = <"> *LHEX <">
entity-digest       = <"> *LHEX <">
LHEX                = "0" | "1" | "2" | "3" | "4" | "5" | "6" | "7" |
                      "8" | "9" | "a" | "b" | "c" | "d" | "e" | "f"
```

The client returns the `response-digest` containing the digest results along with the necessary information such as username, realm, and request URI, for the server to calculate the digest and verify it against the client's digest value.

When verified, the server may optionally return the `Authentication-info` header as described earlier in the chapter. This header can be especially useful for servers who wish to implement one-time nonce values by always returning the `nextnonce` value to the client for the next request.

Both the server and client may optionally include an `entity-digest` when allowed by the protocol. This `entity-digest` is an MD5 digest performed over the entity body and certain headers. This can be used by the recipient to verify the accuracy and integrity of the entity body and message headers. If included, it is calculated by:

```
entity-digest = <"> KD (H(A1), unquoted nonce-value ":" Method ":"
                        date ":" entity-info ":" H(entity-body)) <">
                        ; format is <"> *LHEX <">

date = = rfc1123-date               ; see Section 3.3.1 of [2]
entity-info = H(
          digest-uri-value ":"
          media-type ":"            ; Content-type, see Section 3.7 of [2]
          *DIGIT ":"                ; Content length, see 10.12 of [2]
          content-coding ":"        ; Content-encoding, see 3.5 of [2]
          last-modified ":"         ; last modified date, see 10.25 of [2]
          expires                   ; expiration date; see 10.19 of [2]
          )

last-modified   = rfc1123-date      ; see Section 3.3.1 of [2]
expires         = rfc1123-date
```

If a particular header field is not present within a given request or response message, the digest value is calculated with an empty value for that header.

Digest can be subject to some security concerns, which should be understood by clients and servers. The first concern is for *replay attacks*. A replay attack occurs when an eavesdropper listens for the client's authorization request and subsequently tries to use this information to pass itself off as the authorized client. The inclusion of IP addresses and timestamps in the server's calculation of nonce values helps to prevent this. The second form of attack is the *man in the middle* attack. In this attack, a compromised proxy can try to uncover the client's password and usernames for various realms. This can be as simple as substituting Basic Authentication challenges for Digest challenges. The last attack is the *spoofing by counterfeit servers* attack. This involves a server posing as a trusted server and attempting to compromise passwords or information from the client. Implementors should refer to the complete discussion of these attacks as presented in the Digest specification.

6.4 Implementation

In this section we will look at how a server might build responses to typical HTTP requests using the same www.example.com server as in Chapter 3.

6.4.1 GET and HEAD

For our first example, let's look at the following request message:

```
GET /public/products.html HTTP/1.1
Host: www.example.com
User-Agent: JoeBrowser/1.1
From: phethmon@hethmon.com
Accept-Encoding:
Accept: text/html, text/plain
If-Modified-Since: Fri, 15 Nov 1996 04:33:29 GMT
```

In order to service this request, the server must do a few things. The first step will be to resolve the given request-URI to the actual resource on the machine. For most general purpose servers, this is usually provided through a mapping directive in a configuration file. The accompanying server on the CD uses a directive of the form:

```
PathAlias / h:/www/htdocs/
PathAlias /images h:/www/images/
```

So once the request-URI is parsed from the request line, the server must do simple pattern matching to determine the actual disk location of the resource. Once located, the server must check to see if the user can retrieve the resource without authentication. Given that our example is in the public document tree, no authentication is required.

Now the HTTP server must decide whether any of the request headers modify the GET method. In our example, the client has included a conditional header: If-Modified-Since. (See Figure 6.1.) The server must then check the given date against the current date of the resource. The method used in the example server is to convert all dates to time_t values. This way, all date values are expressed in seconds, relative to the epoch date of January 1, 1970. Manipulating and comparing dates expressed in this way is very convenient.

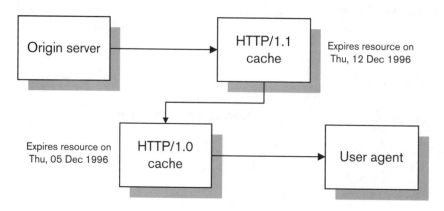

Figure 6.1   Response chain with caches

If the resource has been modified since the given date, then the server simply returns the resource with a 200 status code:

```
HTTP/1.1 200 OK
Date: Thu, 28 Nov 1996 16:09:21 GMT
Server: 3wd/1.1
ETag: "849196010"
Last-Modified: Thu, 28 Nov 1996 15:46:23 GMT
Cache-Control: max-age=604800
Expires: Thu, 05 Dec 1996 16:09:21 GMT
Content-Type: text/html
Content-Length: 3488

[3488 bytes of entity body]
```

If the resource had not been modified since the `If-Modified-Since` date, then a `304` response would be sent:

```
HTTP/1.1 304 Not Modified
Date: Thu, 28 Nov 1996 16:09:21 GMT
Server: 3wd/1.1
ETag: "848032384"
Last-Modified: Fri, 15 Nov 1996 04:33:29 GMT
Cache-Control: max-age=1209600
Expires: Thu, 05 Dec 1996 16:09:21 GMT
```

The two responses mentioned also show the approach of giving HTTP/1.1 caches more leeway than HTTP/1.0 caches. The `Expires` header is set to a constant one week past the date of the response while the `max-age` directive varies on the age of the resource. The newer resource receives a `max-age` value of 1 week, while the older resource received a `max-age` value of 2 weeks, on the theory that a resource which has not changed recently is not likely to change as soon in the future. The server also provides entity tags in the responses. For our simple file based server, the entity tag is given as the last modified date in seconds since the epoch date. This is a reasonable entity tag because we can be confident on a file-based and manually updated server, that no single resource is likely to be updated twice within a single second. If your resources are subject to being updated twice within a single second, then this approach cannot be used. Entity tags must be guaranteed unique across different instances of a resource.

The use of entity tags and last modified dates in conditional requests brings us up to the whole issue of handling the `If` headers. Upon closely examining the protocol specification, one finds the use of `If` headers is allowed generally on any request. Furthermore, there are no restrictions on using more than one `If` header in a single request. This leads to the ability for a client to specify a paradox of `If` headers. For an example, consider a client specifying an `If-Modified-Since` time of x and an `If-Unmodified-Since` time of y. There are circumstances where both headers could be used in a single request, perhaps to only perform an action on a resource with a timestamp between certain hours. But, it also leads to a client's being able to specify time x as being less than or equal to time y:

```
If-Modified-Since: Thu, 28 Nov 1996 17:01:00 GMT
If-Unmodified-Since: Thu, 28 Nov 1996 16:01:00 GMT
```

We have a paradox of conditions here. It is not possible to satisfy both conditions at once. In circumstances such as this, the developer must use common sense and reject the request outright with a `400 Bad Request` response. Another potential conflict is between the `If-Match` and `If-None-Match` headers. These both accept entity tags as a value. If the same entity tag is given in both headers, in the same request, then a conflict exists and should be responded to with a `400` response also.

6.4.2 GET and byte range requests

Our next example here is to show how a client may request a byte range retrieval of a resource and how the server responds to it. First, we'll assume the client is once again browsing our favorite Web site at `www.example.com`. In the course of the client's browsing, it sends a request of the form:

```
GET /public/products.html HTTP/1.1
Host: www.example.com
User-Agent: JoeBrowser/1.1
From: zach@zacaroo.com
If-Match: "729473730912"
Range: bytes=0-300,1200-1250,1500-
```

In this request message, the client indicates the exact resource to send back by the use of the `If-Match` request header. This header includes an entity tag to match against the current resource before performing the requested operation. A `Range` header is also included, listing the three byte ranges for which the client is asking. (See Figure 6.2.)

Upon validating the entity tag sent by the client, together with the current entity tag for the resource, the server must then

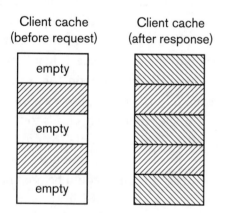

Figure 6.2   Client cache

parse the `Range` header to find the requested byte ranges. The code to parse out the byte ranges is presented in Chapter 8 hereof as part of the HTTP/1.1 server explanation. Once having determined what to send back, the server must begin to do so. The response headers would consist of:

```
HTTP/1.1 206 Partial Content
Server: 3wd/1.1
Date: Tue, 03 Dec 1996 01:45:12 GMT
Last-Modified: Mon, 02 Dec 1996 13:03:13 GMT
ETag: "729473730912"
Cache-Control: max-age=1209600
Content-Type: multipart/byteranges; boundary="a284jvxwo84384dd830"

--a284jvxwo84384dd830
Content-Type: text/html
Content-Range: bytes 0-300/2000

[301 bytes of entity body]
--a284jvxwo84384dd830
Content-Type: text/html
Content-Range: bytes 1200-1250/2000

[50 bytes of entity body]
--a284jvxwo84384dd830
Content-Type: text/html
Content-Range: bytes 1500-1999/2000

[499 bytes of entity body]
--a284jvxwo84384dd830--
```

This is the most complex way to send back byte ranges to a client. When sending back multiple byte ranges, the server must construct a MIME-like header showing the boundary element, which will delimit the different pieces. Within each piece, the server includes the Content-Type showing the media type of this particular part (although all parts of the resource should be the same type, proper syntax requires it in each part) and the Content-Range showing the particular place in the overall entity in which this part belongs.

The definition of multipart types is defined in RFC 1521 at the moment. It is included on the CD enclosed herewith and worth looking over for the general discussion of multipart types and selection of boundary markers. Specifically, therein is shown a boundary marker delimited by double quote marks. The double quote marks are not part of the boundary, but instead serve as a quoting mechanism similar to their use in entity tags.

6.4.3 GET and content negotiation

In this example let us consider a client which uses the `Accept-*` headers to try and receive the best possible representation for the user. To do this the client sends the following request:

```
GET /public/sales.html HTTP/1.1
Host: www.example.com
User-Agent: JoeBrowser/2.2
From: zach@zacaroo.com
Accept: text/html, text/plain;q=0.8
Accept-Charset: ISO-8859-1, UNICODE-1-1;q=0.5
Accept-Language: en, en-gb;q=0.7, fr;q=0.2
```

Breaking down this request, the client is relaying several pieces of information to the server. First, for media types, the client is expressing a first preference for text/html. The text/plain type can be sent, but is considered 20% less favorable than text/html. For character sets, ISO-8859-1 has the highest preference and unicode-1-1 is acceptable after a 50% markdown. The client lists two variations of English as the preferred natural language, but will also accept French if absolutely necessary.

When the server receives this request, it compares these values against the various documents it may store to serve this URI. Consider whether the server has the following variations of the resource available:

- Media types:
  - text/html
  - text/plain
  - application/pdf
- Character sets
  - ISO-8859-1
  - ISO-8859-2
- Languages
  - English
  - Spanish
  - French

The server has a document with which to respond across all combinations of these parameters. So, after performing server-driven negotiation, it would send this response message:

```
HTTP/1.1 200 OK
Server: 3wd/1.1
Date: Tue, 03 Dec 1996 02:40:56 GMT
Last-Modified: Mon, 25 Nov 1996 13:03:22 GMT
ETag: "dks936npe210eqq584"
Cache-Control: max-age=1209600
Vary: Accept, Accept-Charset, Accept-Language
Content-Type: text/html; charset=ISO-8859-1
Content-Language: en
Content-Length: 5288

[5288 bytes of entity data]
```

In this response, the server has indicated the parameters over which the server-driven negotiation has occurred in the `Vary` header. The server must include this field whenever it performs server-driven negotiation in order for cache agents to properly cache the response. The server further includes the appropriate `Content-*` headers describing the entity.

6.5 *Finishing*

This chapter presents the last of the protocol information about HTTP/1.1. In the next chapter we will look into more code examples by presenting sockets and a socket class.

chapter 7

Sockets

7.1 *The socket*

The socket is the basic mechanism used by programs to communicate in the TCP/IP world. In simple terms, it is a communications link between two programs across a TCP/IP network. Sockets have their beginnings in BSD UNIX from around 1982. At that time, the Internet was developing into the form as we know it today. The Defense Advanced Research Projects Agency (DARPA) had funded the ARPANET, beginning in the 1970s. The original ARPANET connected military, university, and research sites across the United States with a packet-switched network. This network consisted mainly of leased telephone lines, although it did include experimentation with radio networks and satellite communications.

In the early 1980s, BSD UNIX was growing in popularity among university computer science departments. To encourage the use of the new TCP/IP protocols that DARPA research had created, they made an implementation of them available at a low cost. DARPA funded Bolt Beranek and Newman, Inc., to implement TCP/IP on a UNIX system and the University of California at Berkeley did likewise to integrate TCP/IP into its BSD UNIX software. By doing this, DARPA was able to reach most computer science departments in the United States and ensure the success of the socket and TCP/IP protocols.

The `sockaddr` structure defined in the `<sys\socket.h>` header file defines a socket address. Also used with the `sockaddr` structure are `struct in_addr` and `struct sockaddr_in`.

```
#include <sys\socket.h>
struct sockaddr
{
  u_short sa_family;    /* address family */
  char    sa_date[14];  /* protocol specific information */
};

#include <netinet\in.h>
struct in_addr
{
  u_long s_addr;  /* 32 bit host address, network byte order */
};

struct sockaddr_in
```

```
{
  short    sin_family;        /* AF_INET family */
  u_short  sin_port;          /* 16 bit port number */
  struct   in_addr sin_addr;  /* 32 bit host address */
  char     sin_zero[8];       /* set to zero, not used */
};
```

The `sa_family` field of the `sockaddr` structure defines which addressing family is being used with the socket. `AF_INET` is the address family we will be using. Other families include `AF_UNIX`, `AF_NS`, and `AF_IMPLINK`. When the `sockaddr` structure is used with the `AF_INET` family, it is overlaid with the `sockaddr_in` structure. In simple terms, this means that the socket calls expect a structure of type `sockaddr`. When using the calls with the `AF_INET` family, use the `sockaddr_in` structure and cast it to the `sockaddr` structure in the function call.

In the `sockaddr_in` structure, `sin_family` corresponds to the `sa_family` field of the `sockaddr` structure and is always set to `AF_INET`. `sin_port` is the 16-bit port number in network byte order, while `sin_addr` is the 32-bit host address in network byte order. `sin_zero` is not used and is set to zero. In a typical server application, the `sin_port` field will be set to the well-known port number for the server, while the `sin_addr` field will be set to `INADDR_ANY`. By setting the host address to `INADDR_ANY`, the system will accept connections from any internet interface. The client program is only slightly different, in that it will set the specific `sin_addr` field to the host address of the server to which it wishes to connect.

7.2 Setting up the server socket

The first API call to be used is `socket()`.

```
#include <sys\types.h>
#include <sys\socket.h>

int socket(int family, int type, int protocol);
```

`family` is set to `AF_INET`, as outlined in the last section. `type` specifies the type of socket to be created. The possible values are `SOCK_STREAM`,

SOCK_DGRAM, and SOCK_RAW. For this book, we will be using the SOCK_STREAM only. The combination of AF_INET and SOCK_STREAM yield a TCP socket. With SOCK_DGRAM, a UDP socket would be created, while SOCK_RAW gives access to the IP protocol. The protocol field is typically set to zero, which means the system selects the correct protocol based on the first two parameters. The return value from socket() will be –1 in case of error, or will return the socket number otherwise.

Once a socket is allocated in a server application, the next API to be logically used is bind().

```
#include <sys\types.h>
#include <sys\socket.h>

int bind(int s, struct sockaddr *addr, int addrlen);
```

The bind call is used to assign a name to a socket. s is the socket number previously allocated while addr is the protocol specific structure holding the address. The size of the structure is specified in the addrlen parameter. With TCP, the structure used is of type struct sockaddr_in. bind() is used to tell the system that your application wants any messages received for the given address. For a server application such as FTPD or HTTPD, use the well known port address of these servers in the call. You may specify any port for the bind call, given the operating system restrictions. UNIX systems restrict the ports below 1024 to the superuser (root) only. If the port is already in use by another process, the call to bind will fail. The exception to this is, if the socket option SO_REUSEADDR has been set, using the setsockopt() call. By setting this option, the system will give control of the port to your program, taking it away from the previous process using the port. A positive return value indicates success.

Once our server is bound to a port, the socket must be set to passive mode in order to accept connections from the clients. To accomplish this, the listen() call is used:

```
#include <sys\types.h>
#include <sys\socket.h>

int listen(int s, int backlog);
```

As before, s is the socket number, `backlog` is the maximum number of requests the system will queue. For most systems, the maximum allowed is five. To make the program more flexible, the constant SOMAXCONN can be used. This constant is defined in the header files to the current maximum value allowed. Once a socket is placed in passive mode, it cannot be used to initiate connections, but only accept them. A positive value indicates success.

One last call is needed by the server in order to establish connections: `accept()`:

```
#include <sys\types.h>
#include <sys\socket.h>

int accept(int s, struct sockaddr *client, int *addrlen);
```

The `accept()` call causes the calling process to either accept a connection from a client or be blocked until such a connection occurs. If the call returns successfully, a new socket will have been created that is connected to the client. The new socket number is the return value from `accept()`. At this point, you will have created what many books call a 5-tuple. A 5-tuple is simply the set of data that defines a unique connection between two processes across a TCP/IP socket. It consists of the following: a socket number, a server IP address, a server port, a client IP address, and a client port.

These four calls are all that is necessary to create a minimal server. The following example shows just that:

```
#include <sys\types.h>
#include <sys\socket.h>
#include <netinet\in.h>

void main(int argc, char *argv[])
{
  int  s,     // our socket
       rc,    // return code
       c,     // client socket
       len;   // length of structure
  struct sockaddr_in server, client;

  s = socket(AF_INET, SOCK_STREAM, 0);  // create a socket
  if (s < 0)
    {
```

```
      cerr << "Error! Cannot create socket." << endl;
      return;
   }

len = sizeof(struct sockaddr_in);
bzero(server, len);  // clear the data
server.sin_family = AF_INET;
server.sin_port = htons(7777);
server.sin_addr = INADDR_ANY;
rc = bind(s, (struct sockaddr *) &server, len);
if (rc < 0)
   {
      cerr << "Error! Bind failed." << endl;
      return;
   }

rc = listen(s, SOMAXCONN);  // change to passive socket
if (rc < 0)
   {
      cerr << "Error! Listen failed." << endl;
      return;
   }

for( ; ; )
   {
      bzero(&client, len);
      c = accept(s, (struct sockaddr *)&client, &len);
      if (c < 0)
        {
           cerr << "Error! Accept failed." << endl;
           return;
        }

      // do some work with new socket c to client
      close(c);
   }
}
```

This example follows the API calls as outlined previously. A socket is allocated first, using the `socket()` call. If successful, the socket is bound to port 7777 using the `bind()` call. The use of port 7777 is an arbitrary one, as any port could be used. Port 7777 is above the range of the reserved and well-known ports for such services as HTTP and SMTP (80 and 25 respectively). The line

```
server.sin_port = htons(7777);
```

does introduce one concept not yet mentioned. In the TCP/IP world, the range of machines goes from PCs to supercomputers using various CPUs. To overcome the problem of the machine representation of an integer being different on a Motorola 68040 than on an Intel Pentium Pro, the concept of network byte order is used. Network byte order uses big endian notation such as on the Motorola 68000 series of processors. On machines that use big endian notation, `htons()` will be defined as a null macro. For machines that use the little endian notation, it will swap the byte ordering. It is always a good idea to use the byte swapping routines even if you know the machine you're targeting is big endian. With the proliferation of processors and the ability of operating systems to run on many platforms, you never know where your code will end up.

Once the `bind()` call completes, the socket is placed into passive mode with the `listen()` call. At this point, the server is ready to accept incoming connections. A loop is used to cycle the server through the accept cycle. The cycle starts by clearing the data structure used for the client information. `accept()` is then called to complete the connection. Upon successful completion of the `accept()` call, the necessary processing between the client and server takes place. Depending on the operating system, this processing would take place by starting a new process (UNIX), or by starting a new thread (OS/2 and NT). For a very simple server, the processing could take place in the same process as the accept call, but that would risk the possibility of dropping a waiting connection.

7.3 Setting up the client socket

The procedure for setting up the client program starts out the same as for the server, that is, a socket is allocated with the `socket()` call. After that, the client is ready to establish a connection with a server. The call used to do this is `connect()`.

```
#include <sys\types.h>
#include <sys\socket.h>

int connect(int s, struct sockaddr *server, int len);
```

As before, s is the socket handle from the socket() call. server is the struct sockaddr_in structure. It specifies the server to which it wishes to connect by filling in the address and port fields. The last parameter, len, is the size of parameter two. When connect completes successfully, a connection is established between the client and server with another 5-tuple. A negative return value indicates failure.

The following example shows a simple client:

```
#include <sys\types.h>
#include <sys\socket.h>
#include <netinet\in.h>

// this program expects the server address as a parameter

void main(int argc, char *argv[])
{
   int  s,   // the socket handle
        rc;  // return code
   struct sockaddr_in server;

   if (argc != 2)
     {
       cerr << "Error! Incorrect number of arguments." << endl;
       return;
     }

   s = socket(AF_INET, SOCK_STREAM, 0);
   if (s < 0)
     {
       cerr << "Error! Cannot create socket." << endl;
       return;
     }

   bzero(&server, sizeof(struct sockaddr_in);
   server.sin_family = AF_INET;
   server.sin_port = htons(7777);
   server.sin_addr = inet_addr(argv[1]);  // use command line address

   rc = connect(s, (struct sockaddr *) &server,
              sizeof(struct sockaddr_in));
   if (rc < 0)
     {
       cerr << "Error! Connect failed." << endl;
       return;
     }
```

```
  // do some processing of data between client and server

  close(s);
}
```

While simple, this example shows the four basic steps that a client application must perform. The first step is to create a socket. Next a connection must be made to the server. The actual data processing is performed and the last step is to close the socket.

7.4 Data transmission

Since we are dealing with stream sockets, the data transmission which occurs is simply a byte stream. There are no inherent records or signals for the end of a message, hence the application must supply it. The typical signal for the end of a data transmission in the Internet protocols is the Telnet end-of-line sequence. This sequence is defined as a carriage return, followed by a line feed. You will note this is also the end-of-line marker for OS/2 and NT. TCP/IP has several different APIs available for sending and receiving data. The two that we'll be using in this book are:

```
#include <sys\types.h>
#include <sys\socket.h>

int send(int s, char *msg, int len, int flags);
int recv(int s, char *msg, int len, int flags);
```

In both calls, the first parameter s refers to the socket number on which to perform the operation. msg is the buffer holding the data to be sent, for send(), or the buffer area to receive the data, for recv(). The next parameter, len, holds the length of the data for send(), and the length of the message buffer for recv(). The flags parameter is used to modify the behavior of the calls. Some of the flags available include MSG_OOB and MSG_PEEK. MSG_OOB refers to placing out-of-bound data in-bound while MSG_PEEK is used for the recv() call in order to receive the waiting data, but not consume it. The data is left for later calls to read.

Before we delve into the use of these calls, one point of TCP communications needs to be addressed. When a process transmits data using the `send()` call, it will request a certain number of bytes to be sent. However, there is no guarantee that the number of bytes requested to be sent will be the number of bytes actually sent. So, it may be necessary to resend part of the buffer because it was not sent on the first call. Likewise, when receiving data using the `recv()` call, you may allocate a buffer of 1024 bytes and set your length to that number. To the protocol stack, the length is just the maximum length you will accept. You will only receive the number of bytes available. Multiple `recv()`s will be needed to insure receiving the number of bytes your process needs.

Now we see the need for the Telnet end-of-line sequence in Web and Internet protocols. The processes which are communicating need a way to signal each other that the command has ended. The easiest way to accomplish this is to have a special function to read lines from the socket. The next example shows the `RecvLine()` function which does this:

```
#include <sys\types.h>
#include <sys\socket.h>

// Receive a command line terminated by a telnet eol sequence

int RecvLine(int iSocket, char *szBuf, int iLen)
{
    int  iBytesRead,
         iIdx,
         bNotDone;

    iBytesRead = recv(iSocket, &szBuf[0], 1, 0);
    iIdx = 1;
    bNotDone = TRUE;

    while (bNotDone == TRUE)
      {
        iBytesRead = recv(iSocket, &szBuf[iIdx], 1, 0);
        if (iBytesRead < 0)
          {
            return ( -1 );  // error receiving
          }

        iIdx++;
        if ( (szBuf[iIdx - 2] == '\r') &&
```

```
            (szBuf[iIdx - 1] == '\n')      )
          {
            bNotDone = FALSE;   // got telnet eol
          }
        if (iIdx == iLen)
          {
            return ( -1 ); // error, buffer too small
          }
      }

   szBuf[iIdx - 2] = NULL;   // append null termination
   return ( TRUE );
}
```

This example shows a simple way to receive a command line typically used in Internet protocols such as HTTP, FTP, or SMTP. The function takes three arguments which are the same as the first three arguments of recv(). The fourth argument of recv() is not used and is left at 0. It starts by reading a single character from the socket. Since our aim is to read until we have a telnet end-of-line sequence, we must have a minimum of two characters. The first character is read outside of the loop to ensure that we have at least two when we check. We next enter the reading loop. A character is read and the return code is checked for an error. If there is no error, then the string is checked for the end-of-line sequence. We also check for a possible overrun of the message buffer. Finally, once the end-of-line sequence has been read, the buffer is null terminated at the end of the message. We discard the end-of-line sequence.

The drawback of this approach is that receiving one character at a time is an expensive operation. A much better approach would be to receive as many characters as are available and then inspect the buffer until the end-of-line sequence is reached. In order to accomplish this effectively, a C++ class could be used to encapsulate the socket. With the class approach, you can easily maintain a buffer of data for each socket used in the system. Fortunately, most command lines are small, less than a few dozen characters. For an efficient implementation, I would recommend using C++ classes and we'll do that later in this chapter.

Now, let us take a look at how we would use the send() and recv() functions in our simple client:

```
#include <sys\types.h>
#include <sys\socket.h>
```

```
#include <netinet\in.h>
#include <iostream.h>
#include <string.h>

// this program expects the server address as a parameter

void main(int argc, char *argv[])
{
  int s,                      // the socket handle
      rc;                     // return code
  char szBuf[256];            // data buffer
  struct sockaddr_in server;  // server address

  if (argc != 2)
    {
      cerr << "Error! Incorrect number of arguments." << endl;
      return;
    }

  s = socket(AF_INET, SOCK_STREAM, 0);
  if (s < 0)
    {
      cerr << "Error! Cannot create socket." << endl;
      return;
    }

  bzero(&server, sizeof(struct sockaddr_in);
  server.sin_family = AF_INET;
  server.sin_port = htons(7777);
  server.sin_addr = inet_addr(argv[1]);   // use command line address

  rc = connect(s, (struct sockaddr *) &server,
               sizeof(struct sockaddr_in));
  if (rc < 0)
    {
      cerr << "Error! Connect failed." << endl;
      return;
    }

  // do some processing of data between client and server
  strcpy(szBuf, "HELLO\r\n");
  rc = send(s, szBuf, strlen(szBuf), 0);
  if (rc < 0)
    {
      cerr << "Error! Send failed." << endl;
      return;
    }
```

```
rc = RecvLine(s, szBuf, 256);
if (rc < 0)
   {
     cerr << "Error! RecvLine failed." << endl;
     return;
   }

if (strcmp(szBuf, "OK") != 0)
   {
     cerr << "Error! Unknown reply from server." << endl;
     return;
   }

strcpy(szBuf, "GOODBYE\r\n");
rc = send(s, szBuf, strlen(szBuf), 0);
if (rc < 0)
   {
     cerr << "Error! Send failed." << endl;
     return;
   }

rc = RecvLine(s, szBuf, 256);
if (rc < 0)
   {
     cerr << "Error! RecvLine failed." << endl;
     return;
   }

if (strcmp(szBuf, "OK") != 0)
   {
     cerr << "Error! Unknown reply from server." << endl;
     return;
   }

close(s);
}
```

This example is the same as our first client example, only with the addition of code to exchange messages with the server. The logic is simple. Once the client is connected to the remote server, a simple greeting is sent. The client then checks for the server's response. If it receives the OK reply it expects, it then sends a closing message of GOODBYE. The OK reply is expected again and checked before the client closes the connection to the server.

On the server side, things have changed only slightly:

```
#include <sys\types.h>
#include <sys\socket.h>
#include <netinet\in.h>
#include <iostream.h>
#include <string.h>

void main(int argc, char *argv[])
{
  int s,            // our socket
      rc,           // return code
      c,            // client socket
      len;          // length of structure
  struct sockaddr_in server, client;

    s = socket(AF_INET, SOCK_STREAM, 0);   // create a socket
  if (s < 0)
     {
       cerr << "Error! Cannot create socket." << endl;
       return;
     }

  len = sizeof(struct sockaddr_in);

  bzero(server, len);  // clear the data
  server.sin_family = AF_INET;
  server.sin_port = htons(7777);
  server.sin_addr = INADDR_ANY;
  rc = bind(s, (struct sockaddr *) &server, len);
  if (rc < 0)
     {
       cerr << "Error! Bind failed." << endl;
       return;
     }

  rc = listen(s, SOMAXCONN);   // change to passive socket
  if (rc < 0)
     {
       cerr << "Error! Listen failed." << endl;
       return;
     }

  for( ; ; )  // forever
     {
       bzero(&client, len);
       c = accept(s, (struct sockaddr *)&client, &len);
       if (c < 0)
          {
```

```
                    cerr << "Error! Accept failed." << endl;
                    return;
                }

            // do some work with new socket c to client
            TalkToClient(c);
        }
}

// -------------------------------------------------------------

void TalkToClient(int iSocket)
{
    int iRc,
        bNotDone;
    char szBuf[256],
         szOk[] = "OK",
         szErr[] = "ERR";
    bNotDone = TRUE;

    while (bNotDone == TRUE)
        {
            iRc = RecvLine(iSocket, szBuf, 256);
            if (iRc < 0)
                {
                    cerr << "Error! RecvLine failed." << endl;
                    bNotDone = FALSE;
                }
            if (strcmp(szBuf, "HELLO") == 0)
                {
                    iRc = send(iSocket, szOk, strlen(szOk), 0);
                    if (iRc < 0)
                        {
                            cerr << "Error! Send failed." << endl;
                            bNotDone = FALSE
                }
            else if (strcmp(szBuf, "GOODBYE") == 0)
                {
                    iRc = send(iSocket, szOk, strlen(szOk), 0);
                    if (iRc < 0)
                        {
                            cerr << "Error! Send failed." << endl;
                            bNotDone = FALSE
                        }
                    bNotDone = FALSE;  // close connection on GOODBYE
```

```
        }
     else // unknown message
        {
           send(iSocket, szErr, strlen(szErr), 0);
           bNotDone = FALSE;
        }
     }

   close(iSocket);
}
```

The revised server example has a function `TalkToClient()` added to it to handle all communications with the connecting clients. In this function, the server goes into a loop, receiving messages from the remote client. Upon receiving the HELLO message, the server responds with an OK reply. If the GOODBYE message is received, then the OK reply is sent and the Boolean flag is marked FALSE to end the connection. If the server receives any other messages, then the ERR reply is sent and the connection is closed.

Although the example server does no real work, it does model the work flow of a real server. Connections are accepted in a loop and a function handles the work. In a real server, the difference would be that another process or thread would be used to handle the work function. Under OS/2, the typical code would look like this:

```
_beginthread(TalkToClient, 0, 8192, (void *)NULL);
```

This function starts a new thread of execution on the `TalkToClient()` function. Under Linux, the `fork()` call is used to start a new process:

```
if (fork() == 0)
  {
    close(s);
    TalkToClient(c);
    return;
  }
```

Either method produces the same results. Another thread of execution handles the connection to the currently connected client so that the server can go back to accepting more connections.

7.5 Utility routines

The `htons()` function was mentioned briefly before. Other than this function, several others exist for TCP/IP programming. The first to mention includes:

```
#include <sys\types.h>
#include <sys\socket.h>

u_short htons(short int i);
u_long htonl(long int i);
short int ntohs(u_short i);
long int ntohl(u_long i);
```

The first function, `htons()`, has already been discussed. The second function, `htonl()`, works the same as `htons()` except that it operates on `long` values. The function takes a `long` value on the local machine and translates it to network byte order. As before, on big endian machines, this translates to a null macro. It should still be used in all code for portability. The next two functions work the other way. They take values in network byte order and translate them to the local machine byte ordering. `ntohs()` handles `short` values, while `ntohl()` handles the `long` values.

These functions will always be used when dealing with parameters to the various socket calls and data structures. All socket calls and data structures expect values in network byte order. If supplying a constant value to a socket call, such as the port number, be sure to use the appropriate byte swapping routine.

7.6 Host name and address routines

To deal with the many ways addresses can be written, several function calls are available. The first two handle address translation to and from dotted decimal notation and 32-bit addresses:

```
#include <sys\types.h>
#include <sys\socket.h>
```

```
#include <netinet\in.h>
#include <arpa\inet.h>

u_long inet_addr(char *addr);
char * inet_ntoa(struct in_addr in);
```

inet_addr() provides a way to translate from a dotted decimal notation character string to the 32-bit Internet address. This means that you can take an address such as 128.169.15.22 and translate it to the machine form that the TCP/IP stack needs. When starting out with the network byte order address and wanting the dotted decimal notation, the inet_ntoa() is used. There are other functions which provide similar services. However, these two provide the bulk of what is routinely used.

The next two functions provide host information based on the struct hostent data structure:

```
#include <netdb.h>

struct   hostent
{
  char *h_name;
  char **h_aliases;
  int h_addrtype;
  int h_length;
  char **h_addr_list;
  #define h_addr h_addr_list[0]
};

struct hostent * gethostbyaddr(char *addr, int len, int domain);
struct hostent * gethostbyname(char *hostname);
```

First, let us talk about the fields in the struct hostent structure. The first field is h_name and contains the official hostname. h_aliases contains a list of aliases for the host. Currently, the h_addrtype is always set to AF_INET and the h_length is set to 4. A list of Internet addresses is found in the h_addr_list field. h_addr is defined for backward compatibility. For the Internet addresses with which we are dealing, the h_addr_list[0], h_addr_list[1], and so forth, point to in_addr structures.

When using gethostbyaddr(), addr will point to a network byte order address, typically a in_addr structure. The second parameter, len, contains the length and the third parameter, domain, is the domain type (set to AF_INET). This call is typically used to gather information about a remote host. A server could use this call to obtain the hostname of the remote client to log. You should note that in today's Internet, not all hosts have hostnames. Don't expect this call to always return a name. Check the value of h_name to make certain that it is current and not null.

The gethostbyname() call and gethostbyaddr(), return the same information. The difference is that you provide it with a hostname such as hops.ag.utk.edu.* A client application would more typically use this call to resolve a name provided by a user to an address to use in the connect() call.

The next call is getpeername():

```
#include <sys\types.h>
#include <sys\socket.h>

int getpeername(int s, struct sockaddr *addr, int len);
```

This call is very useful to server applications. The first parameter refers to the socket number in which you are interested. addr will actually be a struct sockaddr_in for the Internet domain. The final parameter is simply the length of parameter two. Using this call, the server application can determine who the client is, and with whom it was connected in the accept() call. From this information, the hostname can then be determined. For security purposes, the address returned can be checked against a list of allowable addresses. After a call to getpeername(), a call to gethostbyaddr() would be made to determine the hostname.

7.7 NT specifics

Programming under Windows NT uses the standard Winsock interface. Under Winsock, the program must first check to make sure socket services are available, and that the version of Winsock requested is available. Including the individual

---

* Yes it's real.

socket header files is also unnecessary. Just include `winsock.h` to pull in all of the header information:

```
WORD wVersionRequested;
WSADATA wsaData;
wVersionRequested = MAKEWORD(1, 1);

iRc = WSAStartup(wVersionRequested, &wsaData);
if (iRc != 0)
  {
    cerr << "Error!" << endl;
    cerr << "Socket services not available. Exiting." << endl;
    return 1;
  }
```

The foregoing bit of code presented must be used to check for Winsock availability in each program using the Winsock library. The specific version of Winsock requested is placed in `wVersionRequested` using the `MAKEWORD` macro to place one part in the high two bytes and the other part in the lower two bytes of the `WORD` sized variable. `wsaData` holds more specific data.

Once a program is finished, `WSACleanup()` must be called to ensure that the Winsock library releases any resources still allocated for the sockets used by the current program.

7.8 OS/2 specifics

The IBM TCP/IP implementation is virtually the standard BSD style socket we've been discussing. There are some differences however. The first and probably the biggest difference is that sockets under OS/2 are not file handles. This means the standard C library routines `read()` and `write()` do not work. This is the reason for sticking with the standard socket functions `send()` and `recv()` for unfailing data transmission.

Socket handles are also global across OS/2 processes. This means that processes under OS/2 can pass socket handles back and forth. Of course, there is always a catch to situations such as this and IBM is no exception. In the current implementation of TCP/IP, IBM has a few undocumented calls used to pass sockets between processes. These are used by the INETD superserver IBM provides to pass socket handles to the child processes for the various daemons. It will be necessary to add declarations for these calls in your header files if you wish to use them:

```
int _System removesocketfromlist(int s);
void _System addsockettolist(int s);
```

The return value from `removesocketfromlist()` is 1, if successful, and 0, if the socket could not be found. Both calls take, as a single argument, the socket handle. If socket handles ever become file handles under OS/2, these calls are likely to disappear, so use them with great care. The INETD superserver would use the `removesocketfromlist()` call before starting the requested daemon. The daemon started should then call `addsockettolist()` to ascertain the socket number associated with it.

The reason for this is that OS/2 keeps a global list of socket numbers and the process associated with them. When the process ends, if the necessary cleanup was not done by the program, the TCP/IP kernel will clean up for it. This means if the parent program were to end and has not called `removesocketfromlist()`, then the TCP/IP kernel would close the socket which the child process was using.

Another call that is necessary in OS/2 programs that use sockets is that of an initialization call:

```
int sock_init();
```

Since OS/2 doesn't ship in default form with TCP/IP support, this call checks to see that TCP/IP support has been enabled and is working. It should be used before any other socket call in your program.

Another side effect of sockets not being file handles is that `close()` cannot be used to close a socket. Instead, a call to `soclose()` must be made. The syntax is the same as the standard C library `close()`.

The last difference which should be mentioned is that socket calls under OS/2 do not set the global error value `errno`. Instead, TCP/IP maintains its own global error value. This value can be accessed by the following calls:

```
int sock_errno();
void psock_errno(char *msg);
```

The `sock_errno()` call returns the error value associated with the previous socket call. `psock_errno()` is similar to `perrno()`. It prints the socket error plus the message passed to it.

7.9 *The socket class*

Once you start to program in C++ and add in sockets, the next progression is to ask yourself why not create a socket class to handle all of the grunt work? There are many neat things you can do with sockets, once you encapsulate them into a class with persistent data and methods. Some procedures which come to mind include buffering incoming data, combining socket calls, and creating methods for sending files. Let us look next at the class definition we will use throughout the rest of this book:

```
//
// Socket   File: socket.hpp
//
//
// Copyright 1996 Paul S. Hethmon
//
// Prepared for the book "Illustrated Guide to HTTP"
//

//
// Socket Class
//

#ifndef _SOCKET_HPP_
#define _SOCKET_HPP_

#include <memory.h>
#include <string.h>
#include <iostream.h>
#include <fstream.h>

#ifdef __OS2__
   #include <os2.h>
   #define OS2          // This is needed for the socket header files
   #include <types.h>
   #include <netdb.h>
```

```
   #include <sys\types.h>
   #include <sys\socket.h>
   #include <netinet\in_systm.h>
   #include <netinet\in.h>
   #include <netinet\ip.h>
#elif __WINDOWS__
   #include <windows.h>
   #include <winsock.h>
   #define soclose(x) closesocket(x)
   #define bzero(x, y) memset((x), '\0', (y))
#endif

#include "defines.hpp"

// --------------------------------------------------------------------

// Define this to the size of the largest ascii line of
// data your application expects to receive.
#define MAX_SOCK_BUFFER  16384
#define NO_EOL 1
#define REUSE_PORT 1

class Socket
{
  public:

  Socket()
    {
       iLen = sizeof(siUs);
       iSock = -1;
       iErr = 0;
       szOutBuf = new char[MAX_SOCK_BUFFER];
       szBuf1 = new char[MAX_SOCK_BUFFER/2];
       szBuf2 = new char[MAX_SOCK_BUFFER/2];
       iBeg1 = iEnd1 = iBeg2 = iEnd2 = 0;
       iBuf = 1;
       szPeerIp = NULL;
       szPeerName = NULL;
       ulTimeout = 5 * 60;   // 5 minutes default.
    };
  ~Socket()
    {
       if (iSock > -1) soclose(iSock);
       delete [] szOutBuf;
       delete [] szBuf1;
       delete [] szBuf2;
```

```
      if (szPeerIp) delete [] szPeerIp;
      if (szPeerName) delete [] szPeerName;
    };

int Create()                    // Allocate a socket for use
    {
      iSock = socket(AF_INET, SOCK_STREAM, 0);
      return iSock;
    };
int Passive(short int sPort)    // Turn the socket into a passive
    {                           // socket. Do not set SO_REUSEADDR.
      return(Passive(sPort, 0));
    }
int Passive(short int sPort,    // Turn the socket into a passive
            int iReuse);        // socket. Allow setting of
                                // SO_REUSEADDR.
Socket * Accept();              // Listen for connections.
int Connect(char *szBuf, short sPort);// Connect the socket to the
                                // remote host.
int Recv()                      // Receive bytes on this
    {                           // socket.
      return(Recv(MAX_SOCK_BUFFER));
    }
int Recv(int iBytes);           // Receive up to iBytes on this
                                // socket.
int RecvTeol()                  // Receive up to the telnet eol.
    {
      return(RecvTeol(0));      // Include the telnet eol.
    }
int RecvTeol(int iToast);       // Receive up to the telnet eol
                                // and possibly remove the telnet
                                // eol.
int Send(char *szBuf, int iLen)  // Send the buffer on this socket.
    {
      return send(iSock, szBuf, iLen, 0);
    };
int Send(char *szBuf)           // Send the text buffer on this
    {                           // socket.
      return send(iSock, szBuf, strlen(szBuf), 0);
    };
int Send(const char *szBuf)     // Send the text buffer on this
    {                           // socket.
      return send(iSock, (char *)szBuf, strlen(szBuf), 0);
    };
int SendText(char *szFileName);// Send this text file across the
                                // socket.
```

```
    int SendBinary(char *szFileName);// Send this binary file across
                                // the socket.
    int ResolveName();              // Look up the ip address and name
                                // of the peer.
    int Close()                     // Close this socket.
      {
        iBeg1 = iEnd1 = iBeg2 = iEnd2 = 0;
        iBuf = 1;
        memset(szOutBuf, 0, MAX_SOCK_BUFFER);
        memset(szBuf1, 0, MAX_SOCK_BUFFER/2);
        memset(szBuf2, 0, MAX_SOCK_BUFFER/2);
        if (szPeerIp) delete [] szPeerIp;
        if (szPeerName) delete [] szPeerName;
        szPeerIp = NULL;
        szPeerName = NULL;
        ulTimeout = 5 * 60;  // 5 minutes default.
        iErr = soclose(iSock);
        iSock = -1;
        return iErr;
      };

    int iSock;                      // The socket number allocated.
    int iErr;                       // The last error code on a socket
                                // call.
    char *szOutBuf;                 // Used to return data in.
    char *szPeerName;               // The ip name of the peer
                                // connected.
    char *szPeerIp;                 // The ip address of the peer
                                // connected.
    unsigned long ulTimeout;        // The timeout for receives in
                                // seconds.

    protected:

    struct sockaddr_in siUs;    // Our address
    struct sockaddr_in siThem;  // Their address
    short int sPortUs;          // Our port
    short int sPortThem;        // Their port
    int iLen;                   // The size of siUs and siThem
    int iBuf;                   // Active buffer flag.
    char *szBuf1, *szBuf2;      // Internal buffers.
    int iBeg1, iEnd1,           // Buffer markers.
       iBeg2, iEnd2;
};

#endif
```

Let us go over the data members first, since they define the elements with which our interface works. Starting in the `public:` section of the definition, we have defined two integer values, `iSock` and `iErr`. `iSock` is simply the socket number used by this instance of the socket class. It is the same number returned by the normal C `socket()` call. `iErr` contains the last error value reported by a socket call. The next variable, `szOutBuf`, is of particular importance. It provides the space where incoming data is returned to the calling program. Normally, in a `recv()` call, data is returned in the buffer which is passed to the call. Since we're encapsulating the actual call to `recv()`, the socket class needs to provide a data buffer to store the incoming data. This also lets us determine the size of the data buffer, which proves useful to simplify some algorithms in the class methods. The next two hold values for the IP name and address of the remote peer. `szPeerName` holds the peer name while `szPeerIp` holds the IP address. Note that not all Internet hosts have IP names, but all will have IP addresses. The last variable, `ulTimeout`, is used to specify the number of seconds to wait in a `recv()` call before timing out.

These five variables are defined in the `public:` section of the class so that the programmer can have direct access, if need be. The socket class does not provide a method to every possible socket operation. When other socket operations are needed, such as `ioctl()` or `setsockopt()`, the socket number is available for those operations. Exposing `iErr` makes the error information accessible, while access to `szOutBuf` is mandatory.

Entering the `protected` section, we first define to `sockaddr_in` structures to be used for socket operations. Also defined is the variable `iLen`, which holds the size of the structure for the many socket calls which require it as a parameter. `sPortUs` and `sPortThem` hold the values for the port numbers used to connect our system with the remote system.

The last set of variables is used in the buffering of incoming data on the socket. In a typical connection, much of the data received consists of ASCII lines of data terminated (hopefully) by the TELNET end-of-line sequence, the carriage return line feed. Simple implementations will grab a single character at a time in the receive operation until the end-of-line is encountered. The negative effect of this is the hundreds (if not thousands) of times a system call has to be made, imposing a performance penalty. To overcome this, we will use two buffers for incoming data in a round-robin fashion. The `iBuf` variable is the marker for the active buffer, while `szBuf1` and `szBuf2` are the data buffers themselves. The last four variables, `iBeg1`, `iEnd1`, `iBeg2`, and `iEnd2`, are used to index properly into the data buffers.

7.10 The socket class methods

Now that we have defined the data members of our socket class, we need to define the methods we want to have available. The first two methods to be defined are our constructor and destructor. The third method is our method to actually allocate a socket. All three methods are defined inline in the header file:

```
Socket()
   {
     iLen = sizeof(siUs);
     iSock = -1;
     iErr = 0;
     szOutBuf = new char[MAX_SOCK_BUFFER];
     szBuf1 = new char[MAX_SOCK_BUFFER/2];
     szBuf2 = new char[MAX_SOCK_BUFFER/2];
     iBeg1 = iEnd1 = iBeg2 = iEnd2 = 0;
     iBuf = 1;
     szPeerIp = NULL;
     szPeerName = NULL;
     ulTimeout = 5 * 60;   // 5 minutes default.
   };
~Socket()
   {
     if (iSock > -1) soclose(iSock);
     delete [] szOutBuf;
     delete [] szBuf1;
     delete [] szBuf2;
     if (szPeerIp) delete [] szPeerIp;
     if (szPeerName) delete [] szPeerName;
   };
int Create()                     // Allocate a socket for use
   {
     iSock = socket(AF_INET, SOCK_STREAM, 0);
     return iSock;
   };
```

The first thing to note about the `Socket()` constructor is that an actual socket is *not* allocated in it. Some basic housekeeping duties are performed, including allocating internal buffers and calculating the size of the `sockaddr_in` structure. Index values associated with the receive buffers are also initialized to their default values. By constructing the class in this manner, we allow ourselves to easily reuse an instance of the class with multiple sockets. Only the data members which are used across multiple sockets are initialized.

In the destructor method, a final check of the socket number is made to make certain any socket resources in use are freed by the application. In an operating system, such as OS/2 which has a finite number of sockets in the system, it is especially important to make sure the resources are returned to the system pool. The other task charged to the destructor is deallocating the memory used for the internal buffers.

The third method, `Create()`, actually starts to do some real work. `Create()` is used to allocate a socket to the class instance. You should note the socket allocated is a TCP stream socket. For UDP and non-stream sockets, more work would have to be done. We leave it narrow here since our use of sockets is limited to TCP stream sockets. The `iSock` variable is set as well in returning the socket number for error checking.

```
int Passive(short int sPort)        // Turn the socket into a passive
  {                                 // socket.
    return(Passive(sPort, 0));      // Do not set SO_REUSEADDR
  }
int Passive(short int sPort         // Turn the socket into a
          int iReuse);              // passive socket
Socket * Accept();                  // Listen for connections
int Connect(char *szBuf, short sPort);// Connect the socket to the
                                    // remote host
```

Our next three methods start to show the real benefits of using a socket class over standard C socket calls. `Passive()`, `Accept()`, and `Connect()` all encompass several socket calls into a single class method. It not only makes it easier to code, it reduces the chances of errors creeping in.

`Passive()` turns our regular socket into a passive socket to listen for connections, a typical practice for TCP/IP servers. The code required to do this normally takes several lines and a couple of different socket calls. When we turn it into a class method, a one-parameter call is all that is required.

```
int
Socket::Passive(short int sPort, int iReuse)
{
  int optval = 1;

  if (iReuse > 0)  // Force reuse of the address.
    {
    setsockopt(iSock, SOL_SOCKET, SO_REUSEADDR, (char *) &optval,
          sizeof(int));
    }

  sPortUs = sPort;

  bzero((void *)&siUs, iLen);        // make sure everything zero
  siUs.sin_family = AF_INET;
  siUs.sin_port = htons(sPortUs);
  siUs.sin_addr.s_addr = INADDR_ANY;

  // Bind to the given port
  iErr = bind(iSock, (struct sockaddr *) &siUs, iLen);
  if (iErr < 0)
    {
      return iErr;
    }

  // change to passive socket
  iErr = listen(iSock, SOMAXCONN);
  if (iErr < 0)
    {
      return iErr;
    }

  return 0;
}
```

The second parameter of the `Passive()` needs some explaining. When the `bind()` call was first introduced at the beginning of this chapter, we mentioned a bit about the use and reuse of port addresses. TCP/IP stacks set a timeout, typically about two minutes, between reuses of a port address to prevent stray packets from arriving after one application has ended and another has started and thus possibly causing problems for the new application. In practice for servers, you must use the specified port address if you want clients to be able to contact you. The way to force the TCP/IP stack to do this is to use the `setsockopt()` and specify the `SO_REUSEADDR` flag. We provide a way to do this in the `Passive()` call by specifying a positive value for the second parameter, `iReuse`. If this value is positive, then we set the reuse address option before calling `bind()`.

To allow for further ease of using the `Passive()`, we also define it as taking only one parameter which then defaults to the regular implementation without using the `SO_REUSEADDR` flag. We let the compiler take care of the mapping instead of remembering `Passive()` needs two parameters.

From the example code, the first thing necessary to do is to prepare the `sockaddr_in` data structure `siUs`. We first make sure the entire structure is null using the `bzero()` call, just a shorthand way of calling `memset()`. Once done, the necessary fields are set, and `sin_family` is set to the Internet protocol family using the constant `AF_INET`. The port number, `sin_port`, is set using the supplied port number to the `Passive()` call. Also note that the port number is converted from host byte order to network byte order before assigning a value to `sin_port`. We finally set the `s_addr` field to the constant `INADDR_ANY` indicating we'll accept connections on any IP address on this machine.

Once done, a simple call to `bind()` takes care of binding the socket to a port. We use our `iSock` and `iLen` data members which have been previously set by the `Create()` and `Socket()` methods respectively. Our data member `iErr` is used to handle any error return values from `bind()`. If an error does occur, we return from our class method without completing.

The last step is to actually call `listen()` to place the socket into the passive state. The constant `SO_MAXCONN` is used to specify the maximum number of waiting connections. As before, `iErr` is used to hold any error return codes from `listen()`. If an error code is encountered, then the error code is returned to the calling program. On successful completion, a value of 0 is returned.

```
Socket *
Socket::Accept()
{
   Socket *sSock;

   sSock = new Socket();
```

```
bzero(&siThem, iLen);
sSock->iSock = accept(iSock, (struct sockaddr *)&(sSock->siThem),
                      &iLen);
if (sSock->iSock < 0)
  {
     iErr = sSock->iSock;
     delete sSock;
     return NULL;
  }

sSock->szPeerIp = new char[128];
strncpy(sSock->szPeerIp, inet_ntoa(sSock->siThem.sin_addr), 128);

return sSock;
}
```

The `Accept()` call also hides a few implementation details. It functions as a self-contained way to accept an incoming connection and return a new `Socket()` instance when a connection is accepted. The first step is to allocate a new class instance to be used as a return value. Once done, the `siThem` data member is zeroed out in anticipation of being filled by the `accept()` call. Finally, the actual `accept()` call is made and the socket number returned is checked to see if it is valid. If we fail, we deallocate the class instance, set the error variable and return null. On successful completion, we allocate space in the `szPeerIp` character string and save the IP address of the peer which connected to us. The last thing we do is return the new `Socket` class instance.

```
int
Socket::Connect(char *szBuf, short sPort)
{
   struct hostent *heHost;

   heHost = gethostbyname(szBuf);
   if (heHost == NULL)
     {
        return (iErr = 1);
     }

   bzero((void *)&siUs, iLen);       // make sure everything zero
   siUs.sin_family = AF_INET;
   siUs.sin_port = htons(sPort);
   siUs.sin_addr.s_addr = *((u_long *)heHost->h_addr);
```

```
    iErr = connect(iSock, (sockaddr *)&siUs, iLen);
    return (iErr);
}
```

The third method, `Connect()`, handles the client side of operations as opposed to `Passive()` and `Accept()`, which are geared toward servers. `Connect()` accepts two parameters, the first is the hostname with which to connect, and the second is the port number at which to connect. Our next step is to find the network address of the hostname by using the `gethostbyname()` call to return a `hostent` structure. We return an error if we cannot find the network address of the given host. On success, we proceed to fill out the `siUs` variable similar to the `Passive()` call.

The difference between the calls is the address assigned to `s_addr`. This time, we need to specify the host with whom to explicitly connect, and we must be careful about it. You will notice the way in which the value is assigned to the `s_addr` field. The reason is the `s_addr` field is declared to be of type `ulong *` while the `h_addr` field of the `hostent` structure is of type `char *`. We first cast `h_addr` to be of the correct type, and then we must dereference the pointer so the value is copied and not the pointer address.

Once the data structures are ready, a simple call to `connect()` is made to connect to the remote host. If successful, `iErr` will be assigned a value of zero. On error, it will be assigned a value of −1. Either way, the work for the class method is done, so the value is simply returned without checking.

The next two class methods work together to provide buffered storage for incoming data:

```
int Recv()                      // Receive bytes on this socket.
  {
    return(Recv(MAX_SOCK_BUFFER));
  }
int Recv(int iBytes);           // Receive up to iBytes on this
                                // socket.
int RecvTeol()                  // Receive up to the telnet eol.
  {
    return(RecvTeol(0));        // Include the telnet eol.
  }
int RecvTeol(int iToast);       // Receive up to the telnet eol
                                // and possibly remove the telnet
                                // eol.
```

We define two versions of Recv(). The first receives the maximum number of bytes on a socket that the class instance can hold. It simply redirects to the real code, which allows us to specify exactly how many bytes we want to read from the socket. This allows an easy implementation of persistent connections later. Let us look at the code for Recv():

```
// --------------------------------------------------------------
//
// Recv
//
// Receive up to iBytes on this socket.
//

int
Socket::Recv(int iBytes)
{
#ifdef __OS2__
  int fdsSocks[1];
#elif __WINDOWS__
  fd_set fdsSocks;
  struct timeval stTimeout;
#endif

  memset(szOutBuf, 0, MAX_SOCK_BUFFER);

  if ((iBuf == 1) && (iEnd1 != 0))  // Copy the contents of buf 1.
    {
      if (iBytes >= (iEnd1 - iBeg1))  // Copy all the bytes.
        {
          memcpy(szOutBuf, szBuf1 + iBeg1, iEnd1 - iBeg1);
          iErr = iEnd1 - iBeg1;
          iBeg1 = iEnd1 = 0;
          iBuf = 2;
        }
      else  // Only copy the requested number.
        {
          memcpy(szOutBuf, szBuf1 + iBeg1, iBytes);
          iErr = iBytes;     // This many bytes sent back.
          iBeg1 += iBytes;   // Advance to this location.
        }
    }
  else if ((iBuf == 2) && (iEnd2 != 0)) // Copy the contents of buf 2.
    {
      if (iBytes >= (iEnd2 - iBeg2))
        {
```

```
            memcpy(szOutBuf, szBuf2 + iBeg2, iEnd2 - iBeg2);
            iErr = iEnd2 - iBeg2;
            iBeg2 = iEnd2 = 0;
            iBuf = 1;
        }
      else
        {
            memcpy(szOutBuf, szBuf2 + iBeg2, iBytes);
            iErr = iBytes;
            iBeg1 += iBytes;
        }
    }
  else
    {
#ifdef __OS2__
      fdsSocks[0] = iSock;
      iErr = select(fdsSocks, 1, 0, 0, ulTimeout * 1000);
      if (iErr < 1) // Error occured.
        {
            return -1;
        }
#elif __WINDOWS__
      FD_ZERO(&fdsSocks);
      FD_SET(iSock, &fdsSocks);
      stTimeout.tv_sec = ulTimeout;
      iErr = select(1, &fdsSocks, 0, 0, &stTimeout);
      if (iErr < 1) // Error occured.
        {
            return -1;
        }
#endif
      iErr = recv(iSock, szOutBuf, iBytes, 0);
      if (iErr == 0) return -1;
    }

  return iErr;
}


// ----------------------------------------------------------------
```

This function looks to the two internal buffers of the Socket() class, first to see if any data is left over from a previous call to RecvTeol(). The internal buffer flag, iBuf, is checked to see which buffer it points to. Also checked is the corresponding end-of-data flag, either iEnd1 or iEnd2. Once the correct buffer is determined and if data is present in it, then it must check how many bytes to copy from the internal buffer to the public buffer. The `if` statement checks whether to copy the rest of the internal buffer or only the requested number of bytes. The data is copied into `szOutBuf`, using a `memcpy()` call. It is important to note `memcpy()` must be used here. The socket class has no knowledge of whether the incoming data is binary or text, so the buffer pointers must be kept and a byte copying routine used.

On the second call to `Recv()`, the internal buffers will again be checked. If the other internal buffer has data in it, the same procedure is followed. However, once both internal buffers have been emptied, then the `szOutBuf` buffer is filled directly. By handling the receipt of data in this way, we allow ourselves to buffer the data for the `RecvTeol()` call where it is needed while still providing the greatest efficiency when transferring large chunks of binary data.

Whenever we are ready to actually request a `recv()`, we take one additional step to prevent excessive blocking. A call to `select()` is made on the socket to determine if any data is available to be read. The default time-out value specified by the class `ctor` is five minutes. If no data is received before the specified time, then `select()` will return an error and then we return an error to the caller. The caller would normally terminate the connection at this point. Under OS/2, we use the OS/2 style select-call which uses an array of socket numbers, plus the numbers of read, write, and exception sockets to monitor. Under Winsock, we use the familiar BSD style `select()`. Both are functionally equivalent, but use slightly different syntax.

One last note about `Recv()` is that it is the application's responsibility to check how many bytes are returned. It might be less than the requested number and most certainly will be for any request size larger than the internal buffers. The calling function must maintain an algorithm to adjust the number of bytes it requests on each call dynamically as bytes are received.

```
// -------------------------------------------------------------
//
// RecvTeol
//
// Receive a line delimited nominally by the telnet end-of-line
// sequence -- CRLF. This one also accepts just CR or just LF
// also.
//
int
```

```
Socket::RecvTeol(int iToast)
{
  int i;
  int iState = 1,
      idx = 0;
#ifdef __OS2__
  int fdsSocks[1];
#elif __WINDOWS__
  fd_set fdsSocks;
  struct timeval stTimeout;
#endif

  memset(szOutBuf, 0, MAX_SOCK_BUFFER);

  while (iState != 0)
    {
      switch (iState)
        {
          case 1:  // Figure out where to start.
            {
              if ((iEnd1 == 0) && (iEnd2 == 0))    // Both buffers
                {                                  // empty.
                  iState = 2;
                }
              else
                {
                  iState = 3;
                }
              break;
            }
          case 2:  // Fill the buffers with data.
            {
#ifdef __OS2__
              fdsSocks[0] = iSock;
              iErr = select(fdsSocks, 1, 0, 0, ulTimeout * 1000);
              if (iErr < 1) // Error occured.
                {
                  return -1;
                }
#elif __WINDOWS__
              FD_ZERO(&fdsSocks);
              FD_SET(iSock, &fdsSocks);
              stTimeout.tv_sec = ulTimeout;
              iErr = select(1, &fdsSocks, 0, 0, &stTimeout);
              if (iErr < 1) // Error occured.
                {
                  return -1;
```

```
              }
#endif
            iErr = recv(iSock, szBuf1, MAX_SOCK_BUFFER/2, 0);
            if (iErr == -1)   // Error receiving data.
              {
                iState = 0;
                break;
              }
            iBeg1 = 0;
            iEnd1 = iErr;
            if (iErr == MAX_SOCK_BUFFER/2)   // Filled up Buffer 1.
              {
#ifdef __OS2__
                fdsSocks[0] = iSock;
                Err = select(fdsSocks, 1, 0, 0, ulTimeout * 1000);
                if (iErr < 1) // Error occured.
                  {
                    return -1;
                  }
#elif __WINDOWS__
                FD_ZERO(&fdsSocks);
                FD_SET(iSock, &fdsSocks);
                stTimeout.tv_sec = ulTimeout;
                iErr = select(1, &fdsSocks, 0, 0, &stTimeout);
                if (iErr < 1) // Error occured.
                  {
                    return -1;
                  }
#endif
                iErr = recv(iSock, szBuf2, MAX_SOCK_BUFFER/2, 0);
                if (iErr == -1)   // Error receiving data.
                  {
                    iState = 0;
                    break;
                  }
                iBeg2 = 0;
                iEnd2 = iErr;
              }
            iBuf = 1;
            iState = 3;   // Advance to the next state.
            break;
          }
        case 3:   // Look for the EOL sequence.
          {
            if ((iBuf == 1) && (iEnd1 != 0))   // Use Buffer 1 first.
              {
                for ( ; iBeg1 < iEnd1; iBeg1++)
```

```
          {
        szOutBuf[idx] = szBuf1[iBeg1];    // Copy.
        if ((szOutBuf[idx] == '\n') ||
            (szOutBuf[idx] == '\r')      )
          {
            iBeg1++;     // Count the char just read.
            if ((szOutBuf[idx] == '\r') &&
                (szBuf1[iBeg1] == '\n')     )
              {
                // Using CRLF as end-of-line.
                idx++;
                szOutBuf[idx] = szBuf1[iBeg1];
                iBeg1++;                    // Consume LF.0
              }
            szOutBuf[idx + 1] = '\0';// True. Null Line
            iState = 4;              // Goto cleanup & exit.
            break;                   // Break from for loop.
          }
        idx++;                          // Advance to next spot.
        if ((idx+1) == MAX_SOCK_BUFFER) // Out of room.
          {
            szOutBuf[MAX_SOCK_BUFFER] = '\0';
            iState = 4;
            break;
          }
      }
    if (iBeg1 == iEnd1) iBeg1 = iEnd1 = 0;    // Reset.
    if (iState == 3)    iBuf = 2; // EOL not found yet.
  }
else if ((iBuf == 2) && (iEnd2 != 0))  // Use Buffer 2.
  {
    for ( ; iBeg2 < iEnd2; iBeg2++)
      {
        szOutBuf[idx] = szBuf2[iBeg2];    // Copy.
        if ((szOutBuf[idx] == '\n') ||
            (szOutBuf[idx] == '\r')      )
          {
            iBeg2++;          // Count the char just read
            if ((szOutBuf[idx] == '\r') &&
                (szBuf2[iBeg2] == '\n')     )
              {
                // Using CRLF as end-of-line.
                idx++;
                szOutBuf[idx] = szBuf2[iBeg2];
                iBeg2++;
              }
            szOutBuf[idx + 1] = '\0';// True. Null line.
```

```
                        iState = 4;              // Goto cleanup & exit.
                        break;                   // Break from for loop.
                      }
                      idx++;                     // Advance to next spot.
                      if ((idx+1) == MAX_SOCK_BUFFER) // Out of room.
                        {
                          szOutBuf[MAX_SOCK_BUFFER] = '\0';
                          iState = 4;
                          break;
                        }
                    }
                  if (iBeg2 == iEnd2) iBeg2 = iEnd2 = 0;    // Reset.
                  if (iState == 3)     iBuf = 1;  // EOL not found yet.
                }
              else  // Both buffers empty and still no eol.
                {
                  if (idx < MAX_SOCK_BUFFER)
                    {
                      iState = 2;  // Still room. Refill the buffers.
                    }
                  else
                    {
                      iState = 4;  // Out of room. Return.
                    }
                }
              break;
            }
          case 4:  // Cleanup and exit.
            {
              iState = 0;
              break;
            }
        } // End of switch statement.
    } // End of while loop.

  if (iToast > 0)   // Remove the telnet end-of-line before returning.
    {
      while ( (szOutBuf[idx] == '\r') || (szOutBuf[idx] == '\n') )
        {
          szOutBuf[idx] = '\0';
          idx--;
        }
    }

  return (idx + 1);
}
// ---------------------------------------------------------------
```

THE SOCKET CLASS METHODS

The `RecvTeol()` method is designed to efficiently receive lines delimited by either the TELNET end-of-line sequence, a carriage return followed by a line feed, by a line feed, or by a carriage return. We define two interfaces to the function in the header file. The first method is returned as a call to the second, with the second parameter set to zero. This tells the class method to include the TELNET end-of-line characters in the string that is returned. The second implementation leaves it as an option to the programmer. If `iToast` is set greater than zero, then the class method will remove the TELNET end-of-line characters before returning the line.

Many implementations of this function will receive a byte at a time looking for the end-of-line sequence. The implementation here buffers the data it receives and then looks for the end-of-line sequence. In order to do this in an easy manner, two internal buffers are created which are used in a round-robin fashion. In addition, the buffers are half the size of the output buffer, thus easing some of the internal code. The size of these internal buffers is defined at compile time by the `MAX_SOCK_BUFFER` constant. For greatest efficiency, this should be defined at least the size of the biggest line you would expect to receive. The method works fine if lines are larger, but then the calling code will have to check whether or not the end-of-line sequence was found.

The method is implemented as a state machine with four states. (See Figure 7.1.) Each of the states is represented by a `case` statement. The entire switch statement is then encompassed by a `while` statement, which loops until an ending condition is reached. State 1 determines whether data exists in either internal buffer. If data doesn't exist, then the state is moved to State 2. If data does exist, then the state advances to State 3. The presence of data is determined by the value of the end-of-buffer flags. These flags will be non-zero when data is present and zero if the buffer is empty.

State 2 is used to fill the internal buffers with data. To make life easier, neither buffer is filled unless both are empty. As in the `Recv()` method, `select()` is used to determine whether data is present to read and to time-out the connection when it is not. When the buffers are filled by the `recv()` call, `szBuf1` is filled first. If `szBuf1` is filled by the call to `recv()`, then an attempt is made to also fill `szBuf2`. The thinking here is that most text lines received will be shorter than the internal buffer size. In most instances, a single `recv()` call will capture

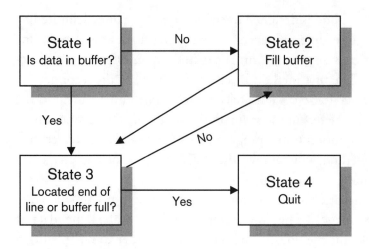

Figure 7.1   Four-state operation

the entire line into the internal buffer. From that point, it is a simple matter to find the end-of-line sequence. If `szBuf1` is filled, then it is likely we will need the data which `recv()` then places in `szBuf2`. Once the buffers are filled, the state advances to State 3.

The hard work is done in State 3. This is where we have to locate the end-of-line sequence. We start by finding out which internal buffer is the current one and if it has any data in it. Once found, we start looking for the end-of-line sequence, character-by-character. The code here looks for either a carriage return, or line feed. Once either is found, we look at the next character in the buffer. If we find a carriage return and line feed in sequence, then we take both, otherwise, just the one we found originally. This allows us to accept either CRLF, CR, or LF as the end-of-line sequence. For HTTP, we must be able to accept all three ways.

Also checked within the loop is whether the out buffer is full. We allow the buffer to fill up to one less than the maximum before stopping the copy sequence and appending the null. In this situation, the calling program must check the buffer for the end-of-line sequence. Good practice dictates the check always be made. Once the condition is reached to stop the copy operation, the state is advanced to State 4.

The other condition for exiting the copying loop is for the internal buffer to run out of data. In this situation, the current internal buffer is reset to mark it

THE SOCKET CLASS METHODS

empty and the buffer flag is set to the other internal buffer. The state stays in State 3 and loops around the `while` loop again to re-enter State 3 and repeat the process for the second internal buffer. If this still does not locate the end-of-line sequence, and both buffers are empty, the last `else` clause will execute, causing the internal buffers to be refilled and the process starts again.

Once State 4 is entered, cleanup activities take place. The `iState` variable is set to zero to cause the enclosing `while` loop to fail and the function to return. The value returned is the number of bytes copied into the out buffer. The ability to buffer data on a per-socket basis is probably the best and most practical reason for using a C++ class.

The final operation is to check if the method call was made using the flag to remove the TELNET end-of-line sequence. If so, we start at the end of the string, looking for either \r or \n. As long as we find either of these characters, we set them to NULL and continue to look for more. This step also takes care to decrement the length value returned.

The next three methods handle sending data and files to the connected peer:

```
int Send(char *szBuf, int iLen)    // Send the buffer on this socket.
  {
    return send(iSock, szBuf, iLen, 0);
  };
int Send(char *szBuf)              // Send the text buffer on this
  {                                // socket.
    return send(iSock, szBuf, strlen(szBuf), 0);
  };
int Send(const char *szBuf)        // Send the text buffer on this
  {                                // socket.
    return send(iSock, (char *)szBuf, strlen(szBuf), 0);
  };
int SendText(char *szFileName);    // Send this text file across the
                                   // socket.
int SendBinary(char *szFileName);  // Send this binary file across the
                                   // socket.
```

The first three methods are simple inlines of the TCP/IP `send()` function. The necessary parameters are filled in for the call and the data is sent. For the first, we require the length of the data to be sent to allow for binary data which may contain the NULL character. The second method for `Send()` can be used for sending text strings. It explicitly finds the length of the string. The third handles const strings. For sending files, we look to the next method:

```
// --------------------------------------------------------------
//
// SendText
//
// Send the specified file across the socket. This assumes
// a text file.
//

int
Socket::SendText(char *szFileName)
{
   ifstream ifIn;
   char *szBuf;

   ifIn.open(szFileName);
   if (! ifIn)
     {
        return -1;
     }

   szBuf = new char[BUFSIZE];
   iErr = 0;
   do
     {
        memset(szBuf, 0, BUFSIZE);
        ifIn.getline(szBuf, BUFSIZE, '\n');
        iErr += send(iSock, szBuf, strlen(szBuf), 0);// The line.
        if ( ifIn.eof() ) break;              // The last line
                                              // doesn't get an
                                              // eol appended.
        iErr += send(iSock, "\r\n", strlen("\r\n"), 0); // The eol.
     }
   while ( ! ifIn.eof() );

   ifIn.close();
   delete [] szBuf;
   return iErr;
}

// --------------------------------------------------------------
```

`SendText()` is a straightforward method to send a text file across the connection. It takes a single argument which is the name of the file to send. The method starts by opening the file. If the file cannot be opened, an error value of −1 is returned. Standard `ifstreams` are used to access the file. Next, memory is dynamically allocated for a buffer to read a file using the `getline()` method of `ifstream`. The function then enters a `while` loop checking for the end-of-file condition for termination. As each line of the file is read, it is sent across the socket connection. Also, for each line sent, a proper TELNET end-of-line sequence is sent. The last line of the file does not get the TELNET end-of-line appended as this would add bytes to the total of the file. The last step is to close the file and delete the temporary buffer. `iErr` is used for the return code.

```
int
Socket::SendBinary(char *szFileName)
{
   ifstream ifIn;
   char *szBuf;

   ifIn.open(szFileName, ios::binary);
   if (! ifIn)
      {
         return -1;
      }

   szBuf = new char[BUFSIZE];

   while ( ! ifIn.eof() )
      {
         ifIn.read(szBuf, BUFSIZE);
         iErr = send(iSock, szBuf, ifIn.gcount(), 0);    // The line
      }

   ifIn.close();
   delete [] szBuf;
   return iErr;
}
```

`SendBinary()` is an almost exact duplicate of the `SendText()` method. A few things need to change in order to accommodate the reading and sending of binary data. The first change is in the `open()` call, where we specify the mode of opening as `ios::binary`. The next change is in the call used to read the data from the file. Where before, we used the `getline()` call, this time we cannot use it, so we must use a call which handles unformatted data, `read()`. The `read()` call simply reads bytes from the file, up to the size specified. In order to account for a different amount of bytes being read than was requested, we must find out how many for the `send()` call. We use the standard `gcount()` call to determine the number of bytes read and thus the number of bytes to send. Once the file is sent, the `ifstream` is closed, the temporary buffer is deleted and we return the `iErr` value.

```
int ResolveName();   // Look up the ip address and name of the peer
```

`ResolveName()` can be used by the calling process to look up the hostname of the machine on the other end of the socket connection:

```
// ----------------------------------------------------------------
//
// ResolveName
//
// Look up the name of the peer connected to this socket.
//

int
Socket::ResolveName()
{
   struct hostent *hePeer;

   if (szPeerIp == NULL)  // Only if we don't have it already.
   {
       szPeerIp = new char[128];
       strncpy(szPeerIp, inet_ntoa(siThem.sin_addr), 128);
     }
   szPeerName = new char[128];
   hePeer = gethostbyaddr((char *)&(siThem.sin_addr),
                       sizeof(struct in_addr), AF_INET);
   if (hePeer != NULL)  // We found the ip name.
     {
        strncpy(szPeerName, hePeer->h_name, 128);
        iErr = 0;        // Good return.
     }
   else                  // No name available for this host.
     {
        strncpy(szPeerName, szPeerIp, 128);
        iErr = -1;       // Bad return.
```

```
    }

  return iErr;
}

// ------------------------------------------------------------------
```

The method first checks to make sure the IP address of the peer connection has been copied into the `szPeerIp` variable. Next it calls `gethostbyaddr()` to obtain the IP name of the peer from the DNS system. The return value must be checked to make certain the lookup succeeded. Many hosts on the Internet today are not assigned IP names and thus, `hePeer` is assigned a `NULL` value. If the call did succeed, then the IP name is copied into `szPeerName`. On failure, the IP address is used instead.

Our last method is `Close()`. It closes the socket and re-initializes the data structures so that the class instance may be used again. Doing it this way, we can avoid the overhead of creating a new instance of the class each time:

```
int Close()                    // Close this socket
  {
    iBeg1 = iEnd1 = iBeg2 = iEnd2 = 0;
    memset(szOutBuf, 0, MAX_SOCK_BUFFER);
    memset(szBuf1, 0, MAX_SOCK_BUFFER/2);
    memset(szBuf2, 0, MAX_SOCK_BUFFER/2);
    if (szPeerIp) delete [] szPeerIp;
    if (szPeerName) delete [] szPeerName;
    szPeerIp = NULL;
    szPeerName = NULL;
    ulTimeout = 10;
    iErr = soclose(iSock);
    iSock = -1;
    return iErr;
  };
```

7.11 Finishing

Now that we have seen how to use sockets and construct a socket class, the following chapter will guide you through a complete HTTP/1.1 server.

chapter 8

The HTTP/1.1 server

Since HTTP/1.1 has not yet reached standard status, the code in appendix hereto is based on the latest Internet Draft 7, dated August 12, 1996, which has been approved by the IESG as a proposed standard, but has not been processed by the RFC editor as this is written. By the time this book is in print, the proposed standard should be available from the Internic. You should retrieve a copy to check if any changes were made necessitating code changes in the server. If changes were necessary, you may contact me at `phethmon@hethmon.com` to learn where to obtain the updated code.

What is presented here is an explanation of the HTTP server on the accompanying CD. In some places, you will be referred to the CD to look at some of the code. The code in those sections is fairly straightforward and the comments in the code should be sufficient. The parts of the code which implement the protocol directly, and are perhaps a bit tricky, are fully explained.

8.1 The configuration file

We'll start by looking over the configuration file which controls how the server behaves:

```
#
# 3wd configuration file
#

ServerRoot h:\book\server1.1

#
HostName Warp.rmt.utk.edu

#
Port 80

#
DNSLookup On

# The offset in minutes between local time and GMT
# Where hhmm is the format. This value plus local time
# should equal GMT.
GMTOffset 0400
```

```
#
Welcome welcome.html

#
AccessLog h:\book\server1.0\access.log

#
ErrorLog h:\book\server1.0\error.log

#
LogTime GMT

# Filename used for read access authorizations
ReadAccessName 3wdread

# Filename used for write access authorizations
WriteAccessName 3wdwrite

#
# PathAlias is used to map document tree aliases to real locations
#
# Up to 128 path aliases allowed.
#
PathAlias /1.0 h:/book/server1.0/
PathAlias /1.1 h:/book/server1.1/
PathAlias /0.9 h:/book/server0.9b/
PathAlias /images h:/book/images/


#
# ExecAlias is used to map cgi-bin aliases to real locations
#
# Up to 128 exec aliases allowed.
#
ExecAlias /cgi-bin h:/book/server1.1/cgi-bin

#
# DeleteDir is used to put store deleted resources
#
DeleteDir h:/book/server1.1/delete/

#
# ExtType is used to map file extensions to the appropriate MIME type.
# MIME types beginning with "text/" are assumed to be text format, all
# others are assumed binary and transmitted as such.
#
# Up to 256 extensions allowed.
```

```
#
ExtType html      text/html
ExtType htm       text/html
ExtType txt       text/plain
ExtType text      text/plain
ExtType readme    text/plain
ExtType me        text/plain
ExtType cmd       text/plain
ExtType doc       text/plain
ExtType faq       text/plain
ExtType cpp       text/plain
ExtType hpp       text/plain
ExtType c         text/plain
ExtType h         text/plain
ExtType jpeg      image/jpeg
ExtType jpg       image/jpeg
ExtType jpe       image/jpeg
ExtType gif       image/gif
ExtType tiff      image/tiff
ExtType tif       image/tiff
ExtType bmp       image/bmp
ExtType au        audio/basic
ExtType wav       audio/x-wav
ExtType wave      audio/x-wav
ExtType snd       audio/basic
ExtType mid       audio/x-midi
ExtType midi      audio/x-midi
ExtType avi       video/avi
ExtType mpeg      video/mpeg
ExtType mpg       video/mpeg
ExtType mpe       video/mpeg
ExtType inf       application/x-view
ExtType pdf       application/pdf
ExtType zip       application/unzip
ExtType exe       application/octet-stream
ExtType ps        application/postscript
ExtType dvi       application/x-dvi
```

Our configuration file starts out, as before, by specifying a default server root, hostname, and DNS lookup. These items are fairly self-explanatory. However the next variable, GMTOffset is used to tell the server the proper time relationship between local time and GMT (or UTC) standard. Due to the variances in support for establishing GMT under OS/2 and NT, we'll depend on the user to tell us the explicit difference in hours and minutes. The Welcome variable gives the default filename to use if one is not specified by the client. `AccessLog` and `ErrorLog` control where the respective access and error files are written. The `LogTime` variable tells the server whether to use local time or GMT within the log files.

In order to implement basic authentication, the server must have a way to determine who has the proper authorization to view or change documents. This includes access for methods such as GET and POST, but also the PUT and DELETE methods. The access permissions need to be able to be specified independently of one another however, so resources may be viewed by anyone, but only updated by those with authorization:

```
# Filename used for read access authorizations
ReadAccessName 3wdread

# Filename used for write access authorizations
WriteAccessName 3wdwrite
```

The former applies only to read access while the latter applies to write access to files. Depending on the operation requested by the client, we check the appropriate permissions:

Also specified in the file is a place to hold *deleted* resources.

```
#
# DeleteDir is used to put store deleted resources
#
DeleteDir h:/book/server1.1/delete/
```

If this keyword is set, when the remote client deletes a file using the DELETE method, the original file will be stored here. The server administrator must then periodically clean up the delete directory. This allows the user to call up in a panic after having deleted the incorrect resource and to have the cool headed administrator say "no problem."

Then we come to one of the more important directives: `PathAlias`. `PathAlias` is used to specify a translation between the paths requested by clients and the actual location in the file system. This lets us use a URL of the form:

```
http://warp.rmt.utk.edu/1.1
```

This would in turn map to:

```
h:\book\server1.1
```

In use, we can set up different roots for various document trees. It also allows us to optimize some client caching by putting all of our image files in the same directory which can be located by the same relative URL. Given images are some of the biggest items your server will be sending, and the byte savings can be quite large when the same images are repeated on multiple pages.

Our next directive, `ExecAlias`, does the same thing for our CGI scripts as `AliasPath` did for documents. The format is the same as for `AliasPath`. The last directive in the file is used to tell the server what the proper MIME types are for various files in the system. The `ExtType` directive gives the file extension and the proper MIME type to return for it. It allows us to specify that files named `Readme` can be returned as plain text. It will likewise match a filename without an extension.

The source to read and parse the configuration file is presented in `config.cpp` on the CD. The code presented in it is simple and therefore will be skipped here.

8.2 The main program

Now let us take a look at the main function for the server:

```
// ------------------------------------------------------------------

volatile int iAccessLock = 0;   // Ram semaphore for access logfile.
volatile int iErrorLock = 0;    // Ram semaphore for error logfile.
void Stop(int iSig);

// ------------------------------------------------------------------
//
// main()
//
// Our main function and entry point
//
```

```
int main(int argc, char *argv[])
{
  int iPort = WWW_PORT;
  int i,
    iRc;
  char szCmd[512];
  BOOL bNotDone = TRUE;

#ifdef __OS2__
  iRc = sock_init();          // Make sure socket services are available
  if (iRc != 0)
    {
      cerr << "Error!" << endl;
      cerr << "Socket services not available. Exiting." << endl;
      return 1;
    }
#elif __WINDOWS__
  WORD wVersionRequested;
  WSADATA wsaData;
  wVersionRequested = MAKEWORD(1, 1);

  iRc = WSAStartup(wVersionRequested, &wsaData);
  if (iRc != 0)
    {
      cerr << "Error!" << endl;
      cerr << "Socket services not available. Exiting." << endl;
      return 1;
    }
#endif

  iRc = ReadConfig("3wd.cf");
  if ( iRc )
    {
      cerr << "Error!" << endl;
      cerr << "Error reading configuration file. Exiting." << endl;
      return 1;   // Exit on error.
    }

  i = 1;
  while (i < argc)          // Check the command line args
    {
      if (strcmp(argv[i], "-p") == 0)
        {
          // Set the port to user requested
          sPort = (short) atoi(argv[i + 1]);
```

```
            i += 2;
        }
    else                  // Unknown arg, ignore it
        {
            cout << "Unknown argument \"" << argv[i]
                << "\" ignored." << endl;
            i++;
        }
    }

    signal(SIGABRT, (_SigFunc)Stop);
    signal(SIGBREAK, (_SigFunc)Stop);
    signal(SIGINT, (_SigFunc)Stop);
    signal(SIGTERM, (_SigFunc)Stop);

    cout << "w3d> Starting server on port number " << iPort << "."
        << endl;

    Server();

#ifdef __WINDOWS__
    WSACleanup();  // Cleanup for windows sockets.
#endif

    // Now we're done
    return 0;
}

// ------------------------------------------------------------------
//
// Stop
//
// Handle the signals and stop the server.

void Stop(int iSig)
{
#ifdef __WINDOWS__
    WSACleanup();  // Cleanup for windows sockets.
#endif

    exit(0);
}

#endif

// ------------------------------------------------------------------
```

Before our main function, we declare two important variables. iAccess-Lock and iErrorLock are used as RAM semaphores for controlling access to both the access log and error log respectively. Since we're using threads to handle each connection, we must serialize access to the log files. These integer values are used with the fast RAM semaphore functions provided by Visual Age C++. We must take care to initialize the values to zero so the semaphores are free initially.

We start our main function by initializing our socket support for OS/2 with the sock_init() call or for Windows with the WSAStartup() call. Both calls serve to initialize socket support under the respective operating systems.

After this, we read the configuration file using the standard name 3wd.cf. If there is an error, we print out a short error message to standard error and exit. The reading of the configuration file is set before checking the command line arguments on purpose. We want to allow any command line arguments to override the values in the configuration file. To simplify our programming, the global variables are set before we check the command line. This way we do not have to keep a separate set of possible command line variables to hold those values while the configuration file is read.

In the next section, we then read the command line arguments:

```
i = 1;
while (i < argc)          // Check the command line args
  {
    if (strcmp(argv[i], "-p") == 0)
      {
        // Set the port to user requested
        sPort = (short) atoi(argv[i + 1]);
        i += 2;
      }
    else                  // Unknown arg, ignore it
      {
        cerr << "Unknown argument \"" << argv[i]
             << "\" ignored." << endl;
        i++;
      }
  }
```

The first thing to do is to skip over argv[0], as it contains the program name. Our index variable i is set to 1 to start. A while loop is used until i has been incremented past the value of argc, thus checking all of the command line arguments. For our server, the only argument we're supporting is for an alternate port. We look for a -p and if found, use the next argument as the port number. Once that is done, we must increment our index value by 2 to allow for the -p and the port number. Any other argument is ignored and a short error message is sent to standard error.

The next four lines set up the signal handlers to catch a break signal from the user. This is used to allow the server to clean up after itself before closing. Once those are set up, then we call the `Server()` function to actually handle the incoming connections from the client. If `Server()` returns, as would happen on an error condition, then `WSACleanup()` is called for the Winsock version to clean up any remaining sockets. OS/2 will automatically clean up sockets when the program ends. Also shown in the code listing is the signal handler itself, `Stop()`. It is simply called whenever an exception is caught and proceeds to make sure `WSACleanup()` is called for the Winsock version.

8.3 The server

The next part of the server is the function used to listen for requests from clients. This is contained in the function `Server()`:

```
// -------------------------------------------------------------------
//
// This function accepts the incoming connections spawning the threads
// to handle the actual work.
//

void Server()
{
   Socket sSock,         // Our server socket for listening
          *sClient;      // The client socket
   int iRc;              // Integer return code

   cout << "w3d> Using port number " << sPort << "."
        << endl << "w3d> ";

   if (! sSock.Create())    // If failure
     {
       cerr << "Error." << endl;
```

```
        cerr << "Cannot create socket to accept connections." << endl;
        return;
    }

  sSock.Passive(sPort, REUSE_PORT); // Go to passive model

  for ( ; ; )                       // Forever
    {
      sClient = sSock.Accept();  // Listen for incoming connections

      if (sClient != NULL)
        {
          // We established a good connection, start a
          // thread to handle it
          iRc = _beginthread(W3Conn, 0, STACKSIZE, (void *)sClient);
          if ( iRc == -1 )
            {
              // Failure to start thread. Close the connection.
              sClient->Close();
              delete sClient;
            }
        }
    }
}

// ----------------------------------------------------------------
```

Using our socket class, the code here is very simple. The first thing we do is announce on what port we're listening. Next, we create a socket using sSock.Create() from our socket class. If we fail, we announce that and return, otherwise a call to sSock.Passive(sPort, REUSE_PORT) puts our socket into listen mode. We specify the REUSE_PORT option to make sure our daemon receives the port from the TCP/IP stack.

Now at this point, we're ready to accept incoming connections. We start an infinite for loop and wait for a connection in the sSock.Accept() call. Accept() will return a pointer to a new Socket class instance when a connection is made. We verify that the class instance is valid and then call _beginthread() to handle the connection.

Our next operation is to start a secondary thread to actually handle the incoming HTTP connections. We use the C library call _beginthread(). If you are not familiar with using threads in your programs, then a short explanation is in order. Each thread in a program operates as an independent order of execution. They do share a common address space and any global variables are accessible by any thread in the process. This gives both advantages and disadvantages. By sharing a common address space, threads are sometimes referred to as a lightweight process. Each operates independently, but does not require a separate process, just its own stack and processor context. But just as this is an advantage, it also means if one thread causes an exception, all threads in the process will fail.

Our call to `_beginthread()` requires four arguments for the IBM Visual Age C++ compiler. Other compilers may support a different number of arguments. Check your compiler's documentation for details. The first argument is the address of the function to start. This function must be declared using the `_Optlink` calling convention. The second argument is a holdover from OS/2 1.x days when the address of the bottom of the stack was needed. Stack allocation is now handled automatically by OS/2. The third parameter is the size of the stack for the thread. As mentioned previously, the stack allocation is handled automatically, so we specify a generous size. The last parameter is a pointer which is passed as the only argument to the function. This is where we can pass thread specific information. Since only 4 bytes are passed by the system, a pointer to a data structure is a common argument to pass. The code here passes a `NULL` value since we have no need to pass a parameter to the server thread.

Our call to `_beginthread()` here specifies starting `W3Conn()` and passing it a pointer to the `Socket` class instance as a parameter to the new thread. This gives us a tidy package with which to start the connection. Our last bit of work here is to make sure a new thread was actually started to handle the connection. If the call failed, we close the socket and delete the class instance.

The next function is `W3Conn()`. This is the function with which the new thread starts executing in order to serve the incoming request:

```
// ------------------------------------------------------------------
//
// W3Conn
//
// This is our worker thread to handle the actual request.
//
void _Optlink W3Conn(void *arg)
{
  Socket *sClient;
```

```
   char *szRequest, *szUri, *szVer;
   int iRc;

   sClient = (Socket *)arg;            // Get the pointer to the socket

   // Resolve the IP Name if requested.
   if (bDnsLookup == TRUE)
      {
         sClient->ResolveName();
         }

   szRequest = new char[SMALLBUF];
   szUri = new char[SMALLBUF];
   szVer = new char[SMALLBUF];

   iRc = sClient->RecvTeol(NO_EOL);   // Get the message

   // Parse the components of the request
   sscanf(sClient->szOutBuf, "%s %s %s", szRequest, szUri, szVer);

   if (stricmp(szVer, "http/1.0") == 0)
      {
         DoHttp10(sClient, szRequest, szUri);
         }
   else if (stricmp(szVer, "http/1.1") == 0)
      {
         iRc = DoHttp11(sClient, szRequest, szUri);
         while (iRc == TRUE)  // Do persistent connections.
           {
              sClient->RecvTeol(NO_EOL);
              sscanf(sClient->szOutBuf, "%s %s %s", szRequest,
                    szUri, szVer);
              iRc = DoHttp11(sClient, szRequest, szUri);
           }
      }
   else  // Treat this request as a HTTP/0.9 request.
      {
         DoHttp09(sClient, szRequest, szUri);
         }
   delete [] szRequest;
   delete [] szUri;
   delete [] szVer;
   delete sClient;
   return;

// ----------------------------------------------------------------
```

When we find `szVer` equal to HTTP/1.1, we call the function `DoHttp11()` to actually process the request:

```
iRc = DoHttp11(sClient, szRequest, szUri);
while (iRc == TRUE)  // Do persistent connections.
  {
    sClient->RecvTeol(NO_EOL);
    sscanf(sClient->szOutBuf, "%s %s %s", szRequest,
          szUri, szVer);
    iRc = DoHttp11(sClient, szRequest, szUri);
  }
```

Since persistent connections are the default behavior for HTTP/1.1, we loop over the connection until the client tells us it wants to close. The return value from `DoHttp11()` will be `FALSE` when the client sends the `Connection: close` header to us. Inside our loop, we simply grab the request line, parse it out and call `DoHttp11()` each time.

8.4 *The authorization model*

Before we go further, let us take a look at what is required to support the separate read and write accesses. First from the header file `util.hpp`:

```
// ------------------------------------------------------------
//
// Authorization codes.
//

#define ACCESS_OK       1  // Allow access.
#define ACCESS_DENIED   2  // Need authorization.
#define ACCESS_FAILED   3  // Credentials failed.

#define WRITE_ACCESS    1  // Check write access
#define READ_ACCESS     2  // Check read access
```

The defines here are used within the server to define the different failure codes and types of access requested. Whenever a client makes a request, the server calls the `CheckAuth()` function to determine if access is allowed. If an access file is present, then this function does the necessary work to determine whether or not the current request is granted access.

```
// -----------------------------------------------------------------
//
// CheckAuth()
//
// This function will scan the directory tree for an access file.
// If found it will either verify the authorization if present in the
// Headers variable and return a challenge otherwise.
//

int CheckAuth(char *szPath, Headers *hInfo, int iType)
{
  char *szTmpPath, *szPtr,
       *szName;
  int l,
    iRc;
  BOOL bNotFound = TRUE;
  struct stat sBuf;

  if (iType == READ_ACCESS)  // Check for read or write access.
    {
      szName = szReadAccess;
    }
  else
    {
      szName = szWriteAccess;
    }

  szTmpPath = strdup(szPath);

  l = strlen(szTmpPath) - 1;

  // Look for the access filename.
  while (bNotFound)
    {
      while ((l > 0) && (szTmpPath[l] != '/'))
        {
          szTmpPath[l] = NULL;
          l--;
        }

      if (l == 0) break;  // Stop. No more path left.
      l--; // Go before the "/" for the next attempt.
```

```
        strcat(szTmpPath, szName);    // Create filename.
        iRc = stat(szTmpPath, &sBuf);
        if (iRc == 0)                 // We found the file.
          {
            iRc = CheckFile(szTmpPath, hInfo);
            bNotFound = FALSE;
            continue;
          }
    }
  delete [] szTmpPath;

  if (bNotFound == TRUE) // No access file found. Return ok.
    {
      return (ACCESS_OK);
    }

  return (iRc);
}

// ------------------------------------------------------------------
```

The first step after starting the function now is to check the value of iType
passed in. If we match the READ_ACCESS value, we assign szName to point to
szReadAccess. For matching WRITE_ACCESS, we use szWriteAccess instead.
The CheckFile() function is called to verify the given username and password
against what is in the access file. The function can be found in the util.cpp file
on the CD.

8.5 Request and response headers

With HTTP/1.1, the number of headers defined by the protocol has gone up
tremendously. In order to handle the increased number and to just handle the
increased amount of data in general that we track during each transaction, we
have created a class called Headers. Herewith is part of the headers.hpp
include file:

```
// ------------------------------------------------------------------
//
// The Headers class contains most of the information used during
// a connection with a client. The header lines, the method, the
```

```
// URI, and various other bits used to service a request.
//

class Headers
{
  public:

  Headers();
  ~Headers();
  int RcvHeaders(Socket *sClient);
  int CheckHeaders();
  int FindRanges(int iSize);

  char *szMethod,
       *szUri,
       *szVer,
       *szQuery,
       *szAuthType,
       *szRemoteUser,
       *szAccept,
```

The `Headers` class contains the complete set of information pertaining to a single HTTP request. Most data members mimic an HTTP/1.1 header and as such, just hold that information. A few are there to hold other information pertaining to the request and we'll go over them also. The first two member functions we examine relative thereto are the constructor and destructor:

```
// --------------------------------------------------------------
//
// Headers
//
// The ctor initializes most values to NULL for safety and easy
// checking.
//

Headers::Headers()
{
  szMethod = NULL;
  szUri = NULL;
  szVer = NULL;
  szQuery = NULL;
  szAuthType = NULL;
  szRemoteUser = NULL;
  szAccept = NULL;
  szAcceptCharset = NULL;
```

```
szAcceptEncoding = NULL;
szAcceptLanguage = NULL;
szAge = NULL;
szAllow = NULL;
szAuth = NULL;
szCacheControl = NULL;
szConnection = NULL;
szContentBase = NULL;
szContentEncoding = NULL;
szContentLanguage = NULL;
szContentLength = NULL;
szContentLocation = NULL;
szContentMD5 = NULL;
szContentRange = NULL;
szContentType = NULL;
szDate = NULL;
szETag = NULL;
szExpires = NULL;
szFrom = NULL;
szHost = NULL;
szIfModSince = NULL;
szIfMatch = NULL;
szIfNoneMatch = NULL;
szIfRange = NULL;
szIfUnmodSince = NULL;
szLastMod = NULL;
szLocation = NULL;
szMaxForwards = NULL;
szPragma = NULL;
szPublic = NULL;
szRange = NULL;
szReferer = NULL;
szRetryAfter = NULL;
szServer = NULL;
szTransferEncoding = NULL;
szUpgrade = NULL;
szUserAgent = NULL;
szVary = NULL;
szVia = NULL;
szWarning = NULL;
szWWWAuth = NULL;
szDate = NULL;
szRealm = NULL;
ttIfModSince = 0;
ttIfUnmodSince = 0;
bPersistent = TRUE;
ulContentLength = 0;
```

```
    szIfMatchEtags = NULL;
    szIfNoneMatchEtags = NULL;
    rRanges = NULL;
    iRangeNum = 0;
    bChunked = FALSE;
}


// ----------------------------------------------------------------
//
// ~Headers
//
// The dtor deletes any memory stored in the class instance.
//

Headers::~Headers()
{
    int i;

    if (szMethod) delete [] szMethod;
    if (szUri) delete [] szUri;
    if (szVer) delete [] szVer;
    if (szQuery) delete [] szQuery;
    if (szAuthType) delete [] szAuthType;
    if (szRemoteUser) delete [] szRemoteUser;
    if (szAccept) delete [] szAccept;
    if (szAcceptCharset) delete [] szAcceptCharset;
    if (szAcceptEncoding) delete [] szAcceptEncoding;
    if (szAcceptLanguage) delete [] szAcceptLanguage;
    if (szAge) delete [] szAge;
    if (szAllow) delete [] szAllow;
    if (szAuth) delete [] szAuth;
    if (szCacheControl) delete [] szCacheControl;
    if (szConnection) delete [] szConnection;
    if (szContentBase) delete [] szContentBase;
    if (szContentEncoding) delete [] szContentEncoding;
    if (szContentLanguage) delete [] szContentLanguage;
    if (szContentLength) delete [] szContentLength;
    if (szContentLocation) delete [] szContentLocation;
    if (szContentMD5) delete [] szContentMD5;
    if (szContentRange) delete [] szContentRange;
    if (szContentType) delete [] szContentType;
    if (szDate) delete [] szDate;
    if (szETag) delete [] szETag;
    if (szExpires) delete [] szExpires;
    if (szFrom) delete [] szFrom;
    if (szHost) delete [] szHost;
    if (szIfModSince) delete [] szIfModSince;
```

```
if (szIfMatch) delete [] szIfMatch;
if (szIfNoneMatch) delete [] szIfNoneMatch;
if (szIfRange) delete [] szIfRange;
if (szIfUnmodSince) delete [] szIfUnmodSince;
if (szLastMod) delete [] szLastMod;
if (szLocation) delete [] szLocation;
if (szMaxForwards) delete [] szMaxForwards;
if (szPragma) delete [] szPragma;
if (szPublic) delete [] szPublic;
if (szRange) delete [] szRange;
if (szReferer) delete [] szReferer;
if (szRetryAfter) delete [] szRetryAfter;
if (szServer) delete [] szServer;
if (szTransferEncoding) delete [] szTransferEncoding;
if (szUpgrade) delete [] szUpgrade;
if (szUserAgent) delete [] szUserAgent;
if (szVary) delete [] szVary;
if (szVia) delete [] szVia;
if (szWarning) delete [] szWarning;
if (szWWWAuth) delete [] szWWWAuth;
if (szDate) delete [] szDate;
if (szRealm) delete [] szRealm;
if (szIfMatchEtags)
    {
      for (i = 0; szIfMatchEtags[i] != NULL; i++)
        {
          delete [] (szIfMatchEtags[i]);
        }
      delete [] szIfMatchEtags;
    }
  if (szIfNoneMatchEtags)
    {
      for (i = 0; szIfNoneMatchEtags[i] != NULL; i++)
        {
          delete [] (szIfNoneMatchEtags[i]);
        }
      delete [] szIfNoneMatchEtags;
    }
  if (rRanges != NULL) delete [] rRanges;
}

// ------------------------------------------------------------------
```

The ctor function is very simple. It makes certain everything has a default value. The reason for this is to make our coding easier when using the class. We want to be able to check for the presence of a particular header by checking if it has a value. By explicitly assigning NULL to the character pointers, we can use logical expressions such as:

```
if (h->szAccept != NULL)
```

This leads to an easy-to-understand programming style and coding. If we did not initialize the pointers to NULL, it would be likely that an expression such as this would be true, but for h->szAccept to point just about anywhere in the system would cause a crash as soon as we tried to use it.

We also initialize several byte counters and time counters to 0 to signify being empty. Likewise, assigned are default values for a couple of Booleans. bPersistent tells us whether or not to keep alive the connection with the client while bChunked tells us whether to receive a chunked encoding from the client.

The destructor is also rather straightforward. It just checks for allocated memory and frees any it finds. The only tricky parts are handling the memory deallocation for szIfMatchEtags and for szIfNoneMatchEtags. Both of these are pointers to pointers, so we must be sure to free all the memory. To do this, we loop through the array values of each, and free the character strings stored there. Once all of the substrings are taken care of, we free the main pointer to pointers. The rRange variable is similar, but only one-dimensional in nature, so only a single delete operation is needed.

The RcvHeaders() function is next:

```
// ------------------------------------------------------------------
//
// RcvHeaders()
//
// Receive the rest of the headers sent by the client.
//

int
Headers::RcvHeaders(Socket *sClient)
{
    char *szHdr,
         *szTmp,
         *szBuf;
    int iRc, i;

    szHdr = new char[SMALLBUF];
```

```
      do
        {
          iRc = sClient->RecvTeol(NO_EOL);   // Get the message.
          if (iRc < 0) break;
          if (sClient->szOutBuf[0] == NULL) break;

          szTmp = sClient->szOutBuf;
          if (! isspace(szTmp[0]) ) // Replace the header if not
                                    // continuation.
            {
              i = 0;
              while ((*szTmp != ':') && (*szTmp)) // Until the
                {                                 // delimiter.
                  szHdr[i] = *szTmp; // Copy.
                  i++;               // Advance.
                  szTmp++;
                }
              szHdr[i] = NULL;   // Properly end string.
              strlwr(szHdr);     // Lowercase only.
            }
          szTmp++;            // Go past the ':' or ' '.
          while ((*szTmp == ' ') && (*szTmp))
            {
              szTmp++;   // Eliminate leading spaces.
            }

          switch(szHdr[0])
            {
              case 'a':
                {
                  if (strcmp(szHdr, "accept") == 0)
                    {
                      if (szAccept)
                        {
                          szBuf = new char[strlen(szAccept) +
                                       strlen(szTmp) + 2];
                          sprintf(szBuf, "%s,%s", szAccept, szTmp);
                          delete [] szAccept;
                          szAccept = szBuf;
                        }
                      else
                        {
                          szAccept = strdup(szTmp);
                        }
                    }
                  else if (strcmp(szHdr, "accept-charset") == 0)
                    {
```

```
      if (szAcceptCharset)
        {
          szBuf = new char[strlen(szAcceptCharset) +
                       strlen(szTmp) + 2];
          sprintf(szBuf, "%s,%s", szAcceptCharset, szTmp);
          delete [] szAcceptCharset;
          szAcceptCharset = szBuf;
        }
      else
        {
          szAcceptCharset = strdup(szTmp);
        }
    }
  else if (strcmp(szHdr, "accept-encoding") == 0)
    {
      if (szAcceptEncoding)
        {
          szBuf = new char[strlen(szAcceptEncoding) +
                       strlen(szTmp) + 2];
          sprintf(szBuf, "%s,%s", szAcceptEncoding,
                szTmp);
          delete [] szAcceptEncoding;
          szAcceptEncoding = szBuf;
        }
      else
        {
          szAcceptEncoding = strdup(szTmp);
        }
    }
  else if (strcmp(szHdr, "accept-language") == 0)
    {
      if (szAcceptLanguage)
        {
          szBuf = new char[strlen(szAcceptLanguage) +
                       strlen(szTmp) + 2];
          sprintf(szBuf, "%s,%s", szAcceptLanguage,
                szTmp);
          delete [] szAcceptLanguage;
          szAcceptLanguage = szBuf;
        }
      else
        {
          szAcceptLanguage = strdup(szTmp);
        }
    }
  else if (strcmp(szHdr, "authorization") == 0)
    {
```

```
            if (szAuth) delete [] szAuth;
            szAuth = strdup(szTmp);
         }
      break;
   }
case 'c':
   {
      if (strcmp(szHdr, "connection") == 0)
         {
            if (szConnection) delete [] szConnection;
            szConnection = strdup(szTmp);
            if (stricmp(szConnection, "close") == 0)
               {
                  bPersistent = FALSE;
               }
         }
      else if (strcmp(szHdr, "content-length") == 0)
         {
            if (szContentLength) delete [] szContentLength;
            szContentLength = strdup(szTmp);
            ulContentLength = atol(szContentLength);
         }
      else if (strcmp(szHdr, "content-type") == 0)
         {
            if (szContentType) delete [] szContentType;
            szContentType = strdup(szTmp);
         }
      break;
   }
case 'd':
   {
      if (strcmp(szHdr, "date") == 0)
         {
            if (szDate) delete [] szDate;
            szDate = strdup(szTmp);
         }
      break;
   }
case 'f':
   {
      if (strcmp(szHdr, "from") == 0)
         {
            if (szFrom) delete [] szFrom;
            szFrom = strdup(szTmp);
         }
      break;
   }
```

```
case 'h':
  {
    if (strcmp(szHdr, "host") == 0)
      {
        if (szHost) delete [] szHost;
        szHost = strdup(szTmp);
      }
    break;
  }
case 'i':
  {
    if (strcmp(szHdr, "if-modified-since") == 0)
      {
        if (szIfModSince) delete [] szIfModSince;
        szIfModSince = strdup(szTmp);
        ttIfModSince = ConvertDate(szIfModSince);
      }
    else if (strcmp(szHdr, "if-match") == 0)
      {
        if (szIfMatch)
          {
            szBuf = new char[strlen(szIfMatch) +
                            strlen(szTmp) + 2];
            sprintf(szBuf, "%s,%s", szIfMatch, szTmp);
            delete [] szIfMatch;
            szIfMatch = szBuf;
          }
        else
          {
            szIfMatch = strdup(szTmp);
          }
      }
    else if (strcmp(szHdr, "if-none-match") == 0)
      {
        if (szIfNoneMatch)
          {
            szBuf = new char[strlen(szIfNoneMatch) +
                            strlen(szTmp) + 2];
            sprintf(szBuf, "%s,%s", szIfNoneMatch, szTmp);
            delete [] szIfNoneMatch;
            szIfNoneMatch = szBuf;
          }
        else
          {
            szIfNoneMatch = strdup(szTmp);
          }
      }
```

```
        else if (strcmp(szHdr, "if-range") == 0)
          {
            if (szIfRange) delete [] szIfRange;
            szIfRange = strdup(szTmp);
          }
        else if (strcmp(szHdr, "if-unmodified-since") == 0)
          {
            if (szIfUnmodSince) delete [] szIfUnmodSince;
            szIfUnmodSince = strdup(szTmp);
            ttIfUnmodSince = ConvertDate(szIfUnmodSince);
          }
      break;
    }
  case 'r':
    {
      if (strcmp(szHdr, "range") == 0)
        {
          if (szRange) delete [] szRange;
          szRange = strdup(szTmp);
        }
      else if (strcmp(szHdr, "referer") == 0)
        {
          if (szReferer) delete [] szReferer;
          szReferer = strdup(szTmp);
        }
      break;
    }
  case 't':
    {
      if (strcmp(szHdr, "transfer-encoding") == 0)
        {
          if (szTransferEncoding)
            delete [] szTransferEncoding;
          szTransferEncoding = strdup(szTmp);
          if (stricmp(szTransferEncoding, "chunked") == 0)
            {
              bChunked = TRUE;
            }
        }
      break;
    }
  case 'u':
    {
      if (strcmp(szHdr, "upgrade") == 0)
        {
          if (szUpgrade) delete [] szUpgrade;
          szUpgrade = strdup(szTmp);
```

```
                }
            else if (strcmp(szHdr, "user-agent") == 0)
              {
                 if (szUserAgent) delete [] szUserAgent;
                 szUserAgent = strdup(szTmp);
              }
            break;
          }
      }
    }
  while (sClient->szOutBuf[0] != NULL);

  delete [] szHdr;

  // Now determine if we received any etags.
  if (szIfMatch != NULL) szIfMatchEtags = Etag(szIfMatch);
  if (szIfNoneMatch != NULL) szIfNoneMatchEtags =
      Etag(szIfNoneMatch);

  return iRc;
}

// -------------------------------------------------------------
```

This member function is basically an expanded version of the
RcvHeaders() function found in the HTTP/1.0 server. We start out by allocating memory for our internal buffer and then entering the loop:

```
szHdr = new char[SMALLBUF];

do
  {
    iRc = sClient->RecvTeol(NO_EOL);   // Get the message.
    if (iRc < 0) break;
    if (sClient->szOutBuf[0] == NULL) break;
```

The first step in the loop is to receive a line from the client. We do this, and specify to leave off the end-of-line marker. After receiving the line, we must check for any error condition which would end the loop. The first is checking for an error when reading bytes from the socket. If an error was encountered by the Socket class, then a return code of −1 is sent back. The next check is not for an error condition, but for the blank line after the headers. The Socket instance will have read the end-of-line marker, but will not return anything else on the line. We break out of the loop for either condition.

Next we must separate the header tag from its value, while checking for headers which may have been continued across multiple lines:

```
szTmp = sClient->szOutBuf;
if (! isspace(szTmp[0]) )     // Replace the header if not
   {                          // continuation.
     i = 0;
     while ((*szTmp != ':') && (*szTmp))  // Until the delimiter.
        {
           szHdr[i] = *szTmp; // Copy.
           i++;               // Advance.
           szTmp++;
        }
     szHdr[i] = NULL;  // Properly end string.
     strlwr(szHdr);    // Lowercase only.
   }
szTmp++;              // Go past the ':' or ' '.
while ((*szTmp == ' ') && (*szTmp))
   {
     szTmp++;  // Eliminate leading spaces.
   }
```

Using `szTmp` for convenience, we assign it to point to the input buffer. We then check to see if the line just read is a continuation line. It is a continuation line if the first character of the line is a white space character. If it is not a continuation line, then we must find the first ":" character in the line which marks the break between the header name and the value. While we look for it, we copy the header name into the `szHdr` buffer. Once found, `szHdr` has a NULL appended to it, and then it is converted to lowercase for comparison purposes. Outside of the `if` statement, `szTmp` is advanced until the first non-white space character in the string is found.

By constructing the code in this manner, we gain something important. We always have the header value stored in local storage between lines of input. When handling continuation lines, we have to know what header name was used on the previous line so we may append to it. If we simply made `szHdr` point to the beginning of `sClient->szOutBuf`, then the header name would be lost when we grabbed the next line. If the next line was a continuation, then we would be in a bind. So we save the value in local storage and if we find a continuation line, we don't assign a new value to `szHdr`. We still have the previous one to use.

At this point, we have both the header name and the header value. Now we must figure out which header we just read and store it. To do this in an efficient way, we use a combination `switch` and `if-else` tree to determine the header:

```
switch(szHdr[0])
    {
    case 'a':
        {
        if (strcmp(szHdr, "accept") == 0)
            {
            // Do some processing.
            }
        else if (strcmp(szHdr, "accept-charset") == 0)
            {
            // Do some processing.
            }
        break;
        }
    case 'c':
        {
            // And so on.
```

This shortened version shows the basic outline of how it is handled. The `switch` statement keys on the first character in the header name. This allows us to divide the subsequent `if-else` trees into at least twenty-six different structures, although for HTTP/1.1 headers, we don't use all twenty-six letters. Instead, with the correct `case` statement, we only have, at most, five comparisons to make to determine which header it is. To improve the hit ratio slightly, we could order the comparisons within the `case` statements in the frequency in which we expect to see the header. The current order is pretty close anyway, so the gain would probably not be worth it over keeping the alphabetic order for maintenance.

When we match on a comparison, there are a couple of different constructs we use to save the values. The first is for a header which may be continued over multiple lines.

```
if (szAccept)
    {
    szBuf = new char[strlen(szAccept) + strlen(szTmp) + 2];
    sprintf(szBuf, "%s,%s", szAccept, szTmp);
    delete [] szAccept;
```

```
      szAccept = szBuf;
  }
else
  {
     szAccept = strdup(szTmp);
     }
```

We start here by checking to ascertain if the header has already been assigned a value. If it has, then we're adding to what is currently saved. To do this, we allocate a new buffer large enough to hold the current value, plus the new value. You must also take care to leave enough space for the ending NULL, plus the comma between the values. The next line uses `sprintf()` to join the lines together, putting a comma in between them. We then `delete` the old value and assign the newly created buffer to the header variable. If there is not a value assigned to the header variable yet, we simply use `strdup()` to assign one.

The next way in which we save a value is to utilize those which cannot span multiple lines:

```
if (strcmp(szHdr, "connection") == 0)
  {
    if (szConnection) delete [] szConnection;
    szConnection = strdup(szTmp);
    if (stricmp(szConnection, "close") == 0)
      {
        bPersistent = FALSE;
      }
  }
```

Using this code, we check to see if the header variable has already been assigned a value. If it has, we `delete` the current value and then assign a new one using `strdup()`. Also shown here is an additional check done for the value of `szConnection`. If we find the `Connection` header, we check to see if its value is `close`. If it is, then `bPersistent` is assigned a value of FALSE so the persistent connection ends in `W3Conn()`.

Other headers which will require additional processing include `Content-Length`, `If-Modified-Since`, `If-Unmodified-Since`, and `Transfer-Encoding`. When we encounter these headers, we convert the value to our internal use value which may be either a length, time, or Boolean flag.

Once outside of the receiving loop, only a couple of housekeeping chores are left. The first is to free the dynamically allocated memory used in szHdr. After that, we check for entity tags:

```
// Now determine if we received any etags.
if (szIfMatch != NULL) szIfMatchEtags = Etag(szIfMatch);
if (szIfNoneMatch != NULL) szIfNoneMatchEtags =
                            Etag(szIfNoneMatch);
```

The private member function Etag separates out the individual entity tags into the character arrays where we can use them:

```
// -------------------------------------------------------------
//
// Etag
//
// Retrieve the etags sent by the client.
//

char **
Headers::Etag(char *szTags)
{
   char *szPtr, *szStart, **szEtags, cTmp;
   int i, j;

   // Find out how many tags are expected.
   i = 0;
   szPtr = szTags;
   while (*szPtr != NULL)
      {
         if (*szPtr == ',') i++;
         szPtr++;
      }

   // A minimum of 2. One for a tag and one for a NULL marker.
   i += 2;
   szEtags = new char * [i];
   for (j = 0; j < i; j++)
      {
         szEtags[j] = NULL;
      }

   j = 0;
   szPtr = szTags;
   while (*szPtr != NULL)
```

```
    {
      while ( (isspace(*szPtr)) && (*szPtr != NULL) )
        {
           szPtr++;
        }
      if (*szPtr == NULL) continue;  // Escape.
      szStart = szPtr;
      if (*szPtr == 'W') szPtr += 2; // Bypass weak indicator.
      if (*szPtr == '*')
        {
           szEtags[j] = strdup("*");   // Match any.
           break;
        }
      szPtr++;  // Advance past the <"> mark.
      while ( (*szPtr != '"') && (*szPtr != NULL) )
        {
           szPtr++;  // Look for end of etag.
        }
      if (*szPtr == NULL) continue;  // Escape.
      szPtr++;          // Past the ending <"> mark.
      cTmp = *szPtr;    // Save character temporarily.
      *szPtr = NULL;    // Mark end of string of current etag.
      szEtags[j] = strdup(szStart);  // Save it.
      j++;              // Count it.
      *szPtr = cTmp;    // Restore character.
      while ( (*szPtr != ',') && (*szPtr != NULL) )
        {
           szPtr++; // Advance to start of next etag or end-of-line.
        }
      if (*szPtr == ',') szPtr++;
    }

  return szEtags;
}


// --------------------------------------------------------------
```

This little function goes back to nasty C pointers to accomplish its work. The first thing to do is to find out how many entity tags to expect. To do this, we count the number of commas found. This may end up counting more than are actually present, since a comma could be contained within an entity tag. What we do assure ourselves of is not undercounting, which is more important. Once we have counted the number of commas, we add 2 to the value to allow for a minimal case where we only have a single tag (so there would have been no commas counted). The extra is for one to be NULL and thus mark the end of the array. Memory is then allocated for the array of pointers present and each one is set to NULL.

We start out the main part of the program by setting some initial values and entering a loop:

```
j = 0;
szPtr = szTags;
while (*szPtr != NULL)
  {
    while ( (isspace(*szPtr)) && (*szPtr != NULL) )
      {
        szPtr++;
      }
    if (*szPtr == NULL) continue;  // Escape.
```

The variable j is used as our index value into the array of entity tags and is initialized to 0. We also set our temporary pointer to the beginning of the line of entity tags. Once in the loop, we have it continue until the end of the line is reached (as indicated by *szPtr being NULL). The first step taken in the loop is to eliminate any leading white space characters from the string. Once out of that loop, we check for NULL again and break if we find it.

```
szStart = szPtr;
if (*szPtr == 'W') szPtr += 2; // Bypass weak indicator.
if (*szPtr == '*')
  {
    szEtags[j] = strdup("*");  // Match any.
    break;
  }
szPtr++;  // Advance past the <"> mark.
```

At this point, we have found the start of an entity tag, so we assign the szStart pointer to remember where it begins. The next line checks for a weak entity tag indicator. Our server does not generate weak entity tags, so any we receive will be spurious. Now we check for the special case entity tag of ` * `. If we find it, we simply do a strdup() into the next available spot of the szEtags array and break out of the loop. Even if there are more, it doesn't matter since ` * ` matches anything. On a normal entity tag, szPtr would point to the beginning quote mark of the entity tag, so we advance past it. Now we have found the start, so we need to look for the end of the entity tag:

```
while ( (*szPtr != '"') && (*szPtr != NULL) )
   {
     szPtr++;   // Look for end of etag.
   }
if (*szPtr == NULL) continue;  // Escape.
szPtr++;          // Past the ending <"> mark.
```

The `while` loop goes through the line looking for the ending quote mark of the entity tag. Once we break out of the loop, we check for a NULL value for safety and then, if possible, advance past the ending quote mark we just found. At this point we have `szStart` pointing to the beginning quote mark of the entity tag and `szPtr` pointing to the character just after the ending quote mark. Now we need to save the entity tag:

```
cTmp = *szPtr;    // Save character temporarily.
*szPtr = NULL;    // Mark end of string of current etag.
szEtags[j] = strdup(szStart);  // Save it.
j++;              // Count it.
*szPtr = cTmp;    // Restore character.
```

In order to save the entity tag, but not trounce on any subsequent values, we save the character `szPtr` which currently points to the temporary variable `cTmp`. Next, we assign NULL to `*szPtr` thus ending the string pointed to by `szStart`. We can simply use `strdup()` on the next line to save the value and then restore the string to the original state on the final line.

In the last section of code within the loop, we advance `szPtr` past the next comma:

```
while ( (*szPtr != ',') && (*szPtr != NULL) )
   {
     szPtr++; // Advance to start of next etag or end-of-line.
   }
if (*szPtr == ',') szPtr++;
```

When the loop starts up again, it will either be at the end of the line and quit, or it will be at the start of the next entity tag. Once out of the loop, we simply return `szEtags` as the result. The destructor for the class will take care of freeing the memory later.

The next public member function of the `Headers` class is `CheckHeaders()`. This function does some consistency checks on the header fields received from the client. There are a few ways in which clients can send conflicting header information. An example would be sending an `If-Match` and `If-None-Match` header with the same entity tag. Both cannot be valid at the same time. The only time this is likely to happen is when the client is in some sort of error state, or just plain broke. However, the server must be capable of handling any legal and illegal combination of headers. In this example, both headers may be present and both may have the same entity tag and it would be legal. What it means however, is beyond the scope of the protocol and our server rejects it outright. Let us take a look at the entire function now:

```
// --------------------------------------------------------------
//
// CheckHeaders
//
// Check the headers received for inconsistent headers.
//

int
Headers::CheckHeaders()
{
    int i, j;

    // Check for the host header first.
    if (szHost == NULL) return FALSE;

    // First check to make sure the If-Unmodified-Since time
    // is not before the If-Modified-Since time.
    if ((szIfModSince != NULL) && (szIfUnmodSince != NULL))
      {
        if (ttIfModSince <= ttIfUnmodSince)
          {
            return FALSE;
          }
      }

    // Now check for etags which match between If-Match and
    // If-None-Match.
```

```
   if ((szIfMatch != NULL) && (szIfNoneMatch != NULL))
     {
        for (i = 0; szIfMatchEtags[i] != NULL; i++)
          {
            for (j = 0; szIfNoneMatchEtags[j] != NULL; j++)
              {
                if (strcmp(szIfMatchEtags[i],
                        szIfNoneMatchEtags[j]) == 0)
                  {
                    return FALSE;
                  }
              }
          }
     }

   return TRUE;
}

// ------------------------------------------------------------------
```

The first check made in `CheckHeaders()` is for the `Host` header. This header is required in all HTTP/1.1 requests. When it is not found, the server must generate an error message to the client. The function returns `FALSE` when a condition fails. The next possible and sometimes troublesome inconsistency involves the `If-Modified-Since` and `If-Unmodified-Since` headers:

```
// First check to make sure the If-Unmodified-Since time
// is not before the If-Modified-Since time.
if ((szIfModSince != NULL) && (szIfUnmodSince != NULL))
   {
     if (ttIfUnmodSince <= ttIfModSince)
        {
          return FALSE;
        }
   }
```

If both headers are present, we must check to make sure the client has not specified a paradox of time by presenting the `If-Unmodified-Since` time-stamp before the `If-Modified-Since` timestamp. If they do use this new time keeping method, we reject the headers.

The last consistency check done is among the entity tags if both `If-Match` and `If-None-Match` are present:

```
// Now check for etags which match between If-Match and
// If-None-Match.
if ((szIfMatch != NULL) && (szIfNoneMatch != NULL))
  {
    for (i = 0; szIfMatchEtags[i] != NULL; i++)
      {
        for (j = 0; szIfNoneMatchEtags[j] != NULL; j++)
          {
            if (strcmp(szIfMatchEtags[i],
                  szIfNoneMatchEtags[j]) == 0)
              {
                return FALSE;
              }
          }
      }
  }
```

For this check we loop through both sets of entity tags, making comparisons between them. Though fairly processor intensive, it is unlikely both are present to begin with. If both are present, it is unlikely that there would be many tags defined for either one. So the match-checking should be fairly quick and definitely necessary. Again, if we do find a match, we return FALSE to signal that the header check failed.

The last member function is FindRanges(). Once again we have a fairly involved function using numerous pointers to do the work. The HTTP/1.1 protocol allows a great deal of flexibility in specifying ranges. This flexibility for the clients results in considerable work for the server:

```
// -------------------------------------------------------------
//
// FindRanges
//
// Locate and store the ranges sent by the client.
//

int
Headers::FindRanges(int iSize)
{
  char *szBuf, *szTmp;
  int i, iNum, iLength, iIdx,
      bError;

  if (szRange == NULL) return 1;  // Nothing to do.
```

```
bError = FALSE;
szTmp = szRange;
iNum = 1;
while (*szTmp != NULL)   // Count the number of ranges.
   {
      if (*szTmp == ',') iNum++;
      szTmp++;
   }

rRanges = new Range[iNum];   // Space for them.
szBuf = new char[SMALLBUF];

// Now pull out the range numbers.
iIdx = 0;
szTmp = strchr(szRange, '=');
szTmp++;
while (*szTmp != NULL)
   {
      if (isdigit(*szTmp)) // Found range start.
         {
            i = 0;
            while (isdigit(*szTmp))   // Advance past the digits.
               {
                  szBuf[i] = *szTmp;
                  i++;
                  szTmp++;
               }
            szBuf[i] = NULL;           // Mark NULL and grab the start.
            rRanges[iIdx].iStart = atoi(szBuf);

            if (*szTmp != '-') bError = TRUE; // Wrong format.
            szTmp++;
            if (isdigit(*szTmp))      // Found range end.
               {
                  i = 0;
                  while (isdigit(*szTmp)) // Advance past the digits.
                     {
                        szBuf[i] = *szTmp;
                        i++;
                        szTmp++;
                     }
                  szBuf[i] = NULL;       // Mark NULL and grab the end.
                  rRanges[iIdx].iEnd = atoi(szBuf);
               }
            else  // Use end-of-file as range end.
               {
```

```
                    rRanges[iIdx].iEnd = iSize - 1;
                  }
                iIdx++;   // Advance to next spot.
              }
          else if (*szTmp == '-')   // No start range given.
            {
                szTmp++;
                if (isdigit(*szTmp) != TRUE) bError = TRUE;
                i = 0;
                while (isdigit(*szTmp)) // Grab number of bytes.
                  {
                      szBuf[i] = *szTmp;
                      i++;
                      szTmp++;
                  }
                szBuf[i] = NULL;
                i = atoi(szBuf);
                // The start will be so i bytes from the end of the file.
                rRanges[iIdx].iStart = iSize - i - 1;
                rRanges[iIdx].iEnd = iSize - 1;
                iIdx++;
            }
          else
            {
                szTmp++;
            }
      }

    delete [] szBuf;
    iRangeNum = iIdx;

    if (bError == TRUE) // Error in ranges.
      {
          delete [] rRanges;
          rRanges = NULL;
          iRangeNum = 0;
          return 1;
      }
    return 0;
}

// ----------------------------------------------------------------
```

The first check necessary in this function is to make certain we received a
Range header from the client. If we didn't, we can quit and return immediately.
Otherwise we initialize a few data structures to start:

```
bError = FALSE;
szTmp = szRange;
iNum = 1;
while (*szTmp != NULL)   // Count the number of ranges.
   {
      if (*szTmp == ',') iNum++;
      szTmp++;
   }

rRanges = new Range[iNum];   // Space for them.
szBuf = new char[SMALLBUF];
```

The first variable we set is our error flag, bError. Due to the complexity of the function, it is easier to set a flag when there is an error and worry about it at the end. The default, of course, is no error. Next we count the number of ranges sent by the client by counting the number of commas in szRange. We initialize our counter to 1 as a minimum. Following the counting, we allocate the required number of Range instances in an array to hold the range values sent by the client. We also allocate temporary memory for the function here.

The main portion of the function takes part in a while, which keys on the NULL at the end of the string:

```
// Now pull out the range numbers.
iIdx = 0;
szTmp = strchr(szRange, '=');
szTmp++;
while (*szTmp != NULL)
   {
```

iIdx is our counter for the number of range values found and is initialized to 0. We next find the start of the byte ranges by looking for the equal sign in the string. By definition, the equal sign comes just after the token bytes in the string. szTmp is then advanced by one, which should be the start of the first byte range. The loop itself continues until the end of the string marker has been finally found.

Inside the loop we first check for a byte range which starts with a number:

```
if (isdigit(*szTmp)) // Found range start.
   {
      i = 0;
      while (isdigit(*szTmp))  // Advance past the digits.
```

```
      {
         szBuf[i] = *szTmp;
         i++;
         szTmp++;
      }
   szBuf[i] = NULL;            // Mark NULL and grab the start.
   rRanges[iIdx].iStart = atoi(szBuf);
```

The isdigit() function tells us whether or not we have a range start. When we do, we must look for the end of the current number. The while loop continues as long as we have numbers in a row. We store the number in szBuf inside the loop and once outside, append the NULL. The last line then stores the number in numerical form in the current rRange array. At this point we must find out whether we have an open specification, which means from this byte marker until the end of the file, or a closed range:

```
if (*szTmp != '-') bError = TRUE; // Wrong format.
szTmp++;
if (isdigit(*szTmp))  // Found range end.
   {
      i = 0;
      while (isdigit(*szTmp))  // Advance past the digits.
         {
            szBuf[i] = *szTmp;
            i++;
            szTmp++;
         }
      szBuf[i] = NULL;            // Mark NULL and grab the end.
      rRanges[iIdx].iEnd = atoi(szBuf);
   }
else  // Use end-of-file as range end.
   {
      rRanges[iIdx].iEnd = iSize - 1;
   }
iIdx++;  // Advance to next spot.
```

The first check done is for correctness of format. There must be a "-" character as the next character. Anything else is an error and sets our error flag to TRUE. szTmp is then advanced past the "-" and we test whether or not the next character is a digit. If it is a digit, then the client has specified an ending range number and we must grab it, just as we grabbed the beginning number. This time, the end number is stored as the iEnd member of rRanges. This gives us a complete byte range. If there was not a digit there, then the end-of-file is saved as the end of the byte range. Our function has as its parameter the byte size of the file. We save the file size −1 as the ending byte marker. The reason for one less is that byte counting starts at 0 in HTTP/1.1. The counter, iIdx, is then advanced to the next spot in the array.

If the first character tested was not a digit, the only other valid possibility is for it to start with a "−" which means to send the last so-many bytes of the file. If the client specified −500 as a byte range, then we would routinely send the last 500 bytes of the file:

```
else if (*szTmp == '-')   // No start range given.
   {
     szTmp++;
     if (isdigit(*szTmp) != TRUE) bError = TRUE;
     i = 0;
     while (isdigit(*szTmp)) // Grab number of bytes.
        {
          szBuf[i] = *szTmp;
          i++;
          szTmp++;
        }
     szBuf[i] = NULL;
     i = atoi(szBuf);
     // The start will be i bytes from the end of the file.
     rRanges[iIdx].iStart = iSize - i - 1;
     rRanges[iIdx].iEnd = iSize - 1;
     iIdx++;
   }
```

In this section, we advance past the "−" we just found and then check to make sure there is a number coming up next. If there is not a number, we have encountered another syntax error and set the error flag. Otherwise we grab the number of bytes by advancing through the while loop until we run out of numbers. Once out, we convert the number we found to a numerical value and store it in i. The beginning byte range in this case will be found by subtracting the number given from the file size and then subtracting one more for the HTTP/1.1 indexing. The end of the file is found by subtracting 1 from the file size and we then advance our array index to the next available spot.

The default `else` statement, if we didn't find a digit or dash first, is to advance the pointer by 1. This takes care of any white space, although none should be present. Outside of the loop, we only have a few housekeeping duties:

```
delete [] szBuf;
iRangeNum = iIdx;

if (bError == TRUE) // Error in ranges.
   {
     delete [] rRanges;
     rRanges = NULL;
     iRangeNum = 0;
     return 1;
   }
return 0;
```

The first statement outside of the loop frees our locally allocated memory, especially important in a multithreaded server program. The next statement saves the number of byte ranges found in the member variable `iRangeNum`. We then check to see if the error flag was set while searching for byte ranges. If it were, `rRanges` is freed and marked `NULL`. We also set `iRangeNum` to 0 to make sure no inadvertent accesses are made on `rRanges`. Using normal C library style returns, we return 1 on failure and 0 on success.

8.6 HTTP/1.1

In `W3Conn()`, the thread will call the `DoHttp11()` function to handle a HTTP/1.1 level request. This function determines the exact request and handles direction of other functions to return the proper response to the client:

```
// --------------------------------------------------------------
//
// DoHttp11()
//
// This function handles our HTTP/1.1 requests.
//

int DoHttp11(Socket *sClient, char *szMethod, char *szUri)
{
```

```
int iRc,
    iRsp,
    iType,
    iMethod;
char *szReq,
     *szPath,
     *szCgi,
     *szTmp,
     *szSearch;
Headers *hInfo;
long lBytes = 0;
BOOL bExec = FALSE,
     bCgi = FALSE,
     bPersistent;

szReq = strdup(sClient->szOutBuf);   // Save the request line.
iRsp = 200;
szSearch = NULL;
szPath = NULL;
szCgi = NULL;
hInfo = new Headers();
iMethod = CheckMethod(szMethod);   // The request method.

// First, check for TRACE method.
if (iMethod == TRACE)
  {
    // Do a trace, saving connection.
    bPersistent = DoTrace(sClient, hInfo);
    DeHexify(szReq);
    WriteToLog(sClient, szReq, iRsp, hInfo->ulContentLength);
    delete [] szReq;
    delete hInfo;
    return bPersistent;
  }

hInfo->RcvHeaders(sClient);   // Grab the request headers.
bPersistent = hInfo->bPersistent;   // Find out if close
                                    // was requested.
iRc = hInfo->CheckHeaders(); // Make sure none are inconsistent.
if (iRc == FALSE)            // Bad request.
  {
    iRsp = SendError(sClient,
          "Missing Host header or incompatible headers detected.",
          400, HTTP_1_1, hInfo);
    DeHexify(szReq);
    WriteToLog(sClient, szReq, iRsp, hInfo->ulContentLength);
    delete [] szReq;
```

```
         delete hInfo;
         return bPersistent;
      }

   // Check for a query in the URI.
   if ((szTmp = strchr(szUri, '?')) != NULL)
      {
         // Break up the URI into document and and search parameters.
         *szTmp = NULL;   // Append NULL to shorter URI.
         szTmp++;           // Let szTmp point to the query terms.
         szSearch = strdup(szTmp);
         hInfo->szQuery = strdup(szSearch);
         if (strchr(szSearch, '=') != NULL)
            {
               bCgi = TRUE;   // Only a cgi request can contain an
                           // equal sign.
            }
      }

   DeHexify(szUri);                 // Remove any escape sequences.
   hInfo->szMethod = strdup(szMethod);   // Save a few items.
   hInfo->szUri = strdup(szUri);
   hInfo->szVer = strdup(HTTP_1_1);
   szPath = ResolvePath(szUri); // Check for path match.
   szCgi = ResolveExec(szUri);   // Check for exec match.

   // Now key on the request method and URI given.
   if ( (iMethod == OPTIONS) && (szPath != NULL) )
      {
         iRsp = DoOptions(sClient, szPath, hInfo, GET);
      }
   // OPTIONS with a match on Cgi Path.
   else if ( (iMethod == OPTIONS) && (szCgi != NULL) )
      {
         iRsp = DoOptions(sClient, szCgi, hInfo, POST);
      }
   // Generic OPTIONS.
   else if (iMethod == OPTIONS)
      {
         iRsp = DoOptions(sClient, "*", hInfo, UNKNOWN);
      }
   // Any POST request.
   else if (iMethod == POST)
      {
         iRsp = DoExec11(sClient, iMethod, szCgi, szSearch, hInfo);
      }
```

```
   // A GET or HEAD to process as a CGI request.
   else if ( (bCgi == TRUE) &&
           ((iMethod == GET) || (iMethod == HEAD)) )
     {
       iRsp = DoExec11(sClient, iMethod, szCgi, szSearch, hInfo);
     }
   // Any PUT request.
   else if (iMethod == PUT)
     {
       iRsp = DoPut(sClient, hInfo, szPath, szCgi);
     }
   // Any valid DELETE request.
   else if ((iMethod == DELETE) && (szPath != NULL))
     {
       iRsp = DoDelete(sClient, szPath, hInfo);
     }
   // The default, probably a simple GET or HEAD.
   else if (szPath != NULL)
     {
       iRsp = DoPath11(sClient, iMethod, szPath, szSearch, hInfo);
     }
   // Error Condition.
   else
     {
       iRsp = SendError(sClient, "Resource not found.", 404,
                   HTTP_1_1, hInfo);
     }


   // This request now finished. Log the results.
   DeHexify(szReq);
   WriteToLog(sClient, szReq, iRsp, hInfo->ulContentLength);
   delete [] szReq;
   delete hInfo;
   if ( (szSearch != NULL) && (bCgi == FALSE) )
     {
       unlink(szPath);        // The temporary search file.
       delete [] szSearch;
     }
   if (szPath) delete [] szPath;
   if (szCgi) delete [] szCgi;

   return bPersistent;
}

// ----------------------------------------------------------------
```

This function starts out allocating memory, as and when needed, and initializing some variables:

```
szReq = strdup(sClient->szOutBuf);   // Save the request line.
iRsp = 200;
szSearch = NULL;
szPath = NULL;
szCgi = NULL;
hInfo = new Headers();
```

We save the request line in szReq, set the default response code to 200, assign NULL to three strings, and create a new instance of the Headers class for this request. A note here about use of persistent connections: within W3Conn() is where the loop occurs to handle persistent connections. This function is called for each request which comes in. It would have been possible to loop within this function instead, but the coding for looping outside the function is much simpler. Also important is to know for certain that we won't make a mistake in coding and mix up parts of multiple requests. All of the data structures used are created new for each request which comes in. The performance hit is worth it for the clarity of coding and ease of future maintenance.

Our next step is to determine which method is being used:

```
iMethod = CheckMethod(szMethod);   // The request method.

// First, check for TRACE method.
if (iMethod == TRACE)
   {
     // Do a trace, saving connection.
     bPersistent = DoTrace(sClient, hInfo);
     DeHexify(szReq);
     WriteToLog(sClient, szReq, iRsp, hInfo->ulContentLength);
     delete [] szReq;
     delete hInfo;
     return bPersistent;
   }
```

CheckMethod() is called to determine the method used in the request line. Once we have this information, our first check is for the TRACE method. We check for it first, because of the nature of the TRACE method. When we service it, we must return the headers, as we received them, to the client. Normally we would receive the headers, which will change their exact makeup and order if we use our `Headers` instance to just send them back. Furthermore, there may be headers sent in the message of which our server is not aware. So within the `DoTrace()` function, we simply receive a line and then echo it back to the client. The only thing checked, is for the existence of a `Connection: close` header to determine whether to close the connection afterward or not. Once the function completes and returns here, we go through our normal steps to log the connection and free memory.

Receiving and verifying the headers comes next:

```
hInfo->RcvHeaders(sClient);   // Grab the request headers.
bPersistent = hInfo->bPersistent;   // Find out if close was
                                    // requested.
iRc = hInfo->CheckHeaders(); // Make sure none are inconsistent.
if (iRc == FALSE)            // Bad request.
  {
    iRsp = SendError(sClient,
        "Missing Host header or incompatible headers detected.",
          400, HTTP_1_1, hInfo);
    DeHexify(szReq);
    WriteToLog(sClient, szReq, iRsp, hInfo->ulContentLength);
    delete [] szReq;
    delete hInfo;
    return bPersistent;
  }
```

We use the `Header` class method `RcvHeaders()` as described earlier in the chapter to receive the header lines from the client. Our persistence flag is then assigned, based on `hInfo->bPersistent`. Next, we make a check on the consistency of the headers. If any of the headers causes a problem, we send a `400` response back to the client, indicating an error has occurred. The message we send is a bit generic and could be upgraded if we wanted to have `CheckHeaders()` return an error code instead of a Boolean value. In that case we might return 0 on success, 1 if the `Host` header is missing, and so forth.

The next few lines of code perform our standard query string check on the URI and the assigning of values from the request line to the `hInfo` variable. Now let us take a look at our `if-else` tree which determines which path of execution we take:

```
// Now key on the request method and URI given.
// OPTIONS with a match on Path.
if ( (iMethod == OPTIONS) && (szPath != NULL) )
   {
     iRsp = DoOptions(sClient, szPath, hInfo, GET);
   }
// OPTIONS with a match on Cgi Path.
else if ( (iMethod == OPTIONS) && (szCgi != NULL) )
   {
     iRsp = DoOptions(sClient, szCgi, hInfo, POST);
   }
// Generic OPTIONS.
else if (iMethod == OPTIONS)
   {
     iRsp = DoOptions(sClient, "*", hInfo, UNKNOWN);
   }
```

The first check we make in the tree is for the OPTIONS method. The first branch handles resolving the URI to a path, the second to an executable path, and the third to the generic case of "*". We pass a flag value as the last parameter to tell the DoOptions() function what methods are allowed for a resource. The next couple of branches check for a CGI request:

```
// Any POST request.
else if (iMethod == POST)
   {
     iRsp = DoExec11(sClient, iMethod, szCgi, szSearch, hInfo);
   }
// A GET or HEAD to process as a CGI request.
else if ( (bCgi == TRUE) &&
          ((iMethod == GET) || (iMethod == HEAD)) )
   {
     iRsp = DoExec11(sClient, iMethod, szCgi, szSearch, hInfo);
   }
```

Our first check in this section looks for the POST method. Whenever we receive a POST request, we automatically call the DoExec11() function. The other possibility is for the client to send a GET or HEAD which must be handled by the CGI processor. This keys on the bCgi flag set earlier. The next two cases handle looking for PUT or DELETE:

```
// Any PUT request.
else if (iMethod == PUT)
```

```
    {
       iRsp = DoPut(sClient, hInfo, szPath, szCgi);
    }
// Any valid DELETE request.
else if (iMethod == DELETE)
    {
       iRsp = DoDelete(sClient, szPath, szCgi, hInfo);
    }
```

For the PUT method, we include both szPath and szCgi, since it is possible for the client to update either type of resource. For DELETE, we pass both possible cases to the DoDelete() function. Once inside the function it figures out which one to try and delete. This reduces the number of comparisons we do in the if-else tree.

Thus we have:

```
// A simple GET or HEAD request.
else if (((iMethod == GET) || (iMethod == HEAD)) &&
         (szPath != NULL) )
    {
       iRsp = DoPath11(sClient, iMethod, szPath, szSearch, hInfo);
    }
// Unknown method used.
else if (iMethod == UNKNOWN)
    {
       iRsp = SendError(sClient, "Request method not implemented.",
                  501, HTTP_1_1, hInfo);
    }
// Error Condition.
else
    {
       iRsp = SendError(sClient, "Resource not found.",
                  404, HTTP_1_1, hInfo);
    }
```

The first check is for the common case of a GET or HEAD request. We also must make sure the szPath resolved to a valid resource before executing DoPath11(). If we get past all of the previous cases, then we have two possible error conditions to handle. The first is for an unknown method used by the client. For an unknown method, we use SendError() to send a 501 code back to the client. This indicates our server does not implement or understand the request method. The last and default case will be used when nothing else resolves. The likely cause of this is a request for a non-existent resource by the client. We simply send a generic `401` response for this case.

The rest of the function handles the logging and cleaning up of the resources used by the request. This includes several dynamically allocated arrays, and the `Headers` class instance. The function ends up by returning the `bPersistent` flag to `W3Conn()` where it is checked to determine whether or not to continue the connection at that juncture.

8.7 Finding the method

Something we need to do before exploring the different functions that support the methods is to look at how to determine which method the client is using:

```
// --------------------------------------------------------------------
//
// CheckMethod
//
// Determine which method the client is sending. Remember
// that methods *ARE* case-sensitive, unlike most of HTTP/1.1.
//

int CheckMethod(char *szMethod)
{
  if (strcmp(szMethod, "GET") == 0)
    {
      return GET;
    }
  else if (strcmp(szMethod, "POST") == 0)
    {
      return POST;
    }
  else if (strcmp(szMethod, "HEAD") == 0)
    {
      return HEAD;
    }
  else if (strcmp(szMethod, "OPTIONS") == 0)
    {
      return OPTIONS;
    }
  else if (strcmp(szMethod, "PUT") == 0)
```

```
      {
        return PUT;
      }
   else if (strcmp(szMethod, "DELETE") == 0)
      {
        return DELETE;
      }
   else if (strcmp(szMethod, "TRACE") == 0)
      {
        return TRACE;
      }
   return UNKNOWN;
}

// ---------------------------------------------------------
```

This function is very simple. We just pass in a pointer to the method requested by the client and do a series of `strcmp()` function calls until we find a match. In our header file, we defined the constants for each of the methods for ease of use. We also define an UNKNOWN method in case someone tries something we don't know about. We do one optimization for this function, with the order of the evaluations prioritized in the expected frequency of the requests. We've put GET first and TRACE last. Although minor, it should help a bit.

8.8 TRACE

Now let us take a look at the functions required to support each method starting with TRACE:

```
// ---------------------------------------------------------
//
// DoTrace
//
// Perform a HTTP trace on the request just received.
//

int DoTrace(Socket *sClient, Headers *hInfo)
{
   ofstream ofOut;
   char *szName, szBuf[SMALLBUF], *szTmp;
```

```
struct stat sBuf;
int iRc;
BOOL bPersistent = TRUE;

szName = tmpnam(NULL);   // Request temporary filename.
ofOut.open(szName);
if (! ofOut)
   {
      hInfo->RcvHeaders(sClient);
      bPersistent = hInfo->bPersistent;
      delete hInfo;
      SendError(sClient, "Server error.", 500, HTTP_1_1, hInfo);
      return bPersistent;
   }

while (sClient->szOutBuf[0] != NULL)
   {
      ofOut << sClient->szOutBuf << endl;
      // Look for Connection header.
      szTmp = strchr(sClient->szOutBuf, ':');
      if (szTmp != NULL)
        {
           *szTmp = NULL;
           szTmp++;
           if (stricmp(sClient->szOutBuf, "connection") == 0)
             {
                sscanf(szTmp, "%s", szBuf);
                if (stricmp(szBuf, "close") == 0)
                  {
                     bPersistent = FALSE;
                  }
             }
        }
      sClient->RecvTeol(NO_EOL);
   }
ofOut.close();
iRc = stat(szName, &sBuf);
if (iRc == 0)
   {
      sClient->Send("HTTP/1.1 200 \r\n");
      sClient->Send("Server: ");
      sClient->Send(szServerVer);
      sClient->Send("\r\n");
      szTmp = CreateDate(time(NULL));   // Create a date header.
      if (szTmp != NULL)
        {
```

```
            sClient->Send("Date: ");
            sClient->Send(szTmp);
            sClient->Send("\r\n");
            delete [] szTmp;
          }
       sClient->Send("Content-Type: text/http\r\n");

       hInfo->ulContentLength = sBuf.st_size; // Save the entity size.
       sprintf(szBuf, "Content-Length: %d\r\n", sBuf.st_size);
       sClient->Send(szBuf);
       sClient->Send("\r\n");

       iRc = sClient->SendText(szName);
     }
  unlink(szName);
  return bPersistent;
}


// -------------------------------------------------------
```

The TRACE method is very easy to implement. Whenever it is received, we simply send the headers of the request back to the client as an entity body. Since we're going to send the headers back verbatim, we first open a temporary file in which to store them.

```
szName = tmpnam(NULL);   // Request temporary filename.
ofOut.open(szName);
if (! ofOut)
   {
     hInfo->RcvHeaders(sClient);
     bPersistent = hInfo->bPersistent;
     delete hInfo;
     SendError(sClient, "Server error.", 500, HTTP_1_1, hInfo);
     return bPersistent;
   }
```

The only check made here is to be sure the temporary file was opened successfully. The occurrence would be rare, but for completeness, we go ahead and grab the headers if the file open failed, and then send (or at least try to send) an error reply back to the client. The reason for receiving the headers is twofold: First to clear any incoming data before the next request, and second, to check for the persistent connections header.

Once we have the temporary file open, we start into a loop, saving lines to the temporary file and looking for the `Connection` header:

```
while (sClient->szOutBuf[0] != NULL)
  {
    ofOut << sClient->szOutBuf << endl;
    // Look for Connection header.
    szTmp = strchr(sClient->szOutBuf, ':');
    if (szTmp != NULL)
      {
        *szTmp = NULL;
        szTmp++;
        if (stricmp(sClient->szOutBuf, "connection") == 0)
          {
            sscanf(szTmp, "%s", szBuf);
            if (stricmp(szBuf, "close") == 0)
              {
                bPersistent = FALSE;
              }
          }
      }
    sClient->RecvTeol(NO_EOL);
  }
```

At the top of the loop, we make our check for the end of the headers by looking for a NULL incoming line. Inside the loop, the first step is to save the current line to the temporary file, since we're going to mangle the line in the next step. The next step consists of using `strchr()` to locate the delimiting colon in the header line. If we find it, we NULL it to mark the end of the field name. A comparison is then made for the field name `connection`. If we succeed at this, we pull the field value using `sscanf()` since it will eliminate any white space for us and make the comparison for the `close` token. Finding the token sets the `bPersistent` flag to FALSE. Outside of the `if` statement, the last line in the loop receives another line from the client before we repeat the process.

Outside of the loop, we grab the size of the file using the `stat()` call and then construct the necessary headers to return the message to the client. One note here is to notice the `Content-Type` sent to the client is `text/http`. This media type is specifically defined for the TRACE method by the protocol. Our last step at this stage is to delete the temporary file and return the `bPersistent` flag to end the function.

8.9 OPTIONS

The `DoOptions()` function handles all OPTIONS requests from clients. Depending on the values passed in, it sends the generic response, or one specific, to a plain resource or executable resource:

```
// ---------------------------------------------------------
//
// DoOptions
//
// Figure out the options available for the specified resource.
//

int DoOptions(Socket *sClient, char *szPath, Headers *hInfo, int
iType)
{
  char *szTmp;

  sClient->Send("HTTP/1.1 200 OK \r\n");
  sClient->Send("Server: ");
  sClient->Send(szServerVer);
  sClient->Send("\r\n");
  szTmp = CreateDate(time(NULL));   // Create a date header.
  if (szTmp != NULL)
    {
      sClient->Send("Date: ");
      sClient->Send(szTmp);
      sClient->Send("\r\n");
      delete [] szTmp;
    }
  sClient->Send("Accept-Encodings: \r\n");

  if (strcmp(szPath, "*") == 0)  // General options requested.
    {
      sClient->Send("Allow: GET, HEAD, POST, PUT, DELETE, TRACE\r\n");
      sClient->Send("Accept-Ranges: bytes\n\n");
    }
  else if (iType == GET)
    {
      sClient->Send("Allow: GET, HEAD \r\n");
      sClient->Send("Accept-Ranges: bytes\n\n");
    }
  else if (iType == POST)
    {
```

```
        sClient->Send("Allow: POST \r\n");
    }
  sClient->Send("\r\n");
  hInfo->ulContentLength = 0;

  return 200;
}

// -------------------------------------------------------
```

There are only a couple of things we do in this function to distinguish it from a normal return. The function starts by sending the standard `Server` and `Date` headers. After this, we send the `Accept-Encodings` header, with no value, to signify our server does not accept any type of encoding on the entity body. We next key on the value of `szPath` to decide whether or not to send general options. If the value of `szPath` is the "`*`" character, then the client has asked for the general information on server capabilities. Our response to this is an `Allow` header, which contains all of the methods we accept, plus an `Accept-Ranges` header to signal our acceptance of byte range requests.

When `szPath` is not "`*`", we look at the value of `iType`. Depending on the resolution of the URI which `DoHttp11()` performed, the value passed in will either be `GET` or `POST`. We send the appropriate `Allow` header for each, plus the `Accept-Ranges` header for `GET`. The server does not accept byte ranges for `POST`. The final send is a blank line to signify the end of the headers.

8.10 PUT

The `PUT` method is new for HTTP/1.1. There were some uses of it in HTTP/1.0, but not enough to make the standard. The method is very simple in concept: just accept the entity body in the request and store it as the name in the URI. Be on alert here for the permissions. You don't want to let just anyone write new files all over your server machine. The one aspect of `PUT` and `DELETE` support I would change now would be to make the default behavior not give permission, the exact opposite of our security model. If this were a textbook, I would just tell you it was an exercise for the reader, but since this isn't, I'll tell

you to check with me via email to see if I go back and revise the server. Knowing
me, I probably will. Enough prattling; let us take a look at the function:

```
// ----------------------------------------------------------
//
// DoPut
//
// Save the entity sent as the specified URI.
//
int DoPut(Socket *sClient, Headers *hInfo, char *szPath, char *szCgi)
{
  struct stat sBuf;
  char *szTmp,
       *szExt,
       *szLoc,
       szBuf[PATH_LENGTH],
       szFile[PATH_LENGTH];
  ofstream ofTmp;
  int iRsp = 200,
      iRc,
      iType,
      iIfUnmod,
      iIfMatch,
      iIfNone,
      i, j;
  unsigned long ulRc;
  BOOL bChunked = FALSE;

  // Figure out where to store it.
  if (szPath != NULL)
    {
      szLoc = szPath;
    }
  else if (szCgi != NULL)
    {
      szLoc = szCgi;
    }
  else // Error. Cannot resolve location.
    {
      SendError(sClient, "Location not found.", 404, HTTP_1_1, hInfo);
      return 404;
    }

  iRc = CheckAuth(szLoc, hInfo, WRITE_ACCESS);  // Check for
                                                // authorization.
```

```
if (iRc == ACCESS_DENIED)  // Send request for credentials.
  {
    sClient->Send("HTTP/1.1 401 \r\n");
    sClient->Send("Server: ");
    sClient->Send(szServerVer);
    sClient->Send("\r\n");
    szTmp = CreateDate(time(NULL));  // Create a date header.
    if (szTmp != NULL)
      {
        sClient->Send("Date: ");
        sClient->Send(szTmp);
        sClient->Send("\r\n");
        delete [] szTmp;
      }
    sprintf(szBuf, "WWW-Authenticate: Basic realm=\"%s\"\r\n",
         hInfo->szRealm);
    sClient->Send(szBuf);
    sClient->Send("Content-Type: text/html\r\n");
    sprintf(szBuf, "Content-Length: %d\r\n", strlen(sz401));
    sClient->Send(szBuf);
    sClient->Send("\r\n");
    sClient->Send(sz401);
    return 401;
  }
else if (iRc == ACCESS_FAILED) // Send forbidden response.
  {
    sClient->Send("HTTP/1.1 403 Access Denied\r\n");
    sClient->Send("Server: ");
    sClient->Send(szServerVer);
    sClient->Send("\r\n");
    szTmp = CreateDate(time(NULL));  // Create a date header.
    if (szTmp != NULL)
      {
        sClient->Send("Date: ");
        sClient->Send(szTmp);
        sClient->Send("\r\n");
        delete [] szTmp;
      }
    sClient->Send("Content-Type: text/html\r\n");
    sprintf(szBuf, "Content-Length: %d\r\n", strlen(sz403));
    sClient->Send(szBuf);
    sClient->Send("\r\n");
    sClient->Send(sz403);
return 403;
  }

if (hInfo->szRange != NULL)  // Range not allowed for PUT.
```

```
    {
      SendError(sClient, "Range header not accepted for PUT.", 501,
            HTTP_1_1, hInfo);
      return 501;
    }
  if (hInfo->szIfModSince != NULL)   // If-Modified-Since
    {                                // not allowed for PUT.
      SendError(sClient,
            "If-Modified-Since header not accepted for PUT.",
            501, HTTP_1_1, hInfo);
      return 501;
    }

  // Now check the If headers.
  iIfUnmod = IfUnmodSince(hInfo, sBuf.st_mtime);
  iIfMatch = IfMatch(hInfo, sBuf.st_mtime);
  iIfNone = IfNone(hInfo, sBuf.st_mtime);
  if ((iIfUnmod == FALSE) || (iIfMatch == FALSE) ||
     (iIfNone == FALSE))
    {
      SendError(sClient, "Precondition failed.", 412,
            HTTP_1_1, hInfo);
      return 412;
    }

  // Accept the resource.
  if (hInfo->bChunked == TRUE)
    {
      bChunked = TRUE;
    }
  else if (hInfo->szContentLength == NULL) // They must supply a
    {                                      // length.
      SendError(sClient, "Length required.", 411, HTTP_1_1, hInfo);
      return 411;
    }
  tmpnam(szFile);
  ofTmp.open(szFile, ios::binary);
  if (! ofTmp)
    {
      SendError(sClient, "Local processing error.", 500,
            HTTP_1_1, hInfo);
      return 500;
    }

  if (bChunked == TRUE)
    {
      GetChunked(sClient, ofTmp, hInfo);
```

```
    }
else   // Use Content-Length instead.
  {
    i = 0;
    while (i < hInfo->ulContentLength)   // The actual resource.
      {
        j = sClient->Recv(hInfo->ulContentLength - i);
        i += j;
        ofTmp.write(sClient->szOutBuf, j);
      }
  }
ofTmp.close();

iRc = stat(szLoc, &sBuf);   // Check for the resource.

ulRc = DosCopy(szFile, szLoc, DCPY_EXISTING);
unlink(szFile);   // Remove the temporary always.
if (ulRc != 0)
  {
    SendError(sClient, "Local processing error.", 500,
            HTTP_1_1, hInfo);
    return 500;
  }

if (iRc == 0)   // File exists. Overwrite it.
  {
    sClient->Send("HTTP/1.1 204 No Content\r\n");
    iRsp = 204;
  }
else // New resource
  {
    sClient->Send("HTTP/1.1 201 Created\r\n");
    iRsp = 201;
  }
sClient->Send("Server: ");
sClient->Send(szServerVer);
sClient->Send("\r\n");
szTmp = CreateDate(time(NULL));   // Create a date header.
if (szTmp != NULL)
  {
    sClient->Send("Date: ");
    sClient->Send(szTmp);
    sClient->Send("\r\n");
    delete [] szTmp;
  }
sClient->Send("\r\n");
```

```
   hInfo->ulContentLength = 0;
   return iRsp;
}


// ----------------------------------------------------------------
```

The first step is to figure out where to place the entity. We do this by checking the values of szPath and szCgi:

```
// Figure out where to store it.
if (szPath != NULL)
   {
      szLoc = szPath;
   }
else if (szCgi != NULL)
   {
      szLoc = szCgi;
   }
else // Error. Cannot resolve location.
   {
      SendError(sClient, "Location not found.", 404,
            HTTP_1_1, hInfo);
      return 404;
   }
```

Our if-else tree checks szPath first. If it is not NULL, then we assign our local pointer szLoc to point to it. The next branch checks szCgi, while the final branch sends an error message to the client.

We check for authorization in the next step, as we do for any method that involves retrieving or placing an entity. The steps involved are the same as we've seen in the past, so we won't repeat the code fragment here. From the previous code listing, you can see the call to CheckAuth(), followed by the check of the return value for either ACCESS_DENIED or ACCESS_FAILED. Either one causes an error message to be sent to the client and ends the function.

This next check is a bit different from what we've done before:

```
if (hInfo->szRange != NULL)  // Range not allowed for PUT.
   {
      SendError(sClient, "Range header not accepted for PUT.", 501,
            HTTP_1_1, hInfo);
      return 501;
   }
```

```
if (hInfo->szIfModSince != NULL)  // If-Modified-Since
  {                               // not allowed for PUT.
    SendError(sClient,
            "If-Modified-Since header not accepted for PUT.",
            501, HTTP_1_1, hInfo);
    return 501;
  }
```

With the PUT method, there are a couple of things our server refuses to do. The first of these is support a byte range request for the PUT entity. While it is possible to support a byte range insertion into a file, there are quite a few variables which make it uncertain all of the time. The single biggest obstacle is exactly how to calculate the byte range. If considering the PUT operation as updating a Web page, then you basically want to replace part of it. How many times, in editing anything, do you inadvertently make changes which take up the identical number of bytes as what it replaced? If you were working with fixed length records, as in a database, then it would be possible to define an extension range type which is the index number, and submit updates in that manner. We'll avoid those worms here.

The other item we don't allow is the specification of an If-Modified-Since header. The HTTP/1.1 standard specifically states that this header is used as a modifier to the GET method. If we detect the header as just being present, we return an error message to the client.

Now we must check the other If headers introduced by HTTP/1.1:

```
// Now check the If headers.
iIfUnmod = IfUnmodSince(hInfo, sBuf.st_mtime);
iIfMatch = IfMatch(hInfo, sBuf.st_mtime);
iIfNone = IfNone(hInfo, sBuf.st_mtime);
if ((iIfUnmod == FALSE) || (iIfMatch == FALSE) ||
    (iIfNone == FALSE))
  {
    SendError(sClient, "Precondition failed.", 412,
            HTTP_1_1, hInfo);
    return 412;
  }
```

The three headers represented here, If-Unmodified-Since, If-Match, and If-None-Match, must be checked to make sure none failed. The calls to the respective functions perform the checks and return FALSE when any fail. If any of the three failed, the 412 Precondition Failed code is returned to the client. We'll cover the If functions a bit later in this chapter.

Now we're ready to receive the resource from the client for further processing. In order to do so, we must be able to determine the end of the entity body. The two ways we have available to do this are chunked encoding and the client's specifying a content length:

```
// Accept the resource.
if (hInfo->bChunked == TRUE)
   {
     bChunked = TRUE;
   }
else if (hInfo->szContentLength == NULL)// They must supply
   {                                     // a length.
     SendError(sClient, "Length required.", 411, HTTP_1_1, hInfo);
     return 411;
   }
```

We check for chunked encoding first, by looking at hInfo->bChunked. If it's TRUE, then the client has specified the entity body as being transferred using the chunked method. If not, then we check for the Content-Length header to tell us the number of bytes present. If this one fails, we send a 411 Length Required code to the client and end the function.

A temporary file is opened now to hold the entity body as it is received from the client. We then branch onto receiving methods:

```
if (bChunked == TRUE)
   {
     GetChunked(sClient, ofTmp, hInfo);
   }
else  // Use Content-Length instead.
   {
     i = 0;
     while (i < hInfo->ulContentLength)  // The actual resource.
        {
          j = sClient->Recv(hInfo->ulContentLength - i);
          i += j;
          ofTmp.write(sClient->szOutBuf, j);
        }
   }
```

For the chunked method, another function `GetChunked()` is called. We'll look at it in a moment. For entity bodies specified by a length, the `else` branch goes into a loop trying to receive the specified number of bytes. The construction here is important to note. The `Socket` class `Recv()` function only tries to receive the specified number of bytes, so it may return less. Thus, we must loop through until we get the number we want, and each time we must adjust the number for which we ask. Our temporary file has been opened in binary mode, so a `write()` operation is used where the number of bytes to be written can be easily specified.

Once the entity has been saved to the temporary file, we use the appropriate OS API call to copy the new file over the top of the old one. The `stat()` call just before is to determine whether the file was already there. If the file did exist, we send a `204 No Content` response to the client. If it is a new file, then a `201 Created` is sent. Our `Server` and `Date` headers are sent, followed by the empty line to mark the end of the headers. `hInfo->ulContentLength` is set to zero since no entity was sent and `iRsp` is finally returned.

8.11 If functions

In the last section, we made some calls to the `If` functions, which check the values of the conditional headers which may be present. Let us go ahead and look at them now:

```
// --------------------------------------------------------------
//
// IfModSince
//
// Check whether the file had been modifed since the date
// given by the client.
//

int IfModSince(Headers *hInfo, time_t ttMtime)
{
   if (hInfo->szIfModSince != NULL)
     {
       if ((hInfo->ttIfModSince > 0) &&
           (hInfo->ttIfModSince < ttMtime))
         {
```

```
        return TRUE;
      }
    else
      {
        return FALSE;
      }
  }
  return TRUE;   // Default is TRUE.
}
```

// ---

The first `If` function checks the `If-Modified-Since` header. In this function, we must first look for the header by checking if `hInfo->szIfModSince` is
not NULL. Once found, we make certain the value given by the client is greater
than zero, and that the date given is earlier than the current timestamp on the
file. We return FALSE only if the timestamp check fails.

Our next `If` function, `IfUnmodSince()` is almost a twin:

```
// -----------------------------------------------------------------
//
// IfUnmodSince
//
// Check whether the file has not been modified since the date
// given by the client.
//

int IfUnmodSince(Headers *hInfo, time_t ttMtime)
{
  if (hInfo->szIfUnmodSince != NULL)
    {
      if ((hInfo->ttIfUnmodSince > 0) &&
         (hInfo->ttIfUnmodSince > ttMtime))
        {
          return TRUE;
        }
      else
        {
          return FALSE;
        }
    }
  return TRUE;   // Default is TRUE.
}
```

// ---

The logical difference here from the `IfModSince()` function is the returning of FALSE only when the time given is earlier than the modification time of the file, the exact opposite of before. We are, of course, checking the `If-Unmodified-Since` value for this function.

Next we turn our attention to the entity tags in the `If-Match` header:

```
// ----------------------------------------------------------------
//
// IfMatch
//
// Check the etag of the resource against that given by the client
// for a match.
//

int IfMatch(Headers *hInfo, time_t ttMtime)
{
   int iIfMatch = TRUE,
       i;
   char *szBuf,
        szEtagStar[] = "*";

   // Check to see if any etags match.
   if (hInfo->szIfMatch != NULL)
     {
        iIfMatch = FALSE; // We fail unless we match.
        szBuf = new char[SMALLBUF];
        sprintf(szBuf, "\"%d\"", ttMtime);
        for (i = 0; hInfo->szIfMatchEtags[i] != NULL; i++)
          {
            if (strcmp(hInfo->szIfMatchEtags[i], szBuf) == 0)
              {
                iIfMatch = TRUE;
                break;
              }
            if (strcmp(hInfo->szIfMatchEtags[i], szEtagStar) == 0)
              {
                iIfMatch = TRUE;
                break;
              }
          }
        delete [] szBuf;
     }
   return iIfMatch;
}

// ----------------------------------------------------------------
```

This function is a bit more involved than those which check timestamps. In this function we must compare entity tags over the set of tags sent by the client. In most cases, this should be a single tag, but multiple tags are allowed and the code must handle them. The first check made is to see if an `If-Match` header was found. If it wasn't, a default value of TRUE is returned, meaning the test is satisfactory. It may seem a bit odd at first, but the field is optional, so not having any values is the same as matching one, and we return TRUE.

When the header is present, we default the return value to FALSE. We must match now. A call to `sprintf()` is used to create the entity tag for the comparison test. What we do here is loop through the stored entity tags in the `Header` class. Our `for` loop is conditional on finding the last value to be NULL since we don't save the number of tags, but instead we use a NULL marker. Inside the loop, we must make two comparisons each time. The first is against the entity tag since we created it. The second is against the wildcard entity tag of "*". The first time we find a match, `iIfMatch` is set to TRUE and we break out of the loop immediately to return it to the calling function.

The next `If` function handles checking the `If-None-Match` header. Basically it does the opposite of the previous function. It checks to make sure there is not a match of entity tags:

```
// -----------------------------------------------------------------
//
// IfNone
//
// Check to make sure no etags match the resource.
//

int IfNone(Headers *hInfo, time_t ttMtime)
{
   int iIfNone = TRUE,
       i;
   char *szBuf,
       szEtagStar[] = "*";

   // Check to see if any of the If-None-Match etags match
   if (hInfo->szIfNoneMatch != NULL)
   {
       iIfNone = TRUE;  // We're ok unless we match.
       szBuf = new char[SMALLBUF];
       sprintf(szBuf, "\"%d\"", ttMtime);
```

```
      for (i = 0; hInfo->szIfNoneMatchEtags[i] != NULL; i++)
        {
          if (strcmp(hInfo->szIfNoneMatchEtags[i], szBuf) == 0)
            {
              iIfNone = FALSE;
              break;
            }
          if (strcmp(hInfo->szIfNoneMatchEtags[i], szEtagStar) == 0)
            {
              iIfNone = FALSE;
              break;
            }
        }
      delete [] szBuf;
    }
  return iIfNone;
}

// -------------------------------------------------------------
```

As can be seen, the flow of execution is like the `IfMatch()` function. We first check to see if the header `If-None-Match` was found. Not finding it causes a `TRUE` condition to be returned. Inside the `If` statement, we create the entity tag for the current resource and then compare it to the entity tags sent by the client. A check is also made against the match-all token `"*"`. If a comparison is true here, the function sets the return value to be `FALSE`. The meaning of the header is to fail if we match an entity tag for the subject and current resource, hence `FALSE` must be returned.

8.12 Chunked encoding

The chunked encoding method is a way for an HTTP/1.1 application to send an entity body without explicitly knowing the full length when the transmission starts. It allows the application to send a *chunk* of the entity body, specifying only the length of the current chunk. For applications which dynamically generate responses, it means not having to store the entity body in order to calculate the length anymore. Receiving chunked encoding is fairly simple too:

```
// -----------------------------------------------------------------
//
// GetChunked
//
// Receive the entity using the chunked method.
//

int GetChunked(Socket *sClient, ofstream &ofOut, Headers *hInfo)
{
  BOOL bNotDone = TRUE;
  char *szPtr;
  int iBytes, i, j, l, iFactor;

  while (bNotDone == TRUE)
    {
      sClient->RecvTeol(NO_EOL);  // Grab a line. Should have
                                  // chunk size.
      if (strcmp(sClient->szOutBuf, "0") == 0)
        {
          bNotDone = FALSE;  // The end of the chunks.
          continue;
        }

      szPtr = strchr(sClient->szOutBuf, ';');
      if (szPtr != NULL) *szPtr = NULL;  // Mark end of chunk-size.

      l = strlen(sClient->szOutBuf); // Find last hex digit.
      l--;
      iBytes = 0;
      iFactor = 1;
  // Convert to decimal bytes.
      while (l >= 0)
        {
          iBytes += iFactor * Hex2Dec(sClient->szOutBuf[l]);
          l--;
          iFactor *= 16;
        }
      i = 0;
      // Now receive the specified number of bytes.
      while (i < iBytes)
        {
          j = sClient->Recv(iBytes - i);    // Some data.
          i += j;                           // Total the bytes.
          ofOut.write(sClient->szOutBuf, j); // Save to disk.
        }
```

```
        sClient->RecvTeol(NO_EOL);   // Discard end of chunk marker.
    }

    // Now consume anything in the footer.
    hInfo->RcvHeaders(sClient);
    return 0;
}

// --------------------------------------------------------------
```

The basic form for chunked encoding (as presented in Chapter 2) is:

```
Chunked-Body     = *chunk
                   "0" CRLF
                   footer
                   CRLF
chunk            = chunk-size [ chunk-ext ] CRLF
                   chunk-data CRLF
hex-no-zero      = <HEX excluding "0">
chunk-size       = hex-no-zero *HEX
chunk-ext        = *( ";" chunk-ext-name [ "=" chunk-ext-value ] )
chunk-ext-name   = token
chunk-ext-val    = token | quoted-string
chunk-data       = chunk-size (OCTET)
footer           = *entity-header
```

In pseudo-code, we have a pattern such as:

```
<size in hex>CRLF
<data>CRLF
<size in hex>CRLF
<data>CRLF
...
<0 size>CRLF
<optional footer>CRLF
```

For our algorithm, we want to grab the first line of the entity body as delimited by the carriage return line feed sequence. On this line will be the size of the upcoming chunk specified in Hex. The only restriction on the size is that it cannot be a zero size chunk. The use of the zero size chunk is restricted to indicate the end of the chunked encoding. Once the size is decoded, we must receive the specified number of bytes and then receive the carriage return line feed sequence denoting the end of the chunk. This carriage return line feed is not part of the data, but just a marker between the end of the chunk and the next size specification. This pattern is repeated until the 0 chunk is reached. After the 0 chunk, it is possible for the client to send some additional headers known as footers. Only those headers specified in the protocol for use in the footer may be used here. Finally, an ending carriage return line feed is received to mark the end of the entity body and request.

Our first section of code grabs the chunk size from the client:

```
while (bNotDone == TRUE)
   {
      sClient->RecvTeol(NO_EOL); // Grab a line. Should have
                                 // chunk size.
      if (strcmp(sClient->szOutBuf, "0") == 0)
        {
           bNotDone = FALSE;      // The end of the chunks.
           continue;
        }
```

Using the standard `RecvTeol()` function, the next line of input is read from the client. We make a comparison here to determine if it is the ending chunk by comparing it to 0. If we find the end, our loop flag is set to FALSE and the `continue` statement forces execution to the top of the loop where the conditional will now be false. If we don't find a 0, then we have a hex size for a chunk and must decode it:

```
szPtr = strchr(sClient->szOutBuf, ';');
if (szPtr != NULL) *szPtr = NULL;  // Mark end of chunk-size.

l = strlen(sClient->szOutBuf); // Find last hex digit.
l--;
iBytes = 0;
iFactor = 1;
// Convert to decimal bytes.
while (l >= 0)
   {
      iBytes += iFactor * Hex2Dec(sClient->szOutBuf[l]);
      l--;
      iFactor *= 16;
   }
```

The first two lines here check for the existence of a chunk extension with the size. If a chunk extension is present, then a semicolon will separate it from the size. We simply find the semicolon and NULL it out to end the line. Now we can find the last digit of the hex number by using strlen() and adjusting our C indexing by one. iBytes is initialized to 0 as our byte counter and iFactor to 1 as the adjustment for the base 16 of the hex number.

Inside the loop, we multiply iFactor by the decimal value of the hex digit. As we move from right to left of the hex string, we increase our factor by 16 each time, to allow for the change in place of the hex digits. When our index value reaches 0, we have completed the conversion. The Hex2Dec() function is a simple reworking of the Hex2Char() function used for translating URIs. Instead of returning a character value, it returns the appropriate decimal conversion.

To actually receive the chunk, we use the same construct as in the DoPut() function previously mentioned:

```
i = 0;
// Now receive the specified number of bytes.
while (i < iBytes)
   {
     j = sClient->Recv(iBytes - i);      // Some data.
     i += j;                             // Total the bytes.
     ofOut.write(sClient->szOutBuf, j);  // Save to disk.
   }
```

This loop continues reading bytes from the socket until the specified number of bytes have been read. Since we aren't guaranteed how many bytes will be returned each time, we must adjust our request for bytes on the fly. Once the specified number is read, we grab the carriage return line feed, which marks the end of the chunk, and return to the top of the loop to receive the next chunk. After the last chunk is read and the loop ends, we call hInfo->RcvHeaders() to consume any footers sent by the client.

For completeness, following is the Hex2Dec() as modified from the original Hex2Char() function:

```
// ------------------------------------------------------------------
//
// Hex2Dec
```

```
//
// Convert a hex character to a decimal character.
//

int Hex2Dec(char c)
{
  switch (c)
    {
      case 'A':
      case 'a':
        return 10;
      case 'B':
      case 'b':
        return 11;
      case 'C':
      case 'c':
        return 12;
      case 'D':
      case 'd':
        return 13;
      case 'E':
      case 'e':
        return 14;
      case 'F':
      case 'f':
        return 15;
      default:
        return (c - 48);
    }
}

// ----------------------------------------------------------------
```

8.13 The DELETE method

DELETE is the next method we'll examine. The method allows the client to delete selected resources on the Web server. This could be used to implement a Web management system where users can update and remove pages remotely or perhaps a version control system. Just as in the PUT method, this method must be guarded against unauthorized use since a security hole could wreak havoc with a Web server. Following is the complete function:

```
// ------------------------------------------------------------
//
// DoDelete
//
// This function checks to see if it can delete the resource
// specified by the client.
//

int DoDelete(Socket *sClient, char *szPath, char *szCgi,
             Headers *hInfo)
{
  struct stat sBuf;
  char *szTmp,
       *szExt,
       szBuf[PATH_LENGTH],
       szFile[PATH_LENGTH];
  ofstream ofTmp;
  int iRsp = 200,
      iRc,
      iType,
      iIfMod,
      iIfUnmod,
      iIfMatch,
      iIfNone;

  iRc = CheckAuth(szPath, hInfo, WRITE_ACCESS);   // Check for
                                                  // authorization.
  if (iRc == ACCESS_DENIED)  // Send request for credentials.
    {
      sClient->Send("HTTP/1.1 401 \r\n");
      sClient->Send("Server: ");
      sClient->Send(szServerVer);
      sClient->Send("\r\n");
      szTmp = CreateDate(time(NULL));  // Create a date header.
      if (szTmp != NULL)
        {
          sClient->Send("Date: ");
          sClient->Send(szTmp);
          sClient->Send("\r\n");
          delete [] szTmp;
        }
      sprintf(szBuf, "WWW-Authenticate: Basic realm=\"%s\"\r\n",
              hInfo->szRealm);
      sClient->Send(szBuf);
      sClient->Send("Content-Type: text/html\r\n");
      sprintf(szBuf, "Content-Length: %d\r\n", strlen(sz401));
      sClient->Send(szBuf);
```

```
         sClient->Send("\r\n");
         sClient->Send(sz401);
         return 401;
      }
   else if (iRc == ACCESS_FAILED) // Send forbidden response.
      {
         sClient->Send("HTTP/1.1 403 Access Denied\r\n");
         sClient->Send("Server: ");
         sClient->Send(szServerVer);
         sClient->Send("\r\n");
         szTmp = CreateDate(time(NULL));  // Create a date header.
         if (szTmp != NULL)
            {
               sClient->Send("Date: ");
               sClient->Send(szTmp);
               sClient->Send("\r\n");
               delete [] szTmp;
            }
         sClient->Send("Content-Type: text/html\r\n");
         sprintf(szBuf, "Content-Length: %d\r\n", strlen(sz403));
         sClient->Send(szBuf);
         sClient->Send("\r\n");
         sClient->Send(sz403);
         return 403;
      }

   if (hInfo->szRange != NULL)  // Range not allowed for DELETE.
      {
         SendError(sClient, "Range header not accepted for DELETE.",
                   501, HTTP_1_1, hInfo);
         return 501;
      }
   if (hInfo->szIfModSince != NULL)  // If-Modified-Since
      {                              // not allowed for DELETE.
         SendError(sClient,
                   "If-Modified-Since header not accepted for DELETE.",
                   501, HTTP_1_1, hInfo);
         return 501;
      }

   // Now check the If headers.
   iIfUnmod = IfUnmodSince(hInfo, sBuf.st_mtime);
   iIfMatch = IfMatch(hInfo, sBuf.st_mtime);
   iIfNone = IfNone(hInfo, sBuf.st_mtime);
   if ((iIfUnmod == FALSE) || (iIfMatch == FALSE) ||
       (iIfNone == FALSE))
      {
```

```
        SendError(sClient, "Precondition failed.", 412,
                HTTP_1_1, hInfo);
        return 412;
    }

    if (szDeleteDir != NULL)  // Save the deleted resource.
        {
        // Use the same file extension as the current resource.
        szExt = strrchr(szPath, '.');
        if (szExt != NULL)
            {
            szExt++;
            }
        else
            {
            szExt = "del";
            }
        szTmp = MakeUnique(szDeleteDir, szExt);
        DosCopy(szPath, szTmp, DCPY_EXISTING);
        }
    iRc = unlink(szPath);
    if (iRc == 0) // Resource deleted.
        {
        sClient->Send("HTTP/1.1 204 \r\n");
        iRsp = 204;
        }
    else // Delete failed.
        {
        sClient->Send("HTTP/1.1 500 \r\n");
        iRsp = 500;
        }
    sClient->Send("Server: ");
    sClient->Send(szServerVer);
    sClient->Send("\r\n");
    szTmp = CreateDate(time(NULL));// Create a date header.
    if (szTmp != NULL)
        {
        sClient->Send("Date: ");
        sClient->Send(szTmp);
        sClient->Send("\r\n");
        delete [] szTmp;
        }
    sClient->Send("\r\n");
    hInfo->ulContentLength = 0;
    return iRsp;
}

// ----------------------------------------------------------------
```

The `DoDelete()` function starts by checking for the client's authorization. This check uses the same code as the previous functions so we won't go over it in depth right here. After the authorization is approved, we must start checking the conditional headers to make certain we should complete the request:

```
if (hInfo->szRange != NULL)  // Range not allowed for DELETE.
  {
    SendError(sClient, "Range header not accepted for DELETE.",
          501, HTTP_1_1, hInfo);
    return 501;
  }
if (hInfo->szIfModSince != NULL)  // If-Modified-Since
  {                               // not allowed for DELETE.
    SendError(sClient,
          "If-Modified-Since header not accepted for DELETE.",
          501, HTTP_1_1, hInfo);
    return 501;
  }
```

The first conditionals for which we check are the ones we don't allow. If the client sends a range request with the DELETE method, we reject the request outright. The `hInfo->szIfModSince` variable is also checked to see if header `If-Modified-Since` was sent. Again here, the protocol states it is only valid for GET requests, so we reject it also. The other If headers are checked next:

```
// Now check the If headers.
iIfUnmod = IfUnmodSince(hInfo, sBuf.st_mtime);
iIfMatch = IfMatch(hInfo, sBuf.st_mtime);
iIfNone = IfNone(hInfo, sBuf.st_mtime);
if ((iIfUnmod == FALSE) || (iIfMatch == FALSE) ||
    (iIfNone == FALSE))
  {
    SendError(sClient, "Precondition failed.", 412,
          HTTP_1_1, hInfo);
    return 412;
  }
```

As in the `DoPut()` function, the same checks are made here. We want to make sure the `If-Unmodified-Since`, `If-Match`, and `If-None-Match` headers check out. Our check functions return FALSE if any fail, and we then return the `412 Precondition Failed` response to the client.

What we do next is unique to this function: If a client does delete a resource, we allow the Webmaster to specify in the configuration file to save any deleted resources. This allows for a safety net for the users and makes the Webmaster appear omnipotent to the careless users:

```
if (szDeleteDir != NULL)  // Save the deleted resource.
  {
    // Use the same file extension as the current resource.
    szExt = strrchr(szPath, '.');
    if (szExt != NULL)
      {
        szExt++;
      }
    else
      {
        szExt = "del";
      }
    szTmp = MakeUnique(szDeleteDir, szExt);
    DosCopy(szPath, szTmp, DCPY_EXISTING);
    delete [] szTmp;
  }
```

We check our global flag variable szDeleteDir to determine whether to save a copy of the resource. If we find it defined, this signifies its use to save the resource and tells us where to save it. Inside the If statement, we look for the file extension of the resource using strrchr(), which will find the last occurrence of the dot character in the filename. If we find it, we adjust szExt to point to the start of the extension, and if not, to the string del. The following line creates a unique temporary file for us in the directory we specify, with the extension we provide. This function, MakeUnique(), is one we must provide since the C library functions do not let us pick the directory in which to create the temporary filenames. The last step is to copy the resource to the new filename and then delete the memory for the filename.

The last part of the function is to just complete the action:

```
iRc = unlink(szPath);
if (iRc == 0) // Resource deleted.
  {
    sClient->Send("HTTP/1.1 204 No Content\r\n");
    iRsp = 204;
  }
```

```
else // Delete failed.
  {
    sClient->Send("HTTP/1.1 500 Server Error\r\n");
    iRsp = 500;
  }
```

Using `unlink()`, we delete the requested resource. Based on the return value, we send a `204 No Content` when the delete operation succeeds and a `500 Server Error` when it fails. The remainder of the function returns the `Server` and `Date` headers back to the client.

Let us also look at the `MakeUnique()` function.

```
// -------------------------------------------------------
//
// MakeUnique()
//
// Create a unique filename in the specified directory with the
// specified extension.
//
char * MakeUnique(char *szDir, char *szExt)
{
  ULONG ulNum = 0;
  BOOL bNotUnique = TRUE;
  int iRc;
  char *szFileName;

  szFileName = new char[PATH_LENGTH];

  while (bNotUnique)
    {
      sprintf(szFileName, "%s%08d.%s", szDir, ulNum, szExt);
      iRc = open(szFileName, O_CREAT | O_EXCL | O_WRONLY
                 | O_TEXT, S_IWRITE);
      if (iRc != -1)
        {
          // Success. This file didn't exist before.
          close(iRc);
          bNotUnique = FALSE;
          continue;
        }

      ulNum++;
      if (ulNum > 99999999)
        {
```

```
            delete [] szFileName;
            szFileName = NULL;
            bNotUnique = FALSE;
         }
      }
   return (szFileName);
}


// ------------------------------------------------------------
```

This function is simple in its operation. We start with an empty string, szFileName, and create a filename by concatenating together the directory sent by the client, an integer number controlled by the function, and the extension sent by the client. Once put together, we try to create a new file with a call to open() with the O_CREAT and O_EXCL flags set to make certain we only create the file if it does not already exist.

If the open() call is successful, then we close the new file, set NotUnique to FALSE, and issue a continue statement to have the loop complete. The new filename is then returned to the client. When the open() call fails, we instead increment our counter and run through the loop again. The basic algorithm here is to sequentially increment our integer counter until we find one not in use. Given the possibility of running on a FAT partition, we limit the number of digits we use to 8. This gives us plenty of choices however.

8.14 GET the document

Our final method handler to cover is DoPath11(). This is the function which handles the bulk of the requests of the Web server:

```
// -----------------------------------------------------------------
//
// DoPath11()
//
// This function checks to see if it can return the requested
// document back to the client.
//

int DoPath11(Socket *sClient, int iMethod, char *szPath,
```

```
                char *szSearch, Headers *hInfo)
{
   struct stat sBuf;
   char *szTmp,
        *szExt,
        szBuf[PATH_LENGTH],
        szFile[PATH_LENGTH];
   ofstream ofTmp;
   int iRsp = 200,
       iRc,
       iType,
       iIfMod,
       iIfUnmod,
       iIfMatch,
       iIfNone,
       iIfRange,
       iRangeErr;

   if (szPath[strlen(szPath) - 1] == '/')
     {
       strcat(szPath, szWelcome);  // Append default welcome file.
     }

   iRc = CheckAuth(szPath, hInfo, READ_ACCESS);  // Check for
                                                 // authorization.
   if (iRc == ACCESS_DENIED)  // Send request for credentials.
     {
       sClient->Send("HTTP/1.1 401 \r\n");
       sClient->Send("Server: ");
       sClient->Send(szServerVer);
       sClient->Send("\r\n");
       szTmp = CreateDate(time(NULL));  // Create a date header.
       if (szTmp != NULL)
         {
           sClient->Send("Date: ");
           sClient->Send(szTmp);
           sClient->Send("\r\n");
           delete [] szTmp;
         }
       sprintf(szBuf,
               "WWW-Authenticate: Basic realm=\"%s\"\r\n",
               hInfo->szRealm);
       sClient->Send(szBuf);
       sClient->Send("Content-Type: text/html\r\n");
       sprintf(szBuf, "Content-Length: %d\r\n", strlen(sz401));
       sClient->Send(szBuf);
       sClient->Send("\r\n");
```

```
      sClient->Send(sz401);
      return 401;
   }
else if (iRc == ACCESS_FAILED) // Send forbidden response.
   {
      sClient->Send("HTTP/1.1 403 Access Denied\r\n");
      sClient->Send("Server: ");
      sClient->Send(szServerVer);
      sClient->Send("\r\n");
      szTmp = CreateDate(time(NULL));  // Create a date header.
      if (szTmp != NULL)
        {
           sClient->Send("Date: ");
           sClient->Send(szTmp);
           sClient->Send("\r\n");
           delete [] szTmp;
        }
      sClient->Send("Content-Type: text/html\r\n");
      sprintf(szBuf, "Content-Length: %d\r\n", strlen(sz403));
      sClient->Send(szBuf);
      sClient->Send("\r\n");
      sClient->Send(sz403);
      return 403;
   }

if (szSearch != NULL)  // Do an index search.
   {
      iRc = Index(szPath, szSearch, szFile, hInfo->szUri);
      if (iRc != 0)
        {
           iRc = SendError(sClient, "Resource not found.", 404,
                        HTTP_1_1, hInfo);
           return iRc;
        }
      strcpy(szPath, szFile);
   }

iRc = stat(szPath, &sBuf);
if (iRc < 0)
   {
      iRsp = SendError(sClient, "Resource not found.", 404,
                  HTTP_1_1, hInfo);
      return iRsp;
   }

// Check If headers.
iIfMod = IfModSince(hInfo, sBuf.st_mtime);
```

```
iIfUnmod = IfUnmodSince(hInfo, sBuf.st_mtime);
iIfMatch = IfMatch(hInfo, sBuf.st_mtime);
iIfNone = IfNone(hInfo, sBuf.st_mtime);
iIfRange = IfRange(hInfo, sBuf.st_mtime);
iRangeErr = hInfo->FindRanges(sBuf.st_size);

// Check to make sure any If headers are FALSE.
// Either not-modified or no etags matched.
if ( (iIfMod == FALSE) || (iIfNone == FALSE) )
   {
     sClient->Send("HTTP/1.1 304 Not Modified\r\n");
     iRsp = 304;
   }
// No matching etags or it's been modified.
else if ( (iIfMatch == FALSE) || (iIfUnmod == FALSE) )
   {
     sClient->Send("HTTP/1.1 412 Precondition Failed\r\n");
     iRsp = 412;
   }
// Resource matched so send just the bytes requested.
else if ((iIfRange == TRUE) && (iRangeErr == 0))
   {
     sClient->Send("HTTP/1.1 206 Partial Content\r\n");
     iRsp = 206;
   }
// Resource didn't match, so send the entire entity.
else if ((hInfo->szIfRange != NULL) && (iIfRange == FALSE))
   {
     sClient->Send("HTTP/1.1 200 OK\r\n");
     iRsp = 200;
   }
// Only asked for a byte range.
else if (iRangeErr == 0)
   {
     sClient->Send("HTTP/1.1 206 Partial Content\r\n");
     iRsp = 206;
   }
// Must be a plain jane request.
else
   {
     sClient->Send("HTTP/1.1 200 OK\r\n");
     iRsp = 200;
   }

sClient->Send("Server: ");   // Standard server header.
sClient->Send(szServerVer);
sClient->Send("\r\n");
```

```
   szTmp = CreateDate(time(NULL));   // Create a date header.
   if (szTmp != NULL)
     {
        sClient->Send("Date: ");
        sClient->Send(szTmp);
        sClient->Send("\r\n");
        delete [] szTmp;
     }
   szTmp = CreateDate(sBuf.st_mtime);   // The last modified time
                                        // header.
   if (szTmp != NULL)
     {
        sClient->Send("Last-Modified: ");
        sClient->Send(szTmp);
        sClient->Send("\r\n");
        delete [] szTmp;
     }
sprintf(szBuf, "ETag: \"%d\"\r\n", sBuf.st_mtime); // Entity tag.
sClient->Send(szBuf);

   if ((iRsp == 304) || (iRsp == 412))
     {
        sClient->Send("\r\n");
        return iRsp;   // Don't send anything else.
     }

   if (szSearch != NULL)     // Force search results to text/html type.
     {
        iType = FindType("x.html");
     }
   else
     {
        iType = FindType(szPath); // Figure out the media type to
                                  // return.
     }

   if (iRsp == 206) // Sending partial content.
     {
        // Send byte range to client.
        SendByteRange(sClient, hInfo, szPath, &sBuf, iType, iMethod);
        return iRsp;
     }

   // Send full entity.
   sprintf(szBuf, "Content-Type: %s\r\n", eExtMap[iType].szType);
   sClient->Send(szBuf);
   sprintf(szBuf, "Content-Length: %d\r\n", sBuf.st_size);
```

```
   sClient->Send(szBuf);
   sClient->Send("\r\n");

   if (iMethod == GET)   // Don't send unless GET.
     {
        if (eExtMap[iType].bBinary == TRUE)
          {
             iRc = sClient->SendBinary(szPath);
          }
        else
          {
             iRc = sClient->SendText(szPath);
          }
     }

   return iRsp;
}

// -----------------------------------------------------------------
```

Since this function handles all default GET or HEAD requests, it is possible for the client to not specify a specific resource, but to let the system provide the default. The first bit of code in DoHttp11() takes care of this:

```
if (szPath[strlen(szPath) - 1] == '/')
  {
     strcat(szPath, szWelcome);   // Append default welcome file.
  }
```

We simply check for any path ending in a forward slash and if found, we append the default welcome file name as listed in the configuration file. Note, we do not check here to see if this is valid. We just check to make sure we have a full pathname when looking up the resource.

The security check comes after this point, since we now have a full pathname to check. The difference between this one and the calls in DoPut() and DoDelete() is specifying to check read access with the READ_ACCESS flag. Upon failure here, we either request credentials from the client or deny them access if they supplied credentials which failed.

Once access has been approved, we must check to ascertain whether or not the client requested a simple ISINDEX of the requested resource. This will be true if szSearch is not NULL:

```
if (szSearch != NULL)   // Do an index search.
  {
    iRc = Index(szPath, szSearch, szFile, hInfo->szUri);
    if (iRc != 0)
      {
        iRc = SendError(sClient, "Resource not found.", 404,
                        HTTP_1_1, hInfo);
        return iRc;
      }
    strcpy(szPath, szFile);
  }
```

The Index() function (unchanged from the HTTP/1.0 version) performs the simple search, creates the html output file and stores the filename in szFile. Since the rest of DoHttp11() uses szPath, we copy the contents of szFile into the current szPath.

Now that we have reached this point, we verify the existence of the resource file by using the stat() call. If it develops that the file does not exist, an error message is sent to the client with a 404 Not Found code. Otherwise, it is time to check the If headers, all of them this time:

```
// Check If headers.
iIfMod   = IfModSince(hInfo, sBuf.st_mtime);
iIfUnmod = IfUnmodSince(hInfo, sBuf.st_mtime);
iIfMatch = IfMatch(hInfo, sBuf.st_mtime);
iIfNone  = IfNone(hInfo, sBuf.st_mtime);
iIfRange = IfRange(hInfo, sBuf.st_mtime);
iRangeErr = hInfo->FindRanges(sBuf.st_size);
```

The first four lines are functions we have seen when handling the other request methods. New at this time, are the IfRange() and hInfo->FindRanges() functions. The IfRange() function checks the If-Range header to see if it is present. If it is present, it then verifies whether or not the field value matches the given resource. This field value may either be a date or entity tag for the If-Range header. FindRanges(), as mentioned earlier in the chapter, parses any byte ranges given by the client and stores them in an array of Range class objects.

Next comes the tricky part of HTTP/1.1: Given the multitude of possible headers the client may send for any given request, the order in which the conditionals are checked is important. Depending on the failure condition here, we send different response codes to the client:

```
// Either not-modified or no etags matched.
if ( (iIfMod == FALSE) || (iIfNone == FALSE) )
   {
      sClient->Send("HTTP/1.1 304 Not Modified\r\n");
      iRsp = 304;
   }
```

The first check we make is for those headers which require a 304 response on failure. This is either the If-Modified-Since or If-None-Match headers. If the former fails, it means the resource has not been modified since the date given by the client, hence we don't want to send them another copy. If the latter fails, it means an entity tag sent by the client did match the entity tag of the resource. Remember the If-None-Match means only to perform the action if none of the tags sent match the resource. So if one matches, then we have a failure of the conditional:

```
// No matching etags or it's been modified.
else if ( (iIfMatch == FALSE) || (iIfUnmod == FALSE) )
   {
      sClient->Send("HTTP/1.1 412 Precondition Failed\r\n");
      iRsp = 412;
   }
```

This check is for the If-Match and If-Unmodified-Since headers. If either of these fail, we must return a 412 Precondition Failed response to the client. The If-Match header fails if none of the entity tags sent by the client match the entity tag of the resource. If-Unmodified-Since fails when the resource has been modified since the date given by the client.

The checks in the first two If statements must be done before our other checks. The reason is that these are the checks for failure. The rest of the checks are for success. We don't want to send a success response line to the client and then turn around and fail to send the resource. Now that we have progressed this far, we know we are going to send a resource to the client. It is just a matter of whether it will be a full resource or a byte range that we send back.

```
// Resource matched so send just the bytes requested.
else if ((iIfRange == TRUE) && (iRangeErr == 0))
  {
    sClient->Send("HTTP/1.1 206 Partial Content\r\n");
    iRsp = 206;
  }
```

At this point, we must check to see if we need to send a byte range. The conditions necessary for this to be true are for the client to have sent a valid `Range` header and a valid `If-Range`. `iRangeErr` will be 0 when the client sent a valid byte range request. `iIfRange` will be `TRUE` if the client did not send an `If-Range` header or if the `If-Range` header sent is valid. When both conditions are met, we send the `206 Partial Content` response to the client.

```
// Resource didn't match, so send the entire entity.
else if ((hInfo->szIfRange != NULL) && (iIfRange == FALSE))
  {
    sClient->Send("HTTP/1.1 200 OK\r\n");
    iRsp = 200;
  }
```

The next check is instituted when the client requests a byte range, but the resource has since changed. This uses the `If-Range` header to short circuit the normal error message and instead has us send the complete new resource. These conditions are true when the client did send an `If-Range` header and the `iIfRange` variable is `FALSE`, meaning the field value did not match.

```
// Only asked for a byte range.
else if (iRangeErr == 0)
  {
    sClient->Send("HTTP/1.1 206 Partial Content\r\n");
    iRsp = 206;
  }
```

This check must come after the previous two, since it is basically a default following the client's request for a byte range retrieval. We execute this branch when the client has sent a valid `Range` header and there are no contradictory conditional headers it being basically covered by an unconditional byte range retrieval. Again, for purpose of byte range retrievals, we send a `206 Partial Content` response.

The final default response we send to the client is a `200 OK` response:

```
// Must be a plain jane request.
else
   {
     sClient->Send("HTTP/1.1 200 OK\r\n");
     iRsp = 200;
   }
```

At this time, we start to build and send our standard response headers to the client. This includes the `Server`, `Date`, `Last-Modified`, and `ETag` headers. The first two are constructed as we've seen before. The `Last-Modified` header is built using the `CreateDate()` function and the last modified time from the `sBuf.st_mtime` variable. For the `ETag()`, we simply use the actual value of `sBuf.st_mtime` to construct the entity tag. For our file system based Web server, it provides sufficient uniqueness to qualify as an entity tag. In a system where resources are constantly updated, as something based on real time feeds might be, the last modified timestamp would probably not prove to be sufficiently unique to use as an entity tag. Depending on the system's usage, we might need to use some sort of integer counter which is incremented on changes.

Once the basic response headers are sent, we check the response code:

```
if ((iRsp == 304) || (iRsp == 412))
   {
     sClient->Send("\r\n");
     return iRsp;  // Don't send anything else.
   }
```

If we find a 304 or 412 code, we are finished. Because of conditional headers, we are not sending an entity body to the client, so we just send the final empty line to mark the end of the headers and return the response code.

When we do send an entity body to the client, we must determine the media type of the resource and label it:

```
if (szSearch != NULL)   // Force search results to text/html type.
   {
     iType = FindType("x.html");
   }
else
   {
     iType = FindType(szPath);// Figure out the media type to return.
   }
```

The only special checking to do here is to determine if szSearch is defined. If it is, we have done an index search and must force the media type to text/html since szPath will hold the name of a temporary file and will not have the html extension. On any other case, we let the FindType() function from the HTTP/1.0 server figure out the media type for us.

Now we must simply transfer the resource to the client. There are two possibilities for this. The first is that we are sending a byte range back to the client, in which case iRsp will be 206. The other possibility is sending the entire resource back to the client:

```
if (iRsp == 206) // Sending partial content.
  {
    // Send byte range to client.
    SendByteRange(sClient, hInfo, szPath, &sBuf, iType, iMethod);
    return iRsp;
  }
```

The first choice checks to see if iRsp is 206. If it is, we then call the function SendByteRange() to figure out which byte ranges to send to the client. iRsp is then returned to end the function. For the default case we first send the Content-Type and Content-Length:

```
// Send full entity.
sprintf(szBuf, "Content-Type: %s\r\n", eExtMap[iType].szType);
sClient->Send(szBuf);
sprintf(szBuf, "Content-Length: %d\r\n", sBuf.st_size);
sClient->Send(szBuf);
sClient->Send("\r\n");
```

The first line creates the Content-Type header using the information from FindType(). The next line sends the buffer to the client and then the Content-Length header is created and sent. The final line sends the empty line to mark the transition from headers to entity. Our last check is to make certain the request method is GET before sending the entity body:

```
if (iMethod == GET)  // Don't send unless GET.
  {
    if (eExtMap[iType].bBinary == TRUE)
      {
        iRc = sClient->SendBinary(szPath);
```

264

```
        }
    else
        {
            iRc = sClient->SendText(szPath);
        }
    }
```

Within the `if` statement, we key on the file type as held in the `eExtMap` array to decide whether to send the file as binary or text data. Once done, `iRsp` is returned to end the function.

8.15 Checking the If-Range

We used the function `IfRange()` in the `DoHttp11()`, but have not seen it yet. This function is used to verify the `If-Range` header, so let us look at it now:

```
// ------------------------------------------------------------------
//
// IfRange
//
// Find out whether the If-Range tag matches the resource.
//

int IfRange(Headers *hInfo, time_t ttMtime)
{
    char *szBuf;
    time_t ttDate;

    // Check the If-Range header. We must have Range also to be valid.
    if ((hInfo->szIfRange != NULL) && (hInfo->szRange != NULL))
        {
        // Figure out whether it is an etag or date.
        if ((hInfo->szIfRange[0] == '"') ||
            (hInfo->szIfRange[2] == '"'))
        {
            szBuf = new char[SMALLBUF];                  // An etag.
            sprintf(szBuf, "\"%d\"", ttMtime);
            if (strcmp(szBuf, hInfo->szIfRange) == 0)
                {
                    delete [] szBuf;
                    return TRUE;  // Match, send them the resource.
                }
```

```
        delete [] szBuf;
      }
    else
      {
        ttDate = ConvertDate(hInfo->szIfRange); // We found a date.
        if (ttDate >= ttMtime)
          {
            return TRUE;  // Match, send them the resource.
          }
      }
  }

  return FALSE; // No match.
}

// ------------------------------------------------------------------
```

This function combines parts of the other If functions we have seen so far. The reason for this is the possibility for either an entity tag or date for the value. Luckily, we only have to check two characters to determine which is which:

```
// Check the If-Range header. We must have Range also to
// be valid.
if ((hInfo->szIfRange != NULL) && (hInfo->szRange != NULL))
  {
    // Figure out whether it is an etag or date.
    if ((hInfo->szIfRange[0] == '"') ||
        (hInfo->szIfRange[2] == '"'))
      {
```

Another check which must be made first in the function is to see whether we have both an If-Range and Range header in the request. An If-Range header without a Range header is invalid and ignored, according to the protocol standard. If this part is satisfactory, we then make our check to determine whether we have an entity tag or date. The check is made on the first and third characters of the string. If either one is a double quote symbol, then we have an entity tag. We must use both since we may have a situation such as this:

```
If-Range: W/"abc"
If-Range: Wed 24, Jul 1996 09:35:27 GMT
```

As can be seen from the example, it is possible for the two to match in the first position, so we must also check the third position where they cannot match if the first position matches.

The entity tag comparison is similar to before:

```
szBuf = new char[SMALLBUF];                    // An etag.
sprintf(szBuf, "\"%d\"", ttMtime);
if (strcmp(szBuf, hInfo->szIfRange) == 0)
   {
     delete [] szBuf;
     return TRUE;  // Match, send them the resource.
   }
delete [] szBuf;
```

The entity tag is constructed and a `strcmp()` made to determine whether there is a match. Note that we do not check the entity tag sent by the client against the "*" case as for `If-Match` or `If-None-Match`. The syntax for `If-Range` only allows an `entity-tag` as a value.

For the date comparison, we convert the date given by the client to a `time_t` value and then make certain it is greater than or equal to the modification time of the resource. When we find a matching condition in either of the two comparisons, a `TRUE` value is returned.

8.16 Transmission of byte ranges

Our last section for this chapter covers the `SendByteRange()` function. Whenever a client requests a byte range retrieval, we must take some extra measures in its transmission. This is especially pertinent when the client sends a multiple byte range request:

```
// ----------------------------------------------------------------
//
// SendByteRange
//
// Send the given byte ranges back to the client.
//
```

```
int SendByteRange(Socket *sClient, Headers *hInfo, char *szPath,
                  struct stat *sBuf, int iType, int iMethod)
{
  ifstream ifIn;
  int iBytes, iCount, iLen,
      i, j;
  char *szBuf, *szBoundary;

  szBuf = new char[SMALLBUF];

  if (hInfo->iRangeNum == 1)  // Simple response, only one part.
    {
      iLen = hInfo->rRanges[0].iEnd - hInfo->rRanges[0].iStart + 1;
      sprintf(szBuf, "Content-Length: %d\r\n", iLen);
      sClient->Send(szBuf);
      sprintf(szBuf, "Content-Type: %s\r\n", eExtMap[iType].szType);
      sClient->Send(szBuf);
      sClient->Send("\r\n");

      if (iMethod == HEAD)  // Don't send an entity.
        {
          delete [] szBuf;
          hInfo->ulContentLength = 0;
          return 0;
        }

      ifIn.open(szPath, ios::binary);  // Open the file, binary mode.
      ifIn.seekg(hInfo->rRanges[0].iStart, ios::beg);
      iCount = 0;
      while (iCount < iLen)
        {
          ifIn.read(szBuf,
                    (SMALLBUF < iLen-iCount ? SMALLBUF : iLen-iCount));
          iBytes = ifIn.gcount();
          iCount += iBytes;
          sClient->Send(szBuf, iBytes);
        }
      ifIn.close();
    }
  else  // Do a multi-part MIME type.
    {
      szBoundary = new char[70];
      srand(sBuf->st_mtime);
      for (i = 0; i < 68; i++)
        {
          j = rand();
          szBoundary[i] = szMime[ j % iNumMime ];
```

```
      }
   szBoundary[69] = NULL;

   sprintf(szBuf,
         "Content-Type: multipart/byteranges; boundary=\"%s\"\r\n",
         szBoundary);
   sClient->Send(szBuf);

   if (iMethod == HEAD)  // Don't send an entity.
      {
        delete [] szBuf;
        hInfo->ulContentLength = 0;
        return 0;
      }

ifIn.open(szPath, ios::binary);  // Open the file, binary mode.

   for (i = 0; i < hInfo->iRangeNum; i++)
      {
        sClient->Send("\r\n--");       // The boundary marker first.
        sClient->Send(szBoundary);
        sClient->Send("\r\n");
        sprintf(szBuf, "Content-Type: %s\r\n",
                eExtMap[iType].szType);
        sClient->Send(szBuf);         // Now content-type.
        sprintf(szBuf, "Content-Range: bytes %d-%d/%d\r\n\r\n",
                hInfo->rRanges[i].iStart,
                hInfo->rRanges[i].iEnd,
                sBuf->st_size);
        sClient->Send(szBuf);         // Now content-range.

        ifIn.seekg(hInfo->rRanges[i].iStart, ios::beg);
        iLen = hInfo->rRanges[i].iEnd -
                hInfo->rRanges[i].iStart + 1;
        iCount = 0;
        // Read the specified number of bytes.
        while (iCount < iLen)
           {
             ifIn.read(szBuf,
                  (SMALLBUF < iLen-iCount ? SMALLBUF : iLen-iCount));
             iBytes = ifIn.gcount();
             iCount += iBytes;
             sClient->Send(szBuf, iBytes);
           }
      }
   sClient->Send("\r\n--");        // The ending boundary marker.
   sClient->Send(szBoundary);
```

```
        sClient->Send("--\r\n");
        delete [] szBoundary;
        ifIn.close();
    }

  delete [] szBuf;
  return 0;
}


// ----------------------------------------------------------------
```

We have two possible paths for sending byte range responses. The first is the simple case where the client only requests a single byte range. This one is handled much as for any response—a `Content-Length` is sent along with a `Content-Type` and the byte range as an entity body. We check for this type by checking for the number of byte ranges:

```
if (hInfo->iRangeNum == 1)  // Simple response, only one part.
  {
    iLen = hInfo->rRanges[0].iEnd - hInfo->rRanges[0].iStart + 1;
    sprintf(szBuf, "Content-Length: %d\r\n", iLen);
    sClient->Send(szBuf);
    sprintf(szBuf, "Content-Type: %s\r\n",
            eExtMap[iType].szType);
    sClient->Send(szBuf);
    sClient->Send("\r\n");
```

If we do find a single byte range request, then we calculate the number of bytes by subtracting the start number from the end number and then adding one. We must add one, since the specification says byte ranges are inclusive. This length and the media type are then sent to the client.

We must next check for a HEAD request:

```
if (iMethod == HEAD)  // Don't send an entity.
  {
    delete [] szBuf;
    hInfo->ulContentLength = 0;
    return 0;
  }
```

Even though we are doing a byte range request, it is still possible for a client to do a HEAD request on it. This might be done by a client to determine how many bytes are left to transfer for a resource before actually requesting the transfer. If it is a HEAD request, we must free our temporary buffer, szBuf, and mark our byte count transferred to the client as zero.

For GET, we send the requested byte count:

```
ifIn.open(szPath, ios::binary);  // Open the file, binary mode.
ifIn.seekg(hInfo->rRanges[0].iStart, ios::beg);
iCount = 0;
while (iCount < iLen)
   {
       ifIn.read(szBuf,
             (SMALLBUF < iLen-iCount ? SMALLBUF : iLen-iCount));
       iBytes = ifIn.gcount();
       iCount += iBytes;
       sClient->Send(szBuf, iBytes);
   }
ifIn.close();
```

We start here by opening the file in binary mode so we can traverse through the file by byte count. Next we use seekg() to position the file pointer at the beginning byte. Now we loop through our read() operation counting bytes and sending them each time. In the read() call, we don't simply request the total length of the byte range, but instead request the smaller of SMALLBUF and iLen - iCount. We must do this in order to not overflow szBuf. We adjust the number of bytes we request each time by the number we read each time. Once we read and send the requested number, the loop ends and we close the file.

For multiple byte ranges, we must do a little more work. When a client requests multiple byte ranges we need a method to reliably separate the parts in the entity. To do this, a special media type of multipart/byteranges is used. This is based on the MIME standard and requires using a boundary marker between the parts and a separate Content-Type and Content-Range for each part. A typical entity body might resemble the following:

```
Content-Type: multipart/byteranges; boundary="mimeboundarymarker"
--mimeboundarymarker
Content-Type: text/plain
Content-Range: bytes 0-4/10

abcde
--mimeboundarymarker
```

```
Content-Type: text/plain
Content-Range: bytes 5-9/10

fghij
--mimeboundarymarker--
```

The basic idea is that the parts are separated by the boundary marker, which is an arbitrary string. The quotes surrounding it are not part of the string but are required when certain characters are present and are always allowed. We always use them for simplicity of the algorithm. A part starts with two dashes followed immediately by the marker and a carriage return line feed. Next come any headers applicable to this part. We use `Content-Type` and `Content-Range`. The `Content-Range` header is required. There is an empty line following the headers and then the actual data starts. The end of the data is signaled by a carriage return line feed, two dashes, and the marker. The carriage return line feed is not part of the data here, but a delimiter. The end of the parts is specified by the same sequence, plus the addition of two dashes after the boundary marker. RFC 1521 goes into more detail on the multipart media types.

First we need to create the boundary marker:

```
szBoundary = new char[70];
srand(sBuf->st_mtime);
for (i = 0; i < 68; i++)
    {
        j = rand();
        szBoundary[i] = szMime[ j % iNumMime ];
    }
szBoundary[69] = NULL;
```

To create the boundary marker, we use the standard random number routines from the C library over the allowable MIME alphabet:

```
// The alphabet used for MIME boundaries.
const
char szMime[] =
"0123456789abcdefghijklmnopqrstuvwxyzABCDEFGHIJKLMNOPQRSTUVWXYZ'()=_
,-./:=?";
```

The alphabet shown here is stretched over two lines due to book limitations, but it is actually a single string in the code. We loop over the length of our boundary calling `rand()` each time. With this number we index into the MIME alphabet using the mod operator to ensure a valid index value. We use the resource's last modification time as the seed number, which should give us sufficiently random behavior. The only qualification on the boundary marker is that it must not be expected to occur within the body part. Using a 69-character string over the entire MIME alphabet should fairly guarantee it.

The boundary marker is then sent to the client:

```
sprintf(szBuf,
        "Content-Type: multipart/byteranges; boundary=\"%s\"\r\n",
        szBoundary);
sClient->Send(szBuf);
```

Once this is done, we check to see whether or not the method used by the client was HEAD. If it was, then we tidy up as before and return from the function. If it was GET, then we open the file and start looping through each of the byte ranges we have. The protocol actually allows combining byte ranges when they overlap, but for simplicity, we'll assume clients won't request the same parts twice and will just send them exactly what they asked for:

```
sClient->Send("\r\n--");        // The boundary marker first.
sClient->Send(szBoundary);
sClient->Send("\r\n");
sprintf(szBuf, "Content-Type: %s\r\n", eExtMap[iType].szType);
sClient->Send(szBuf);           // Now content-type.
sprintf(szBuf, "Content-Range: bytes %d-%d/%d\r\n\r\n",
        hInfo->rRanges[i].iStart, hInfo->rRanges[i].iEnd,
        sBuf->st_size);
sClient->Send(szBuf);           // Now content-range.

ifIn.seekg(hInfo->rRanges[i].iStart, ios::beg);
iLen = hInfo->rRanges[i].iEnd - hInfo->rRanges[i].iStart + 1;
iCount = 0;
// Read the specified number of bytes.
while (iCount < iLen)
   {
     ifIn.read(szBuf,
            (SMALLBUF < iLen-iCount ? SMALLBUF : iLen-iCount));
     iBytes = ifIn.gcount();
     iCount += iBytes;
     sClient->Send(szBuf, iBytes);
   }
```

The code here is designed to construct a single part of the multipart entity body. We start out by sending a \r\n-- which delimits the parts. This serves two purposes here, i.e., the first time through the loop it provides the initial empty line separating the headers from the entity body. On subsequent trips, it provides the carriage return line feed after the part data. Note also that the boundary marker does not include the quote marks when in use, only in the Content-Type header. The Content-Type header for this part is sent next, followed by the Content-Range header. The latter header consists of the unit specifier which is always bytes for us, and then the starting byte marker, a dash, the ending byte marker, a forward slash, and then the total length of the resource. Once the headers are sent, we use the same piece of code as when sending a single part to forward the requested number of bytes.

Once out of the loop, we close the entity body:

```
sClient->Send("\r\n--");       // The ending boundary marker.
sClient->Send(szBoundary);
sClient->Send("--\r\n");
delete [] szBoundary;
ifIn.close();
```

We send the ending boundary marker, the one delimited with two dashes on both ends, and a final carriage return line feed. The memory for szBoundary is freed and the file closed.

The function ends after freeing the memory used by szBuf.

8.17 Finishing

This chapter has covered the basics of an HTTP/1.1 server. You should have a good understanding of how to translate the protocol elements of HTTP/1.1 into working code at this point. In the last chapter, we'll cover how to support the standard CGI interface for both OS/2 and Windows NT.

chapter 9

Common Gateway
Interface support

9.1 Basic functions

The same basic type function we saw for the other methods is used for Common Gateway Interface (CGI) requests. We'll start by presenting the complete function thereof:

```
// ------------------------------------------------------------------
//
// DoExec11()
//
// This function executes our CGI scripts.
//

int DoExec11(Socket *sClient, int iMethod, char *szPath,
             char *szSearch, Headers *hInfo)
{
  struct stat sBuf;
  char *szTmp,
       *szVal,
       *szPtr,
       szBuf[SMALLBUF],
       szFile[PATH_LENGTH];
  int iRsp = 200,
      iRc,
      iType,
      iIfUnmod,
      iIfMatch,
      iIfNone,
      i,
      iCount;
  Cgi *cParms;
  ofstream ofOut;
  ifstream ifIn;

  iRc = CheckAuth(szPath, hInfo, READ_ACCESS);  // Check for
                                                // authorization.
  if (iRc == ACCESS_DENIED)  // Send request for credentials.
    {
      sClient->Send("HTTP/1.1 401 \r\n");
      sClient->Send("Server: ");
      sClient->Send(szServerVer);
      sClient->Send("\r\n");
      szTmp = CreateDate(time(NULL));  // Create a date header.
      if (szTmp != NULL)
```

```
        {
          sClient->Send("Date: ");
          sClient->Send(szTmp);
          sClient->Send("\r\n");
          delete [] szTmp;
        }
      sprintf(szBuf, "WWW-Authenticate: Basic realm=\"%s\"\r\n",
              hInfo->szRealm);
      sClient->Send(szBuf);
      sClient->Send("Content-Type: text/html\r\n");
      sprintf(szBuf, "Content-Length: %d\r\n", strlen(sz401));
      sClient->Send(szBuf);
      sClient->Send("\r\n");
      sClient->Send(sz401);
      return 401;
    }
else if (iRc == ACCESS_FAILED) // Send forbidden response.
  {
    sClient->Send("HTTP/1.1 403 Access Denied\r\n");
    sClient->Send("Server: ");
    sClient->Send(szServerVer);
    sClient->Send("\r\n");
    szTmp = CreateDate(time(NULL));  // Create a date header.
    if (szTmp != NULL)
      {
        sClient->Send("Date: ");
        sClient->Send(szTmp);
        sClient->Send("\r\n");
        delete [] szTmp;
      }
    sClient->Send("Content-Type: text/html\r\n");
    sprintf(szBuf, "Content-Length: %d\r\n", strlen(sz403));
    sClient->Send(szBuf);
    sClient->Send("\r\n");
    sClient->Send(sz403);
    return 403;
  }

iRc = stat(szPath, &sBuf);
if (iRc < 0)
  {
    iRsp = SendError(sClient, "Resource not found.", 404,
                     HTTP_1_1, hInfo);
    return iRsp;
  }

// Check If headers.
```

```
iIfUnmod = IfUnmodSince(hInfo, sBuf.st_mtime);
iIfMatch = IfMatch(hInfo, sBuf.st_mtime);
iIfNone = IfNone(hInfo, sBuf.st_mtime);
// Check to make sure any If headers are FALSE.
// No match on etags or it's been modified or an etag did match.
if ( (iIfMatch == FALSE) || (iIfUnmod == FALSE) ||
     (iIfNone == FALSE) )
  {
    sClient->Send("HTTP/1.1 412 Precondition Failed\r\n");
    iRsp = 412;
  }
// Go ahead and do the CGI.
else
  {
    sClient->Send("HTTP/1.1 200 OK\r\n");
    iRsp = 200;
  }
sClient->Send("Server: ");   // Standard server response.
sClient->Send(szServerVer);
sClient->Send("\r\n");
szTmp = CreateDate(time(NULL));   // Create a date header.
if (szTmp != NULL)
  {
    sClient->Send("Date: ");
    sClient->Send(szTmp);
    sClient->Send("\r\n");
    delete [] szTmp;
  }

if (iRsp == 412)
  {
    hInfo->ulContentLength = 0;   // For the logfile.
    return iRsp;   // Don't send anything else.
  }

// Execute the cgi program here.
cParms = new Cgi();
cParms->hInfo = hInfo;
cParms->sClient = sClient;
cParms->szProg = szPath;
if (iMethod == POST)
  {
    // Grab the posted data.
    cParms->szOutput = NULL;
    tmpnam(szFile);
    strlwr(hInfo->szContentType);
```

```
      szPtr = strstr(hInfo->szContentType, "text/");
      if (szPtr != NULL)   // Receiving text data.
        {
          ofOut.open(szFile);
          iCount = 0;
          // Get the specified number of bytes.
          while (iCount < hInfo->ulContentLength)
            {
              i = sClient->RecvTeol();   // Keep eol for proper byte
              iCount += i;               // count.
              // Remove the end-of-line.
              while ((sClient->szOutBuf[i] == '\r') ||
                     (sClient->szOutBuf[i] == '\n')    )
                {
                  sClient->szOutBuf[i] = NULL;
                  i--;
                }
              ofOut << sClient->szOutBuf << endl;  // Write to temp
            }                                      // file.
        }
      else   // Binary data.
        {
          ofOut.open(szFile, ios::bin);   // Open in binary mode.
          iCount = 0;
          while (iCount < hInfo->ulContentLength)
            {
              i = sClient->Recv(hInfo->ulContentLength - iCount);
              iCount += i;
              ofOut.write(sClient->szOutBuf, i);
            }
        }
      ofOut.close();
      cParms->szPost = szFile;
  }

ExecCgi(cParms);   // Run the cgi program.

stat(cParms->szOutput, &sBuf);
ifIn.open(cParms->szOutput);   // Open the output file.
iCount = 0;
ifIn.getline(szBuf, SMALLBUF, '\n');
// Parse the cgi output for headers.
while (szBuf[0] != NULL)
  {
    iCount += strlen(szBuf) + 2;
    szVal = strchr(szBuf, ':');
```

```
if (szVal == NULL)
  {
    ifIn.getline(szBuf, SMALLBUF, '\n');
    continue;
  }
*szVal = NULL;
szVal++;
strlwr(szBuf);
// Look for and allow proper response headers.
if (strcmp(szBuf, "cache-control") == 0)
  {
    sClient->Send("Cache-Control: ");
  }
else if (strcmp(szBuf, "content-type") == 0)
  {
    sClient->Send("Content-Type: ");
  }
else if (strcmp(szBuf, "content-base") == 0)
  {
    sClient->Send("Content-Base: ");
  }
else if (strcmp(szBuf, "content-encoding") == 0)
  {
    sClient->Send("Content-Encoding: ");
  }
else if (strcmp(szBuf, "content-language") == 0)
  {
    sClient->Send("Content-Language: ");
  }
else if (strcmp(szBuf, "content-location") == 0)
  {
    sClient->Send("Content-Location: ");
  }
else if (strcmp(szBuf, "etag") == 0)
  {
    sClient->Send("Etag: ");
  }
else if (strcmp(szBuf, "expires") == 0)
  {
    sClient->Send("Expires: ");
  }
else if (strcmp(szBuf, "from") == 0)
  {
    sClient->Send("From: ");
  }
else if (strcmp(szBuf, "location") == 0)
  {
```

```
            sClient->Send("Location: ");
          }
      else if (strcmp(szBuf, "last-modified") == 0)
        {
            sClient->Send("Last-Modified: ");
        }
      else if (strcmp(szBuf, "vary") == 0)
        {
            sClient->Send("Vary: ");
        }
      else  // No match. Don't send this unknown header.
        {
            ifIn.getline(szBuf, SMALLBUF, '\n');
            continue;
        }
      sClient->Send(szVal);   // Send the parameter for the header
      sClient->Send("\r\n"); // line.
      ifIn.getline(szBuf, SMALLBUF, '\n');
    }
ifIn.close();
iCount += 2;   // The last CRLF isn't counted within the loop.
sprintf(szBuf, "Content-Length: %d\r\n\r\n",
        sBuf.st_size - iCount);
sClient->Send(szBuf);

if (iMethod != HEAD) // Only send the entity if not HEAD.
  {
    hInfo->ulContentLength = sBuf.st_size - iCount;
    ifIn.open(cParms->szOutput, ios::bin);
    ifIn.seekg(iCount, ios::beg);
    while (!ifIn.eof())
      {
        ifIn.read(szBuf, SMALLBUF);
        i = ifIn.gcount();
        sClient->Send(szBuf, i);
      }
    ifIn.close();
  }
else
  {
    hInfo->ulContentLength = 0;
  }

// Remove the temporary files and memory.
unlink(cParms->szOutput);
delete [] (cParms->szOutput);
if (cParms->szPost != NULL) unlink(cParms->szPost);
```

```
  delete cParms;

  return iRsp;
}

// ------------------------------------------------------------------
```

The first thing `DoExec11()` does *not* do is to resolve the given pathname any further. Whenever we handle a request with the `Do*()` functions, our first check is to append the default welcome file if none has been specified. When executing CGI, we only accept full paths to begin with, hence there is no default CGI script to execute. The first thing it does do is to check for the proper authorization to execute the CGI program with a call to `CheckAuth()`.

The next step is to check for the existence of the CGI program:

```
iRc = stat(szPath, &sBuf);
if (iRc < 0)
  {
    iRsp = SendError(sClient, "Resource not found.", 404,
                     rhInfo);
    return iRsp;
  }
```

We do this after the authorization check so as to not give out information about what scripts may or may not be available in a restricted area. If this check were done first, then the absence of the CGI program would be reported, whether or not the client was authorized to access it.

Since it is possible for a client to attach a conditional header to a CGI request, we must check the conditional headers `If-Unmodified-Since`, `If-Match`, and `If-None-Match`. The functions introduced in the last chapter are used here. If any check comes back false, then we send a `412` response to the client. If the conditionals are true, then a `200` response is sent:

```
// Check If headers.
iIfUnmod = IfUnmodSince(hInfo, sBuf.st_mtime);
iIfMatch = IfMatch(hInfo, sBuf.st_mtime);
iIfNone = IfNone(hInfo, sBuf.st_mtime);

// Check to make sure any If headers are FALSE.
// No match on etags or it's been modified or an etag did match.
if ( (iIfMatch == FALSE) || (iIfUnmod == FALSE) ||
```

```
   (iIfNone == FALSE) )
{
   sClient->Send("HTTP/1.1 412 Precondition Failed\r\n");
   iRsp = 412;
}
```

If a `412` response is sent to the client, then after the `Server` and `Date` headers are sent, we must end the request:

```
if (iRsp == 412)
   {
      hInfo->ulContentLength = 0;  // For the logfile.
      return iRsp;  // Don't send anything else.
   }
```

The basic headers are sent to the client in the next section, `Server` and `Date` in this case. We then start the CGI processing by creating a `Cgi` class instance to hold the necessary information:

```
// Execute the cgi program here.
cParms = new Cgi();
cParms->rhInfo = rhInfo;
cParms->sClient = sClient;
cParms->szProg = szPath;
```

What we store here is the basic information about the request. `cParms->hInfo` holds the pointer to the `Headers` class instance, `cParms->sClient` holds the `Socket` instance pointer, and `cParms->szProg` is the CGI program to execute. If the request method was `POST`, then we must next receive the post data:

```
if (strcmp(szMethod, "POST") == NULL)
   {
      // Grab the posted data.
      cParms->szOutput = NULL;
      tmpnam(szFile);
      strlwr(rhInfo->szContentType);
      szPtr = strstr(rhInfo->szContentType, "text/");
```

A simple `strcmp()` is used to check the method here. When true, we create a temporary file to hold the post data and then check for the media type of the data. The first step in this is to use `strlwr()` to lowercase the string and then `strstr()` to search for `text/` as a key. Whenever we find the substring, then `szPtr` will not be NULL and we know to look for text delimited lines:

```
ofOut.open(szFile);
iCount = 0;
// Get the specified number of bytes.
while (iCount < hInfo->ulContentLength)
  {
    i = sClient->RecvTeol();   // Keep eol for proper byte count.
    iCount += i;
    // Remove the end-of-line.
    i--;   // C indexing adjustment.
    while ((sClient->szOutBuf[i] == '\r') ||
           (sClient->szOutBuf[i] == '\n')   )
      {
        sClient->szOutBuf[i] = NULL;
        i--;
      }
    ofOut << sClient->szOutBuf << endl;  // Write to temp file.
  }
```

The technique used here is similar to what we have used before. The one difference we make this time is how we actually receive the text lines. Most of the time we are not concerned with the marker used to end lines. This time we are, since we must be careful to only receive the specified number of bytes sent by the client. Because of this, our call to `RecvTeol()` does not ask for the end-of-line characters to be stripped. This gives us an accurate count of the actual bytes received, which are added to `iCount`. Then we must remove any end-of-line characters before saving the line to disk. The only gotcha here is to be sure to subtract the value 1 from `i` to allow for C indexing. Once stripped, the line is saved to the file.

For binary data, our algorithm is much simpler:

```
ofOut.open(szFile, ios::bin);   // Open in binary mode.
iCount = 0;
while (iCount < hInfo->ulContentLength)
  {
    i = sClient->Recv(hInfo->ulContentLength - iCount);
    iCount += i;
    ofOut.write(sClient->szOutBuf, i);
  }
```

We need to open the file in binary mode so no end-of-line translation is done. Then we simply loop until we receive the specified number of bytes from the client. Since we do have binary data, we must use `write()` so that we may specify the number of bytes to be written from the buffer each time.

Once the data is received, `ExecCgi()` is called to actually execute the CGI program and save the output. We'll cover it later in the chapter. After it completes, we find out the size of the output file using `stat()` to help determine the content length to send to the client. We start parsing the CGI output for headers next, as follows:

```
iCount = 0;
ifIn.getline(szBuf, SMALLBUF, '\n');
// Parse the cgi output for headers.
while (szBuf[0] != NULL)
  {
    iCount += strlen(szBuf) + 2;
    szVal = strchr(szBuf, ':');
    if (szVal == NULL)
      {
        ifIn.getline(szBuf, SMALLBUF, '\n');
        continue;
      }
    *szVal = NULL;
    szVal++;
    strlwr(szBuf);
    // Look for and allow proper response headers.
    if (strcmp(szBuf, "cache-control") == 0)
      {
        sClient->Send("Cache-Control: ");
      }
```

The first thing we must do is calculate the size of the file without any headers created by the CGI program. So we must count the number of bytes taken up in the file. To do this, we initialize `iCount` to 0 and then count the size of each line read by counting the `strlen()` of each line plus adding 2 bytes for the carriage return line feed, which is stripped by the `getline()`.

To actually parse the CGI headers, we use `strchr()` to search for the delimiting colon. If found we place a NULL there instead, to mark the end of the header label. `szVal` is then advanced by one to the beginning of the field value for later use. `szBuf` is next lowercased for our comparisons in the `if-else` tree.

We parse the CGI headers to verify that the CGI program actually outputs valid headers to the request. Unrecognized headers are not sent to the client. Many servers will let CGI programs bypass the header check by prefixing the name of the CGI program with `nph-` which stands for *no parse headers*. Since HTTP/1.0 signals the end of a request by closing the connection, this is generally not a problem. A valid `Content-Length` header is not required. For HTTP/1.1 and persistent connections, a server should, at minimum, verify the `Content-Length` value lest the client be completely thrown off with respect to subsequent requests:

```
else  // No match. Don't send this unknown header.
  {
    ifIn.getline(szBuf, SMALLBUF, '\n');
    continue;
  }
sClient->Send(szVal);  // Send the parameter for the header line.
sClient->Send("\r\n");
ifIn.getline(szBuf, SMALLBUF, '\n');
```

The last clause in the `if-else` tree is for the unknown header case. If we do not recognize it, it is tossed. If we did find a valid header, then the value pointed to by `szVal` is sent to the client and a new line read from the CGI output file.

Once done with the CGI headers, we must then provide a valid `Content-Length` for the client:

```
iCount += 2;  // The last CRLF isn't counted within the loop.
sprintf(szBuf, "Content-Length: %d\r\n\r\n",
        sBuf.st_size - iCount);
sClient->Send(szBuf);
```

To do this, we must first add 2 bytes for the separating line between the headers and body. Due to the loop construction, the carriage return line feed is not counted. To figure the length, we subtract the total bytes read for the headers (including the ones not sent) from the size of the file returned earlier by `stat()`. This is used to construct the `Content-Length` header with `sprintf()`.

Next, we send the entity body to the client as long as the method used was not `HEAD`:

```
if (strcmp(szMethod, "HEAD") != 0) // Only send the entity if
```

```
{                                          // not HEAD.
  rhInfo->ulContentLength = sBuf.st_size - iCount;
  ifIn.open(cParms->szOutput, ios::bin);
  ifIn.seekg(iCount, ios::beg);
  while (!ifIn.eof())
    {
      ifIn.read(szBuf, SMALLBUF);
      i = ifIn.gcount();
      sClient->Send(szBuf, i);
    }
  ifIn.close();
}
```

The number of bytes sent to the client is then saved for later logging in `hInfo->ulContentLength`. Since we don't know the media type of the output file, we open it in binary mode to prevent any end-of-line transformations. Using `seekg()`, we move the file pointer to the first byte in the file after the headers. This is why we kept such a close byte count on the headers. Now we simply use a `while` loop, keying on the end-of-file condition, to send the rest of the file to the client.

To conclude, we remove any temporary files generated and delete any memory allocated. Finally, the response code is returned to the calling function.

9.2 Executing the CGI program

To actually execute the CGI program, we use a separate function. The reason for this is the difference between how child programs are handled for OS/2 vs. Windows. The OS/2 version of the function is close to a UNIX version, while the Windows version is, well Windows. Let us start by looking at the header file `cgi.hpp` which is the same for both versions.

```
//
// WWW Server  File: cgi.hpp
//
//
// Copyright 1996 Paul S. Hethmon
//
// Prepared for the book "Illustrated Guide to HTTP"
//
```

```
#ifndef _CGI_HPP_
#define _CGI_HPP_

#include "headers.hpp"
#include "socket.hpp"

// -----------------------------------------------------------------
//
// This class organizes the information needed to start a CGI
// process.
//

class Cgi
{
  public:

  Cgi()
    {
      szPost = NULL;
      szOutput = NULL;
    };

  char *szProg;      // The program to execute.
  char *szPost;      // File containing post data.
  char *szOutput;    // File containing output data.
  Headers *hInfo;    // Various info needed.
  Socket *sClient;   // Various info needed.
};

// -----------------------------------------------------------------
//
// Function prototypes.
//

void InitCgi();
int ExecCgi(Cgi *);

// -----------------------------------------------------------------

#endif

// -----------------------------------------------------------------
```

This header file declares the `Cgi` class used to pass parameters to the `ExecCgi()` function. As used in the previous functions, it contains data members pointing to the name of the program to execute, the name of the file holding the posted data, the name of the file containing output, the `Headers` class instance, and the `Socket` class instance. I should point out the header file here is for the HTTP/1.1 server since `Headers` is used instead of `ReqHeaders`. The code provided with this book does contain both files, as needed. The `ctor` for the `Cgi` class just makes sure `szPost` and `szOutput` are `NULL` since the `ExecCgi()` function keys on the values these headers have.

9.3 *The OS/2 version*

We'll start our look at the `ExecCgi()` function with the OS/2 version:

```
// -----------------------------------------------------------------
volatile int iCgiLock = 0;   // Ram semaphore for CGI access.

// The environment variables passed to the cgi process.
char szServerSoftware[64],
     szServerName[64],
     szGatewayInterface[64],
     szServerProtocol[64],
     szServerPort[64],
     szRequestMethod[64],
     szScriptName[64],
     *szQueryString,
     szRemoteHost[64],
     szRemoteAddr[64],
     szAuthType[64],
     szRemoteUser[64],
     szContentType[64],
     szContentLength[64],
     *szEnvs[15];

// -----------------------------------------------------------------
//
// ExecCgi
//
// This function executes the specified cgi program passing it the
// necessary arguments. It then returns the output to the caller
// for them to return it to the client. We protect this function
// internally with a ram semaphore since there is only one
// stdin/stdout stream for all of our threads.
//
```

```
int ExecCgi(Cgi *cParms)
{
  int pIn[2], pOut[2], iNum, iRc;
  FILE *fpin, *fpout;
  FILE *fpPost;
  char szBuf[SMALLBUF],
       *szArgs[2];
  int stdin_save = -1, stdout_save = -1;
  int hfStdin = STDIN, hfStdout = STDOUT;
  ofstream ofOut;

  // Lock all the other threads out.
  while (__lxchg(&iCgiLock, 1) != 0)
    {
      Sleep(1);  // Sleep, not spin.
    }
  _setmode(STDIN, O_BINARY);  // Binary mode for stdin/stdout.
  _setmode(STDOUT, O_BINARY);

  DosDupHandle(STDIN, (PHFILE)&stdin_save);
  DosDupHandle(STDOUT, (PHFILE)&stdout_save);

  // Create the pipe
  DosCreatePipe((PHFILE)&(pIn[0]), (PHFILE)&(pIn[1]), 4096);
  DosCreatePipe((PHFILE)&(pOut[0]), (PHFILE)&(pOut[1]), 4096);

  // Child does not inherit
  DosSetFHState(pIn[0], OPEN_FLAGS_NOINHERIT);
  DosSetFHState(pIn[1], OPEN_FLAGS_NOINHERIT);
  DosSetFHState(pOut[0], OPEN_FLAGS_NOINHERIT);
  DosSetFHState(pOut[1], OPEN_FLAGS_NOINHERIT);

  _setmode(pIn[0],O_BINARY);        // Binary mode on the pipes
  _setmode(pOut[1],O_BINARY);
  _setmode(pIn[0],O_BINARY);        // Binary mode on the pipes
  _setmode(pOut[1],O_BINARY);

  fpout = fdopen(pIn[1], "w");      // create FILE handle
  dup2(pIn[0], hfStdin);
  close(pIn[0]);                    // close the read handle

  fpin = fdopen(pOut[0], "r");      // create FILE handle
  dup2(pOut[1], hfStdout);
  close(pOut[1]);                   // close the write handle

  setbuf(fpin, NULL);               // Turn buffering off.
  setbuf(fpout, NULL);
```

```
// Setting the environment variables.
sprintf(szServerProtocol, "SERVER_PROTOCOL=%s",
        cParms->hInfo->szVer);
sprintf(szRequestMethod, "REQUEST_METHOD=%s",
        cParms->hInfo->szMethod);
sprintf(szScriptName, "SCRIPT_NAME=%s", cParms->hInfo->szUri);
if (cParms->hInfo->szQuery != NULL)
  {
     szQueryString = new char[(strlen(cParms->hInfo->szQuery) + 15)]
     sprintf(szQueryString, "QUERY_STRING=%s",
             cParms->hInfo->szQuery);
  }
else
  {
     szQueryString = new char[15];
     strcpy(szQueryString, "QUERY_STRING");
  }
// Since szQueryString is dynamic memory, we must
// reassign it each time.
szEnvs[7] = szQueryString;
if (cParms->sClient->szPeerName != NULL)
  {
     sprintf(szRemoteHost, "REMOTE_HOST=%s",
             cParms->sClient->szPeerName);
  }
else
  {
     strcpy(szRemoteHost, "REMOTE_HOST");
  }
sprintf(szRemoteAddr, "REMOTE_ADDR=%s", cParms->sClient->szPeerIp);
if (cParms->hInfo->szAuthType != NULL)
  {
     sprintf(szAuthType, "AUTH_TYPE=%s", cParms->hInfo->szAuthType);
     sprintf(szRemoteUser, "REMOTE_USER=%s",
             cParms->hInfo->szRemoteUser);
  }
else
  {
     strcpy(szAuthType, "AUTH_TYPE");
     strcpy(szRemoteUser, "REMOTE_USER");
  }
if (cParms->hInfo->szContentType != NULL)
  {
     sprintf(szContentType, "CONTENT_TYPE=%s",
             cParms->hInfo->szContentType);
  }
else
```

```
    {
      strcpy(szContentType, "CONTENT_TYPE");
    }
  if (strcmp(cParms->hInfo->szMethod, "POST") == 0)
    {
      sprintf(szContentLength, "CONTENT_LENGTH=%d",
            cParms->hInfo->ulContentLength);
    }
  else
    {
      strcpy(szContentLength, "CONTENT_LENGTH=0");
    }

  szArgs[0] = cParms->szProg;   // The program to run.
  szArgs[1] = NULL;
  // Start it.
  spawnvpe(P_NOWAIT, cParms->szProg, szArgs, szEnvs);

  dup2(stdin_save, hfStdin); // Restore stdin/stdout
  dup2(stdout_save, hfStdout);

  if (cParms->szPost != NULL) // Use POST method.
    {
      fpPost = fopen(cParms->szPost, "rb");
      iNum = 1;
      while (iNum > 0)
        {
          iNum = fread(szBuf, sizeof(char), SMALLBUF, fpPost);
          fwrite(szBuf, sizeof(char), iNum, fpout);
        }
      fclose(fpPost);
    }
  fclose(fpout);

  cParms->szOutput = new char[L_tmpnam]; // Create a temporary file
  tmpnam(cParms->szOutput);                     // for the output.
  ofOut.open(cParms->szOutput, ios::bin);
  // Grab all of the output from the child.
  while ( (iNum = fread(szBuf, sizeof(char), SMALLBUF, fpin)) != 0 )
    {
      ofOut.write(szBuf, iNum);
    }
  ofOut.close();
  delete [] szQueryString;
  fclose(fpin);

  // Unlock cgi access.
```

```
    __lxchg(&iCgiLock, 0);

    return (0);
}

// -------------------------------------------------------------
```

Due to the historical design of CGI support, input and output to the child process is handled by controlling standard-in (stdin) and standard-out (stdout) of the child program. Under UNIX, where multiple processes instead of multiple threads are standard, this behavior works fine. Each connection from a client is handled by its own process, which has its own stdin and stdout streams. In this environment, the server creates two pipes, duplicates the server's stdin and stdout to the pipes and then forks to create the child process, which then has its stdin and stdout tied to the pipes in the parent. The key here is duplicating stdin and stdout of the parent to pipes. Since the child inherits the parent's stream handles, the parent can then write to one pipe to write to the child's stdin and read from the other pipe to read the child's stdout.

For a multi-threaded process, this presents a problem, as every thread shares stdin and stdout. With multiple threads trying to control a single stdin and stdout, problems can develop. Our kludgy solution is to protect access to the ExecCgi() function with a RAM semaphore iCgiLock. This uses the same RAM semaphore function as is used in the logging function. To overcome this limitation, we could actually start a stub program which would communicate with the server thread through named pipes, or by using file names passed by the server thread. The stub program could then dupe its stdin and stdout handles to control input and output to the child process. A performance hit would be taken, since two programs would have to be executed for each CGI request, but would gain the ability to simultaneously run CGI programs without fear of mixing input and output between them. As my textbooks always said, "We'll leave this one as an exercise for the reader."

To start this function, we declare a set of global variables to hold the various environment variables needed by the CGI program. Since only one thread will access the function at any given time, this is adequate for our needs. Most of the variables here are declared as static-sized arrays since their sizes are limited. One is not, szQueryString, since we don't know the size until the client sends it to us. Also declared is an array of pointer-to-character strings which will be used in the function call to start the child process.

To start the function, we first obtain the RAM semaphore using `_lxchg()`. Once the semaphore has been obtained, we must do a couple of manipulations with `stdin` and `stdout`:

```
_setmode(STDIN, O_BINARY);   // Binary mode for stdin/stdout.
_setmode(STDOUT, O_BINARY);

DosDupHandle(STDIN, (PHFILE)&stdin_save);
DosDupHandle(STDOUT, (PHFILE)&stdout_save);
```

The first step we must take is to change the mode of `stdin` and `stdout` to binary mode using `setmode()`. The default mode under OS/2 is for the handles to be opened in text mode. Once set to binary, we duplicate `stdin` and `stdout` using the API call `DosDupHandle()`. Once we complete the CGI program, we need the saved values to restore `stdin` and `stdout` to their original values.

Our next step is to create the pipes:

```
// Create the pipe
DosCreatePipe((PHFILE)&(pIn[0]), (PHFILE)&(pIn[1]), 4096);
DosCreatePipe((PHFILE)&(pOut[0]), (PHFILE)&(pOut[1]), 4096);

// Child does not inherit
DosSetFHState(pIn[0], OPEN_FLAGS_NOINHERIT);
DosSetFHState(pIn[1], OPEN_FLAGS_NOINHERIT);
DosSetFHState(pOut[0], OPEN_FLAGS_NOINHERIT);
DosSetFHState(pOut[1], OPEN_FLAGS_NOINHERIT);

_setmode(pIn[0],O_BINARY);          // Binary mode on the pipes
_setmode(pOut[1],O_BINARY);
_setmode(pIn[0],O_BINARY);          // Binary mode on the pipes
_setmode(pOut[1],O_BINARY);
```

Using the API call `DosCreatePipe()`, we create two pipes. One pipe will serve to control `stdin` to the child process, while the second will control `stdout` of the child. Since a child process normally inherits any open file handles from the parent, we use `DosSetFHState()` to set the four pipe handles to a no-inherit state. The idea is, we don't want the child to inherit the pipes, but instead `stdin` and `stdout` which are attached to the pipes. It's a subtle difference, but we must make sure all unneeded file handles are closed so end-of-file conditions occur correctly. The last step shown above is designed to set the four pipe handles to binary mode.

```
fpout = fdopen(pIn[1], "w");      // Create FILE handle
dup2(pIn[0], hfStdin);
close(pIn[0]);                     // Close the read handle

fpin = fdopen(pOut[0], "r");      // Create FILE handle
dup2(pOut[1], hfStdout);
close(pOut[1]);                    // Close the write handle

setbuf(fpin, NULL);                // Turn buffering off.
setbuf(fpout, NULL);
```

We next create a FILE handle from the stdin write pipe pIn[1] using the fdopen() call. This will be the handle we use to write data to stdin of the child process. dup2() is used in the next line to tie stdin of the parent to the read handle of the pipe, pIn[0]. Now, when anything is written to fpout, it will go through the pipe to stdin. Once the child is spawned, the data will go to the child. The third part here is to close the read end of the pipe, pIn[0], since it is no longer needed. These three steps are then repeated for the second pipe to tie the read end of the pipe to stdout from the child process. Finally, we must set off buffering for the FILE handles. This is a necessary step to make certain all data is flushed immediately, else our thread is likely to hang waiting on input which is being buffered by the system.

The next section of the code sets the environment variables used by the CGI program. Each environment variable is set to a value, even if that value is NULL. This keeps any previous values from being used by the current CGI program. One line to note here is the one assigning szEnvs[7]:

```
// Since szQueryString is dynamic memory, we must
// reassign it each time.
szEnvs[7] = szQueryString;
```

As the comment explains, since we dynamically allocate memory for szQueryString each time the function is called, it always points to a different memory address. szEnvs is used to pass the array of environment variables and so we must always reassign the array element, which points to szQueryString.

At this point, our environment setup is complete and we are ready to start the child process:

```
szArgs[0] = cParms->szProg;   // The program to run.
szArgs[1] = NULL;
// Start it.
spawnvpe(P_NOWAIT, cParms->szProg, szArgs, szEnvs);
```

We use `spawnvpe()` to start the child process. It requires four arguments. The first is the specified execution type of the child. We basically have two options available, synchronous and asynchronous execution. In our usage, we do not want to wait on the child, since we need to be able to write data to the child and read data from the child, hence `P_NOWAIT` is used. The next parameter is the program to run. We use `cParms->szProg` as passed in. The third parameter is used to pass command line arguments to the child process. The only one we specify is the program name itself as the system does not default to supplying this. The final parameter is the array of environment variables. Note that the third and fourth parameters require a `NULL` element to mark the end of the array.

At this point in execution the child process has been started and its `stdin` and `stdout` handles are tied to the pipes we created earlier. The next thing we need to do is restore `stdin` and `stdout` of the server to their original state:

```
dup2(stdin_save, hfStdin); // Restore stdin/stdout
dup2(stdout_save, hfStdout);
```

Using the `dup2()` call, we restore `stdin` and `stdout` using the values we saved at the beginning of the function.

Now we are ready to interact with the CGI program. The first item to check is whether there is post data to send to the child. We do this by checking `cParms->szPost` for not being `NULL`:

```
if (cParms->szPost != NULL) // Use POST method.
  {
    fpPost = fopen(cParms->szPost, "rb");
    iNum = 1;
    while (iNum > 0)
      {
        iNum = fread(szBuf, sizeof(char), SMALLBUF, fpPost);
        fwrite(szBuf, sizeof(char), iNum, fpout);
```

```
    }
    fclose(fpPost);
  }
fclose(fpout);
```

To send the data to the child, we open the posted data file in binary mode and then enter a read loop. In the loop we read from the file, up to our buffer size, and then write the same number of bytes to `fpout`. As soon as the number of bytes read is 0, the loop ends. `fpPost` is closed and then outside of the `if` statement, we close `fpout`. By closing `fpout` we have closed the server's handles to the pipe `pIn[]`. When the child process ends, the system will release the pipe.

Now we must read the output from the child:

```
cParms->szOutput = new char[L_tmpnam]; // Create a temporary file
tmpnam(cParms->szOutput);              // for the output.
ofOut.open(cParms->szOutput, ios::bin);
// Grab all of the output from the child.
while ((iNum = fread(szBuf, sizeof(char), SMALLBUF, fpin)) != 0 )
  {
    ofOut.write(szBuf, iNum);
  }
ofOut.close();
```

We start by allocating memory for a temporary filename in the `cParms->szOutput` variable. This must be dynamically allocated so that we may return the value to the calling function. We open the temporary file next, taking care to specify binary mode, and then read the output from the child. We continue reading the output until we receive the end-of-file marker. This is why we must close the read handle of the pipe after duplicating it to `fpin`. If the pipe handle had not been closed, we would not receive the end-of-file marker when the CGI program ended, since there would still be an obstructive open handle to it in the system.

The final steps left are the final cleanup steps. We must close `fpin` so the system will close the last pipe. Temporary memory for `szQueryString` is freed and the RAM semaphore is freed for other processes to access the function. A simple return then returns control to the calling function where `cParms` has all of the data from the CGI program to return to the client.

One other function needs to be mentioned here. During the initialization and startup of the server, we have an initialization function for CGI support. This function strategically assigns the pointers to the environment variable array, `szEnvs`, and initializes four of the environment variables, since they are the same for all requests:

```
// ------------------------------------------------------------------
//
// InitCgi
//
// Initialize some of the global variables needed for the CGI
// processing.
//

void InitCgi()
{
  char *szPtr;

  szEnvs[0] = szServerSoftware;
  szEnvs[1] = szServerName;
  szEnvs[2] = szGatewayInterface;
  szEnvs[3] = szServerProtocol;
  szEnvs[4] = szServerPort;
  szEnvs[5] = szRequestMethod;
  szEnvs[6] = szScriptName;
  szEnvs[7] = szQueryString;
  szEnvs[8] = szRemoteHost;
  szEnvs[9] = szRemoteAddr;
  szEnvs[10] = szAuthType;
  szEnvs[11] = szRemoteUser;
  szEnvs[12] = szContentType;
  szEnvs[13] = szContentLength;
  szEnvs[14] = NULL;

  // These are the same for all requests, so only set once.
  sprintf(szServerSoftware, "SERVER_SOFTWARE=%s", szServerVer);
  sprintf(szServerName, "SERVER_NAME=%s", szHostName);
  strcpy(szGatewayInterface, "GATEWAY_INTERFACE=CGI/1.1");
  sprintf(szServerPort, "SERVER_PORT=%d", sPort);
}

// ------------------------------------------------------------------
```

The version of `ExecCgi()` presented here is the one used in the HTTP/1.1 server. It handles both HTTP/1.0 and HTTP/1.1 requests there. For the

HTTP/1.0 server, the same function is used with two differences. The first difference is in the declaration of the `Cgi` class. For the HTTP/1.0 server, we use `ReqHeaders` instead of a `Headers` class pointer. The second difference is that the server protocol environment variable is set in the `InitCgi()` since only HTTP/1.0 requests are supported. The accompanying code with this the book includes both versions.

9.4 The Windows version

Now let us take a look at the Windows version of `ExecCgi()`:

```
// ----------------------------------------------------------------

volatile int iCgiLock = 0;   // Ram semaphore for CGI access.

// The environment variables passed to the cgi process.
char szServerSoftware[64],
     szServerName[64],
     szGatewayInterface[64],
     szServerProtocol[64],
     szServerPort[64],
     szRequestMethod[64],
     szScriptName[64],
     * szQueryString,
     szRemoteHost[64],
     szRemoteAddr[64],
     szAuthType[64],
     szRemoteUser[64],
     szContentType[64],
     szContentLength[64];

// ----------------------------------------------------------------
//
// ExecCgi
//
// This function executes the specified cgi program passing it the
// necessary arguments. It then returns the output to the caller
// for them to return it to the client. We protect this function
// internally with a ram semaphore since there is only one
// stdin/stdout stream for all of our threads.
//
```

```
int ExecCgi(Cgi *cParms)
{
  HANDLE pIn[2], pOut[2];
  DWORD iNum;
  int iRc, iPost, iRead,
      iEnvLen;
  char szBuf[SMALLBUF],
       *szTmp,
       *szEnvStrings;
  ofstream ofOut;
  SECURITY_ATTRIBUTES saSecAtr;
  STARTUPINFO suInfo;
  PROCESS_INFORMATION piInfo;
  BOOL bRc;

  // Lock all the other threads out.
  while (__lxchg(&iCgiLock, 1) != 0)
    {
      Sleep(1);  // Sleep, not spin.
    }

  // Setting the environment variables.
  iEnvLen = strlen(cParms->hInfo->szQuery) + (13 * 64) + 32;
  szEnvStrings = new char[iEnvLen];
  memset(szTmp, '\0', iEnvLen);
  szTmp = szEnvStrings;

  sprintf(szRequestMethod, "REQUEST_METHOD=%s",
          cParms->hInfo->szMethod);
  memcpy(szTmp, szRequestMethod, strlen(szRequestMethod));
  szTmp += strlen(szRequestMethod) + 1;

  sprintf(szScriptName, "SCRIPT_NAME=%s", cParms->hInfo->szUri);
  memcpy(szTmp, szScriptName, strlen(szScriptName));
  szTmp += strlen(szScriptName) + 1;

  if (cParms->hInfo->szQuery != NULL)
    {
      szQueryString = new char[(strlen(cParms->hInfo->szQuery) + 15)]
      sprintf(szQueryString, "QUERY_STRING=%s",
              cParms->hInfo->szQuery);
    }
  else
    {
      szQueryString = new char[15];
      strcpy(szQueryString, "QUERY_STRING");
    }
```

```
memcpy(szTmp, szQueryString, strlen(szQueryString));
szTmp += strlen(szQueryString) + 1;

if (cParms->sClient->szPeerName != NULL)
   {
     sprintf(szRemoteHost, "REMOTE_HOST=%s",
             cParms->sClient->szPeerName);
   }
else
   {
     strcpy(szRemoteHost, "REMOTE_HOST");
   }
memcpy(szTmp, szRemoteHost, strlen(szRemoteHost));
szTmp += strlen(szRemoteHost) + 1;

sprintf(szRemoteAddr, "REMOTE_ADDR=%s", cParms->sClient->szPeerIp);
memcpy(szTmp, szRemoteAddr, strlen(szRemoteAddr));
szTmp += strlen(szRemoteAddr) + 1;

if (cParms->hInfo->szAuthType != NULL)
   {
     sprintf(szAuthType, "AUTH_TYPE=%s", cParms->hInfo->szAuthType);
     sprintf(szRemoteUser, "REMOTE_USER=%s",
             cParms->hInfo->szRemoteUser);
   }
else
   {
     strcpy(szAuthType, "AUTH_TYPE");
     strcpy(szRemoteUser, "REMOTE_USER");
   }
memcpy(szTmp, szAuthType, strlen(szAuthType));
szTmp += strlen(szAuthType) + 1;
memcpy(szTmp, szRemoteUser, strlen(szRemoteUser));
szTmp += strlen(szRemoteUser) + 1;

if (cParms->hInfo->szContentType != NULL)
   {
     sprintf(szContentType, "CONTENT_TYPE=%s",
             cParms->hInfo->szContentType);
   }
else
   {
     strcpy(szContentType, "CONTENT_TYPE");
   }
memcpy(szTmp, szContentType, strlen(szContentType));
szTmp += strlen(szContentType) + 1;
if (strcmp(cParms->hInfo->szMethod, "POST") == 0)
```

```
    {
      sprintf(szContentLength, "CONTENT_LENGTH=%d",
              cParms->hInfo->ulContentLength);
    }
  else
    {
      strcpy(szContentLength, "CONTENT_LENGTH=0");
    }
  memcpy(szTmp, szContentLength, strlen(szContentLength));
  szTmp += strlen(szContentLength) + 1;

  sprintf(szServerProtocol, "SERVER_PROTOCOL=%s",
          cParms->hInfo->szVer);
  memcpy(szTmp, szServerProtocol, strlen(szServerProtocol));
  szTmp += strlen(szServerProtocol) + 1;

  sprintf(szServerName, "SERVER_NAME=%s", cParms->hInfo->szHost);
  memcpy(szTmp, szServerName, strlen(szServerName));
  szTmp += strlen(szServerName) + 1;

  memcpy(szTmp, szServerSoftware, strlen(szServerSoftware));
  szTmp += strlen(szServerSoftware) + 1;
  memcpy(szTmp, szServerPort, strlen(szServerPort));
  szTmp += strlen(szServerPort) + 1;

  memset(&saSecAtr, 0, sizeof(SECURITY_ATTRIBUTES));
  saSecAtr.nLength = sizeof(SECURITY_ATTRIBUTES);
  saSecAtr.lpSecurityDescriptor = NULL;
  saSecAtr.bInheritHandle = TRUE;

  iRc = CreatePipe(&(pOut[0]), &(pOut[1]),
                   &saSecAtr, 4096);

  // Set the pipe handle to non-inherit.
  DuplicateHandle(GetCurrentProcess(),
                  pOut[0],
                  GetCurrentProcess(),
                  NULL,
                  0,
                  FALSE,
                  DUPLICATE_SAME_ACCESS);

  memset(&suInfo, 0, sizeof(STARTUPINFO));
  suInfo.cb = sizeof(STARTUPINFO);
  suInfo.dwFlags = STARTF_USESTDHANDLES;
  suInfo.hStdInput = NULL;
  suInfo.hStdOutput = (HANDLE)pOut[1];
```

```
suInfo.hStdError = NULL;

if (cParms->szPost != NULL) // Use POST method.
  {
    suInfo.hStdInput = CreateFile(cParms->szPost,
                                  GENERIC_READ,
                                  FILE_SHARE_READ,
                                  &saSecAtr,
                                  OPEN_EXISTING,
                                  FILE_ATTRIBUTE_NORMAL,
                                  0);
  }

CreateProcess((cParms->szProg),    // Command line.
              NULL,
              NULL,                 // Process security attributes.
              NULL,                 // Thread security attributes.
              TRUE,                 // Inherit handles.
              DETACHED_PROCESS,     // Start detached.
              szEnvStrings,         // Environment variables.
              NULL,                 // Current directory default.
              &suInfo,              // Startup information.
              &piInfo);             // Child information.

CloseHandle(piInfo.hThread);   // Close handle to child, not needed.
CloseHandle(pOut[1]);

cParms->szOutput = new char[L_tmpnam]; // Create a temporary file
tmpnam(cParms->szOutput);                     // for the output.
iRead = open(cParms->szOutput, O_WRONLY | O_CREAT | O_BINARY,
             S_IWRITE);
// Grab all of the output from the child.
memset(szBuf, 0, SMALLBUF);
while ( ReadFile(pOut[0], szBuf, SMALLBUF, (LPDWORD)&iNum, NULL) )
  {
    iRc = write(iRead, szBuf, iNum);
    memset(szBuf, 0, SMALLBUF);
  }
close(iRead);
delete [] szQueryString;

CloseHandle(pOut[0]);
if (suInfo.hStdInput != NULL) CloseHandle(suInfo.hStdInput);

// Unlock cgi access.
__lxchg(&iCgiLock, 0);
```

```
   return (0);
}

// -------------------------------------------------------------
```

Under Windows, `ExecCgi()` works in a different manner from the OS/2 version. The big difference is the API call `CreateProcess()` allows you to control the `stdin` and `stdout` handles of the child process. There is no need to duplicate pipe handles to `stdin` and `stdout` of the server. This allows us quite a bit more flexibility since we're not worried about resource contention for the server's `stdin` and `stdout` handles. The overall flow of the function remains close to that of the OS/2 version, but it could be optimized to perform better by making all of the variables local to the function, so the RAM semaphore could be removed. We'll leave this one as an exercise for the reader too.

Our function starts by creating the environmental variable string:

```
// Setting the environment variables.
iEnvLen = strlen(cParms->hInfo->szQuery) + (13 * 64) + 32;
szEnvStrings = new char[iEnvLen];
memset(szTmp, '\0', iEnvLen);
szTmp = szEnvStrings;

sprintf(szRequestMethod, "REQUEST_METHOD=%s",
        cParms->hInfo->szMethod);
memcpy(szTmp, szRequestMethod, strlen(szRequestMethod));
szTmp += strlen(szRequestMethod) + 1;
```

For the `CreateProcess()` call, the environment variables are given in a single character string separated by NULL characters and ending in two NULL characters. We start by allocating space which will be larger than the string we will construct. The only unknown maximum size is the one for the query string. We calculate the length by taking the `strlen()` of the query string and adding a fixed number of bytes for the remaining environment variables. We then set the entire array to NULL using `memset()`. This makes life easier by not having to worry about inserting NULL characters between strings, but they will nevertheless be there by default.

To actually copy the data into `szEnvStrings`, we use a temporary pointer `szTmp`. `szTmp` will always point to the next spot to use in the array. First the full environment string is constructed using `sprintf()`. Next we use `memcpy()` to copy the string into the environment array at the position pointed at by szTmp. We must use memcpy() here since the string will contain NULL characters. We then advance szTmp by the length of the copied string, plus one character. The extra character is to allow for the NULL character between strings. This method is continued for the rest of the environment variables.

Now, due to coding for Windows NT, we must create a SECURITY_ATTRIBUTES structure for some of the API calls. Our interest in providing this data is not to use the security within Windows NT, but to allow for the child process to inherit handles from the server:

```
memset(&saSecAtr, 0, sizeof(SECURITY_ATTRIBUTES));
saSecAtr.nLength = sizeof(SECURITY_ATTRIBUTES);
saSecAtr.lpSecurityDescriptor = NULL;
saSecAtr.bInheritHandle = TRUE;
```

We first null saSecAtr for safety and then assign values to it. The important one here is bInheritHandle which must be true for the child to inherit handles from the parent process. We then use this structure in CreatePipe().

```
iRc = CreatePipe(&(pOut[0]), &(pOut[1]),
                 &saSecAtr, 4096);

// Set the pipe handle to non-inherit.
DuplicateHandle(GetCurrentProcess(),
                pOut[0],
                GetCurrentProcess(),
                NULL,
                0,
                FALSE,
                DUPLICATE_SAME_ACCESS);
```

For our Windows version, we will only be creating a pipe to connect the stdout of the CGI program to the server. Once the pipe is created in inherit mode, we must use DuplicateHandle() to set the inherit attribute of the read handle, pOut[0], to FALSE. While not entirely obvious, you use Duplicate-Handle() to duplicate the pipe handle to itself, in the process changing the inherit flag.

Next, we must set up the STARTUPINFO structure for the CreateProcess() call:

```
memset(&suInfo, 0, sizeof(STARTUPINFO));
suInfo.cb = sizeof(STARTUPINFO);
suInfo.dwFlags = STARTF_USESTDHANDLES;
suInfo.hStdInput = NULL;
suInfo.hStdOutput = (HANDLE)pOut[1];
```

The first thing we do to suInfo is to null the data structure. By doing this, we set all of the different elements to 0 in one call instead of setting each individually. The first element of suInfo to be set is cb. This simply holds the size of the structure. In order for the client to inherit the handles we want to connect to it, dwFlags must be set to a value of STARTF_USESTDHANDLES. If this value is not set, then the child will not pick up the values we assign for stdin and stdout. Though redundant, we next assign a value of NULL to hStdInput. We go ahead and assign the value for clarity in the code. hStdOutput is then assigned to the write handle of the pipe created earlier.

We then check to see if any post data must be passed to the child:

```
if (cParms->szPost != NULL) // Use POST method.
  {
    suInfo.hStdInput = CreateFile(cParms->szPost,
                                  GENERIC_READ,
                                  FILE_SHARE_READ,
                                  &saSecAtr,
                                  OPEN_EXISTING,
                                  FILE_ATTRIBUTE_NORMAL,
                                  0);
  }
```

If there is post data, we open the file to it, assigning the resulting handle to suInfo.hStdInput, the stdin handle of the child process. Again here, one of the parameters is saSecAtr to allow the resulting handle to be inherited by the child process.

Now all of the elements are in place and the child process can be started:

```
CreateProcess((cParms->szProg),   // Command line.
              NULL,
              NULL,                // Process security attributes.
              NULL,                // Thread security attributes.
              TRUE,                // Inherit handles.
```

```
            DETACHED_PROCESS,      // Start detached.
            szEnvStrings,          // Environment variables.
            NULL,                  // Current directory default.
            &suInfo,               // Startup information.
            &piInfo);              // Child information.

CloseHandle(piInfo.hThread);   // Close handle to child,
                               // not needed.
CloseHandle(pOut[1]);
```

We use `CreateProcess()` to spawn the CGI program. The first parameter given to it is the name of the program to start, `cParms->szProg`. The fifth parameter must be set to `TRUE` to let the child process inherit the pipe and file handles. Next, we specify `DETACHED_PROCESS` to start the child in asynchronous mode. The environment string is the seventh parameter while the last two parameters are the startup information and child process information structures.

Once the child has been started, we close the resulting handle to it referenced by `piInfo.hThread` since it is not needed. We also close the handle to the write end of the pipe so we will receive a proper end-of-file condition when the child stops writing output.

The only thing left for us to do now is to wait and read the output from the CGI program:

```
while (ReadFile(pOut[0], szBuf, SMALLBUF, (LPDWORD)&iNum, NULL) )
   {
     iRc = write(iRead, szBuf, iNum);
     memset(szBuf, 0, SMALLBUF);
   }
close(iRead);
```

The loop used here is similar to the one used in the OS/2 version. We've opened a temporary file in binary mode and simply use the API call `ReadFile()` to read from the pipe as long as there is data to read. Any data read is written to the temporary file. Once done, the temporary file is closed.

Now we clean up after ourselves by closing the read handle of the pipe and the handle to the input data if it was opened. We also delete the memory used to hold the query string. Finally, the RAM semaphore is released and we can return to the caller.

9.5 Finishing

There are several aspects of the code presented in this chapter which could be improved. The biggest single is the limitation that only a single thread may execute ExecCgi() at a given time. I left the limitations in the code in order to present the most clear picture of controlling the stdin and stdout of a child process. Most code examples for this are in UNIX programs which are totally different from the environment presented in multithreaded operating systems such as OS/2 and Windows. The exact steps to do and the exact order in which to do them in are critical and hopefully this is made clear.

In the OS/2 and Windows environments, a better approach for CGI support would be to define a standard DLL interface and have the server thread load a DLL and actually run code in it to provide the CGI support. The code would load faster and complete much quicker than starting a separate process. It would be a simple matter to define a structure to hold pointers to all of the things now passed via environment variables. Once defined, this structure could be filled by the server thread, then the DLL could be dynamically loaded and a standard named entry point called to execute. But the standard has been set and it is what we use.

Well, that's pretty much it. We've covered the complete HTTP/1.1 protocol by way of explanations and by code examples. This is probably the time to pick up the RFC again and reread it. After seeing the material presented herein, and reading the RFC, I hope you have gained a better understanding of the protocol procedures which will help you as you administer HTTP servers and develop HTTP applications.

appendix a: HTTP syntax

This appendix presents a summary of the HTTP/1.1 syntax. It is presented in alphabetical order as opposed to the order of the RFC. The syntax included is both what is contained in the HTTP/1.1 specification and the Digest Access Authentication specification. Since they were separate drafts, there is some over-lap in the syntax defined by each. In those instances where the syntax was not quite exact, both definitions are given.

Symbols

```
<"> = <US-ASCII double-quote mark (34)>
```

A

```
A1 = unquoted username-value ":" unquoted realm-value ":"
     password
A2 = Method ":" digest-uri-value
absoluteURI = scheme ":" *( uchar | reserved )
abs_path = "/" rel_path
Accept = "Accept" ":" #( media-range [ accept-params ] )
Accept-Charset = "Accept-Charset" ":"
                 1#( charset [ ";" "q" "=" qvalue ] )
```

309

```
Accept-Encoding = "Accept-Encoding" ":" #( content-coding )
accept-extension = ";" token [ "=" ( token | quoted-string ) ]
Accept-Language = "Accept-Language" ":"
                    1#( language-range [ ";" "q" "=" qvalue ] )
accept-params = ";" "q" "=" qvalue *( accept-extension )
Accept-Ranges = "Accept-Ranges" ":" acceptable-ranges
acceptable-ranges = 1#range-unit | "none"
Age = "Age" ":" age-value
age-value = delta-seconds
algorithm = "algorithm" "=" ( "MD5" | token )
Allow = "Allow" ":" 1#method
ALPHA = UPALPHA | LOALPHA
asctime-date = wkday SP date3 SP time SP 4DIGIT
attribute = token
AuthenticationInfo = "Authentication-info" ":" 1#( digest
                         nextnonce
Authorization = "Authorization" ":" credentials
Authorization = "Authorization" ":" "Digest" digest-response
auth-param = token "=" quoted-string
auth-scheme = token
```

B

```
byte-content-range-spec = bytes-unit SP first-byte-pos "-"
                            last-byte-pos "/" entity-length
basic-cookie = <base64 [7] encoding of user-pass,
                except not limited to 76 char/line>
basic-credentials = "Basic" SP basic-cookie
byte-range-set = 1#( byte-range-spec | suffix-byte-range-spec )
byte-range-spec = first-byte-pos "-" [last-byte-pos]
byte-ranges-specifier = bytes-unit "=" byte-range-set
bytes-unit = "bytes"
```

C

```
Cache-Control = "Cache-Control" ":" 1#cache-directive
cache-directive = cache-request-directive
                  | cache-response-directive
cache-extension = token [ "=" ( token | quoted-string ) ]
cache-request-directive = "no-cache" [ "=" <"> 1#field-name <"> ]
                          | "no-store"
                          | "max-age" "=" delta-seconds
                          | "max-stale" [ "=" delta-seconds ]
                          | "min-fresh" "=" delta-seconds
```

```
                         | "only-if-cached"
                         | cache-extension
cache-response-directive = "public"
                         | "private" [ "=" <"> 1#field-name <"> ]
                         | "no-cache" [ "=" <"> 1#field-name <"> ]
                         | "no-store"
                         | "no-transform"
                         | "must-revalidate"
                         | "proxy-revalidate"
                         | "max-age" "=" delta-seconds
                         | cache-extension
challenge = auth-scheme 1*SP realm *( "," auth-param )
CHAR = <any US-ASCII character (octets 0 - 127)>
charset = token
chunk = chunk-size [ chunk-ext ] CRLF chunk-data CRLF
chunk-ext = *( ";" chunk-ext-name [ "=" chunk-ext-value ] )
chunk-ext-name = token
chunk-ext-val = token | quoted-string
chunk-data = chunk-size(OCTET)
chunk-size = hex-no-zero *HEX
Chunked-Body  = *chunk
                 "0" CRLF
                 footer
                 CRLF
CTL = <any US-ASCII control character
     (octets 0 - 31) and DEL (127)>
comment = "(" *( ctext | comment ) ")"
Connection-header = "Connection" ":" 1#(connection-token)
connection-token = token
Content-Base = "Content-Base" ":" absoluteURI
content-coding = token
Content-Encoding = "Content-Encoding" ":" 1#content-coding
Content-Language = "Content-Language" ":" 1#language-tag
Content-Length = "Content-Length" ":" 1*DIGIT
Content-Location = "Content-Location" ":" ( absoluteURI |
                    relativeURI )
Content-MD5 = "Content-MD5" ":" md5-digest
Content-Range = "Content-Range" ":" content-range-spec
content-range-spec = byte-content-range-spec
Content-Type = "Content-Type" ":" media-type
CR = <US-ASCII CR, carriage return (13)>
credentials = basic-credentials
              | auth-scheme #auth-param
```

```
CRLF = CR LF
ctext = <any TEXT excluding "(" and ")">
```

D

```
Date = "Date" ":" HTTP-date
date = rfc1123-date
date1 = 2DIGIT SP month SP 4DIGIT
        ; day month year (e.g., 02 Jun 1982)
date2 = 2DIGIT "-" month "-" 2DIGIT
        ; day-month-year (e.g., 02-Jun-82)
date3 = month SP ( 2DIGIT | ( SP 1DIGIT ))
        ; month day (e.g., Jun  2)
delta-seconds = 1*DIGIT
digest = "digest" "=" entity-digest
digest-challenge = 1#( realm | [ domain ] | nonce |
                  [ opaque ] |[ stale ] | [ algorithm ] )
digest-response = 1#( username | realm | nonce | digest-uri |
                  response | [ digest ] | [ algorithm ] |
                  opaque )
digest-uri = "uri" "=" digest-uri-value
digest-uri-value = request-uri     ; As specified by HTTP/1.1
DIGIT = <any US-ASCII digit "0".."9">
domain = "domain" "=" <"> 1#URI <">
```

E

```
entity-body = *OCTET
entity-digest = <"> *LHEX <">
entity-digest = <"> KD (H(A1), unquoted nonce-value ":" Method ":"
                  date ":" entity-info ":" H(entity-body)) <">
entity-header = Allow                    ; Section 14.7
            | Content-Base               ; Section 14.11
            | Content-Encoding           ; Section 14.12
            | Content-Language           ; Section 14.13
            | Content-Length             ; Section 14.14
            | Content-Location           ; Section 14.15
            | Content-MD5                ; Section 14.16
            | Content-Range              ; Section 14.17
            | Content-Type               ; Section 14.18
            | ETag                       ; Section 14.20
            | Expires                    ; Section 14.21
            | Last-Modified              ; Section 14.29
            | extension-header
```

```
entity-info = H( digest-uri-value ":"
                 media-type ":"              ; Content-type
                 *DIGIT ":"                  ; Content length
                 content-coding ":"          ; Content-encoding
                 last-modified ":"           ; last modified date
                 expires                      ; expiration date
entity-length = 1*DIGIT
entity-tag = [ weak ] opaque-tag
escape = "%" HEX HEX
ETag = "ETag" ":" entity-tag
Expires = "Expires" ":" HTTP-date
expires = rfc1123-date
extension-code = 3DIGIT
extension-method = token
extension-header = message-header
extra = "!" | "*" | "'" | "(" | ")" | ","
```

F

```
field-content = <the OCTETs making up the field-value
                 and consisting of either *TEXT or combinations
                 of token, tspecials, and quoted-string>
field-name = token
field-value = *( field-content | LWS )
first-byte-pos = 1*DIGIT
footer = *entity-header
fragment = *( uchar | reserved )
From = "From" ":" mailbox
fsegment = 1*pchar
```

G

```
general-header = Cache-Control            ; Section 14.9
               | Connection               ; Section 14.10
               | Date                     ; Section 14.19
               | Pragma                   ; Section 14.32
               | Transfer-Encoding        ; Section 14.40
               | Upgrade                  ; Section 14.41
               | Via                      ; Section 14.44
generic-message = start-line
                  *message-header
                  CRLF
                  [ message-body ]
```

H

```
H(data) = MD5(data)
HEX = "A" | "B" | "C" | "D" | "E" | "F"
      | "a" | "b" | "c" | "d" | "e" | "f" | DIGIT
hex-no-zero = <HEX excluding "0">
Host = "Host" ":" host [ ":" port ]     ; Section 3.2.2
host = <A legal Internet host domain name
        or IP address (in dotted-decimal form),
        as defined by Section 2.1 of RFC 1123>
HT = <US-ASCII HT, horizontal-tab (9)>
HTTP-date = rfc1123-date | rfc850-date | asctime-date
HTTP-message = Request | Response      ; HTTP/1.1 messages
HTTP-Version = "HTTP" "/" 1*DIGIT "." 1*DIGIT
http_URL = "http:" "//" host [ ":" port ] [ abs_path ]
```

I

```
If-Match = "If-Match" ":" ( "*" | 1#entity-tag )
If-Modified-Since = "If-Modified-Since" ":" HTTP-date
If-None-Match = "If-None-Match" ":" ( "*" | 1#entity-tag )
If-Range = "If-Range" ":" ( entity-tag | HTTP-date )
If-Unmodified-Since = "If-Unmodified-Since" ":" HTTP-date
```

K

```
KD(secret, data) = H(concat(secret, ":", data))
```

L

```
language-tag = primary-tag *( "-" subtag )
language-range = ( ( 1*8ALPHA *( "-" 1*8ALPHA ) ) | "*" )
last-byte-pos = 1*DIGIT
Last-Modified = "Last-Modified" ":" HTTP-date
last-modified = rfc1123-date
LF = <US-ASCII LF, linefeed (10)>
LHEX = "0" | "1" | "2" | "3" | "4" | "5" | "6" | "7"
       | "8" | "9" | "a" | "b" | "c" | "d" | "e" | "f"
LOALPHA = <any US-ASCII lowercase letter "a".."z">
Location = "Location" ":" absoluteURI
LWS = [CRLF] 1*( SP | HT )
```

M

```
Max-Forwards = "Max-Forwards" ":" 1*DIGIT
```

```
md5-digest = <base64 of 128 bit MD5 digest as per RFC 1864>
media-range = ( "*/*"
              | ( type "/" "*" )
              | ( type "/" subtype )
              ) *( ";" parameter )
media-type = type "/" subtype *( ";" parameter )
message-header = field-name ":" [ field-value ] CRLF
message-body = entity-body
             | <entity-body encoded as per Transfer-Encoding>
Method = "OPTIONS"
       | "GET"
       | "HEAD"
       | "POST"
       | "PUT"
       | "DELETE"
       | "TRACE"
       | extension-method
month = "Jan" | "Feb" | "Mar" | "Apr"
      | "May" | "Jun" | "Jul" | "Aug"
      | "Sep" | "Oct" | "Nov" | "Dec"
```

N

```
national = <any OCTET excluding ALPHA, DIGIT,
            reserved, extra, safe, and unsafe>
net_loc = *( pchar | ";" | "?" )
net_path = "//" net_loc [ abs_path ]
nextnonce = "nextnonce" "=" nonce-value
nonce = "nonce" "=" nonce-value
nonce-value = quoted-string
```

O

```
OCTET = <any 8-bit sequence of data>
opaque = "opaque" "=" quoted-string
opaque-tag = quoted-string
other-range-unit = token
```

P

```
password = *TEXT
param = *( pchar | "/" )
parameter = attribute "=" value
params = param *( ";" param )
```

```
password = < user's password >
path = fsegment *( "/" segment )
pchar = uchar | ":" | "@" | "&" | "=" | "+"
port = *DIGIT
pseudonym = token
product = token ["/" product-version]
product-version = token
Pragma = "Pragma" ":" 1#pragma-directive
pragma-directive = "no-cache" | extension-pragma
primary-tag = 1*8ALPHA
protocol-name = token
protocol-version = token
Proxy-Authenticate = "Proxy-Authenticate" ":" challenge
Proxy-Authentication = "Proxy-Authentication" ":" "Digest"
                          digest-challenge
Proxy-Authentication-info = "Proxy-Authentication-info" ":"
                          nextnonce
Proxy-Authorization = "Proxy-Authorization" ":" credentials
Proxy-Authorization = "Proxy-Authorization" ":" digest-response
Public = "Public" ":" 1#method
```

Q

```
qdtext = <any TEXT except <">>
query = *( uchar | reserved )
quoted-string = ( <"> *(qdtext) <"> )
quoted-pair = "\" CHAR
qvalue = ( "0" [ "." 0*3DIGIT ] ) | ( "1" [ "." 0*3("0") ] )
```

R

```
Range = "Range" ":" ranges-specifier
range-unit = bytes-unit | other-range-unit
ranges-specifier = byte-ranges-specifier
realm = "realm" "=" realm-value
realm-value = quoted-string
Reason-Phrase = *<TEXT, excluding CR, LF>
received-by = ( host [ ":" port ] ) | pseudonym
received-protocol = [ protocol-name "/" ] protocol-version
Referer = "Referer" ":" ( absoluteURI | relativeURI )
relativeURI = net_path | abs_path | rel_path
rel_path = [ path ] [ ";" params ] [ "?" query ]
Request = Request-Line
          *( general-header
```

```
                     | request-header
                     | entity-header )
                  CRLF
                  [ message-body ]
request-header = Accept
                      | Accept-Charset
                      | Accept-Encoding
                      | Accept-Language
                      | Authorization
                      | From
                      | Host
                      | If-Modified-Since
                      | If-Match
                      | If-None-Match
                      | If-Range
                      | If-Unmodified-Since
                      | Max-Forwards
                      | Proxy-Authorization
                      | Range
                      | Referer
                      | User-Agent
Request-Line = Method SP Request-URI SP HTTP-Version CRLF
Request-URI = "*" | absoluteURI | abs_path
reserved = ";" | "/" | "?" | ":" | "@" | "&" | "=" | "+"
Response = Status-Line
              *( general-header
               | response-header
               | entity-header )
              CRLF
              [ message-body ]
response = "response" "=" response-digest
response-digest = <"> *LHEX <">
response-digest = <"> < KD ( H(A1), unquoted nonce-value ":"
                  H(A2) > <">
response-header = Age
                      | Location
                      | Proxy-Authenticate
                      | Public
                      | Retry-After
                      | Server
                      | Vary
                      | Warning
                      | WWW-Authenticate
```

```
Retry-After = "Retry-After" ":" ( HTTP-date | delta-seconds )
rfc1123-date = wkday "," SP date1 SP time SP "GMT"
rfc850-date = weekday "," SP date2 SP time SP "GMT"
```

S

```
safe = "$" | "-" | "_" | "."
scheme = 1*( ALPHA | DIGIT | "+" | "-" | "." )
segment = *pchar
Server = "Server" ":" 1*( product | comment )
SP = <US-ASCII SP, space (32)>
stale = "stale" "=" ( "true" | "false" )
start-line = Request-Line | Status-Line
Status-Code = "100"     ; Continue
            | "101"     ; Switching Protocols
            | "200"     ; OK
            | "201"     ; Created
            | "202"     ; Accepted
            | "203"     ; Non-Authoritative Information
            | "204"     ; No Content
            | "205"     ; Reset Content
            | "206"     ; Partial Content
            | "300"     ; Multiple Choices
            | "301"     ; Moved Permanently
            | "302"     ; Moved Temporarily
            | "303"     ; See Other
            | "304"     ; Not Modified
            | "305"     ; Use Proxy
            | "400"     ; Bad Request
            | "401"     ; Unauthorized
            | "402"     ; Payment Required
            | "403"     ; Forbidden
            | "404"     ; Not Found
            | "405"     ; Method Not Allowed
            | "406"     ; Not Acceptable
            | "407"     ; Proxy Authentication Required
            | "408"     ; Request Time-out
            | "409"     ; Conflict
            | "410"     ; Gone
            | "411"     ; Length Required
            | "412"     ; Precondition Failed
            | "413"     ; Request Entity Too Large
            | "414"     ; Request-URI Too Large
```

```
               | "415"    ; Unsupported Media Type
               | "500"    ; Internal Server Error
               | "501"    ; Not Implemented
               | "502"    ; Bad Gateway
               | "503"    ; Service Unavailable
               | "504"    ; Gateway Time-out
               | "505"    ; HTTP Version not supported
               | extension-code
Status-Line = HTTP-Version SP Status-Code SP Reason-Phrase CRLF
subtag = 1*8ALPHA
subtype = token
suffix-byte-range-spec = "-" suffix-length
suffix-length = 1*DIGIT
```

T

```
TEXT = <any OCTET except CTLs,
       but including LWS>
token = 1*<any CHAR except CTLs or tspecials>
time = 2DIGIT ":" 2DIGIT ":" 2DIGIT
       ; 00:00:00 - 23:59:59
tspecials = "(" | ")" | "<" | ">" | "@"
            | "," | ";" | ":" | "\" | <">
            | "/" | "[" | "]" | "?" | "="
            |"{" | "}" | SP | HT
transfer-coding = "chunked" | transfer-extension
Transfer-Encoding = "Transfer-Encoding" ":" 1#transfer-coding
transfer-extension = token
type = token
```

U

```
uchar = unreserved | escape
unreserved = ALPHA | DIGIT | safe | extra | national
unsafe = CTL | SP | <"> | "#" | "%" | "<" | ">"
UPALPHA = <any US-ASCII uppercase letter "A".."Z">
Upgrade = "Upgrade" ":" 1#product
URI = ( absoluteURI | relativeURI ) [ "#" fragment ]
User-Agent = "User-Agent" ":" 1*( product | comment )
user-pass = userid ":" password
userid = *<TEXT excluding ":">
username = "username" "=" username-value
username-value = quoted-string
```

V

```
value = token | quoted-string
Vary = "Vary" ":" ( "*" | 1#field-name )
Via = "Via" ":" 1#( received-protocol received-by [ comment ] )
```

W

```
warn-agent = ( host [ ":" port ] ) | pseudonym
              ; the name or pseudonym of the server adding
              ; the Warning header, for use in debugging
warn-code = 2DIGIT
warn-text = quoted-string
Warning = "Warning" ":" 1#warning-value
warning-value = warn-code SP warn-agent SP warn-text
weekday = "Monday" | "Tuesday" | "Wednesday"
          | "Thursday" | "Friday" | "Saturday" | "Sunday"
weak = "W/"
wkday = "Mon" | "Tue" | "Wed"
        | "Thu" | "Fri" | "Sat" | "Sun"
WWW-Authenticate = "WWW-Authenticate" ":" 1#challenge
WWW-Authenticate = "WWW-Authenticate" ":" "Digest"
                    digest-challenge
```

appendix b

HTTP header-field definitions

This appendix contains Section 14 of the HTTP protocol specification. This section defines the syntax and semantics of all standard HTTP/1.1 header fields. For entity-header fields, both sender and recipient refer to either the client or the server, depending on who sends and who receives the entity.

14.1 Accept

The `Accept` request-header field can be used to specify certain media types which are acceptable for the response. `Accept` headers can be used to indicate that the request is specifically limited to a small set of desired types, as in the case of a request for an in-line image.

```
Accept          = "Accept" ":"
                  #( media-range [ accept-params ] )

media-range     = ( "*/*"
                  | ( type "/" "*" )
                  | ( type "/" subtype )
                  ) *( ";" parameter )

accept-params   = ";" "q" "=" qvalue *( accept-extension )

accept-extension = ";" token [ "=" ( token | quoted-string ) ]
```

The asterisk (*) character is used to group media types into ranges, with */*
indicating all media types and type/* indicating all subtypes of that type. The
media-range *may* include media type parameters that are applicable to that
range.

Each media-range *may* be followed by one or more accept-params, beginning with the "q" parameter for indicating a relative quality factor. The first "q"
parameter (if any) separates the media-range parameter(s) from the
accept-params. Quality factors allow the user or user agent to indicate the relative degree of preference for that media-range, using the qvalue scale from 0 to
1 (Section 3.9). The default value is q=1.

Note: Use of the "q" parameter name to separate media type parameters
from Accept extension parameters is due to historical practice. Although this
prevents any media type parameter named "q" from being used with a media
range, such an event is believed to be unlikely given the lack of any "q" parameters in the IANA media type registry and the rare usage of any media type
parameters in Accept. Future media types should be discouraged from register-
ing any parameter named "q". The example:

```
Accept: audio/*; q=0.2, audio/basic
```

should be interpreted as "I prefer audio/basic, but send me any audio type if it is
the best available after an 80% mark-down in quality."

If no Accept header field is present, then it is assumed that the client
accepts all media types. If an Accept header field is present, and if the server
cannot send a response which is acceptable according to the combined Accept
field value, then the server *should* send a 406 (Not Acceptable) response.

A more elaborate example is:

```
Accept: text/plain; q=0.5, text/html, text/x-dvi; q=0.8, text/x-c
```

Verbally, this would be interpreted as `text/html` and `text/x-c` are the preferred media types, but if they do not exist, then send the `text/x-dvi` entity, and if that does not exist, send the `text/plain` entity.

Media ranges can be overridden by more specific media ranges or specific media types. If more than one media range applies to a given type, the most specific reference has precedence. For example:

```
Accept: text/*, text/html, text/html;level=1, */*
```

have the following precedence:

1 `text/html;level=1`
2 `text/html`
3 `text/*`
4 `*/*`

The media type quality factor associated with a given type is determined by finding the media range with the highest precedence which matches that type. For example:

```
Accept: text/*;q=0.3, text/html;q=0.7, text/html;level=1,
text/html;level=2;q=0.4, */*;q=0.5
```

would cause the following values to be associated:

```
text/html;level=1       = 1
text/html               = 0.7
text/plain              = 0.3
image/jpeg              = 0.5
text/html;level=2       = 0.4
text/html;level=3       = 0.7
```

Note: A user agent may be provided with a default set of quality values for certain media ranges. However, unless the user agent is a closed system which cannot interact with other rendering agents, this default set should be configurable by the user.

14.2 Accept-Charset

The `Accept-Charset` request-header field can be used to indicate what character sets are acceptable for the response. This field allows clients capable of understanding more comprehensive or special-purpose character sets to signal that capability to a server which is capable of representing documents in those character sets. The ISO-8859-1 character set can be assumed to be acceptable to all user agents.

```
Accept-Charset = "Accept-Charset" ":" 1#( charset [ ";" "q" "="
                 qvalue ] )
```

Character set values are described in Section 3.4. Each `charset` may be given an associated quality value which represents the user's preference for that `charset`. The default value is `q=1`. An example is:

```
Accept-Charset: iso-8859-5, unicode-1-1;q=0.8
```

If no `Accept-Charset` header is present, the default is that any character set is acceptable. If an `Accept-Charset` header is present, and if the server cannot send a response which is acceptable according to the `Accept-Charset` header, then the server *should* send an error response with the `406` (`Not Acceptable`) status code, though the sending of an unacceptable response is also allowed.

14.3 Accept-Encoding

The `Accept-Encoding` request-header field is similar to `Accept`, but restricts the content-coding values (Section 14.12) which are acceptable in the response.

```
Accept-Encoding  = "Accept-Encoding" ":" #( content-coding )
```

An example of its use is:

```
Accept-Encoding: compress, gzip
```

If no `Accept-Encoding` header is present in a request, the server *may* assume that the client will accept any content coding. If an `Accept-Encoding` header is present, and if the server cannot send a response which is acceptable according to the `Accept-Encoding` header, then the server *should* send an error response with the `406` (`Not Acceptable`) status code.

An empty `Accept-Encoding` value indicates none are acceptable.

14.4 Accept-Language

The `Accept-Language` request-header field is similar to `Accept`, but restricts the set of natural languages that are preferred as a response to the request.

```
Accept-Language = "Accept-Language" ":" 1#( language-range [ ";" "q"
"=" qvalue ] )

language-range  = ( ( 1*8ALPHA *( "-" 1*8ALPHA ) ) | "*" )
```

Each language-range *may* be given an associated quality value which represents an estimate of the user's preference for the languages specified by that range. The quality value defaults to q=1. For example:

```
Accept-Language: da, en-gb;q=0.8, en;q=0.7
```

would mean: "I prefer Danish, but will accept British English and other types of English." A `language-range` matches a language-tag if it exactly equals the tag, or if it exactly equals a prefix of the tag such that the first tag character following the prefix is "-". The special range "*", if present in the `Accept-Language` field, matches every tag not matched by any other range present in the `Accept-Language` field.

Note: This use of a prefix matching rule does not imply that language tags are assigned to languages in such a way that it is always true that if a user understands a language with a certain tag, then this user will also understand all languages with tags for which this tag is a prefix. The prefix rule simply allows the use of prefix tags if this is the case.

The language quality factor assigned to a language-tag by the `Accept-Language` field is the quality value of the longest language-range in the field that matches the language-tag. If no `language-range` in the field matches the tag, the language quality factor assigned is 0. If no `Accept-Language` header is present in the request, the server *should* assume that all languages are equally acceptable. If an `Accept-Language` header is present, then all languages which are assigned a quality factor greater than 0 are acceptable.

It may be contrary to the privacy expectations of the user to send an `Accept-Language` header with the complete linguistic preferences of the user in every request. For a discussion of this issue, see Section 15.7.

Note: As comprehension is highly dependent on the individual user, it is recommended that client applications make the choice of linguistic preference available to the user. If the choice is not made available, then the `Accept-Language` header field must not be given in the request.

14.5 Accept-Ranges

The `Accept-Ranges` response-header field allows the server to indicate its acceptance of range requests for a resource:

```
Accept-Ranges       = "Accept-Ranges" ":" acceptable-ranges

acceptable-ranges = 1#range-unit | "none"
```

Origin servers that accept byte-range requests *may* send:

```
Accept-Ranges: bytes
```

but are not required to do so. Clients *may* generate byte-range requests without having received this header for the resource involved.

Servers that do not accept any kind of range request for a resource *may* send:

```
Accept-Ranges: none
```

to advise the client not to attempt a range request.

14.6 Age

The `Age` response-header field conveys the sender's estimate of the amount of time since the response (or its revalidation) was generated at the origin server. A cached response is fresh if its age does not exceed its freshness lifetime. `Age` values are calculated as specified in Section 13.2.3.

```
Age = "Age" ":" age-value

age-value = delta-seconds
```

Age values are non-negative decimal integers, representing time in seconds. If a cache receives a value larger than the largest positive integer it can represent, or if any of its age calculations overflows, it *must* transmit an `Age` header with a value of 2,147,483,648 (2^{31}). HTTP/1.1 caches *must* send an `Age` header in every response. Caches *should* use an arithmetic type of at least 31 bits of range.

14.7 Allow

The `Allow` entity-header field lists the set of methods supported by the resource identified by the `Request-URI`. The purpose of this field is strictly to inform the recipient of valid methods associated with the resource. An `Allow` header field *must* be present in a `405` (`Method Not Allowed`) response.

```
Allow          = "Allow" ":" 1#method
```

Example of use:

```
Allow: GET, HEAD, PUT
```

This field cannot prevent a client from trying other methods. However, the indications given by the `Allow` header field value *should* be followed. The actual set of allowed methods is defined by the origin server at the time of each request.

The `Allow` header field *may* be provided with a `PUT` request to recommend the methods to be supported by the new or modified resource. The server is not required to support these methods and *should* include an `Allow` header in the response giving the actual supported methods.

A proxy *must not* modify the `Allow` header field even if it does not understand all the methods specified, since the user agent *may* have other means of communicating with the origin server.

The `Allow` header field does not indicate what methods are implemented at the server level. Servers *may* use the `Public` response-header field (Section 14.35) to describe what methods are implemented on the server as a whole.

14.8 Authorization

A user agent who wishes to authenticate itself with a server—usually, but not necessarily, after receiving a `401` response—*may* do so by including an `Authorization` request-header field with the request. The `Authorization` field value consists of credentials containing the authentication information of the user agent for the realm of the resource being requested.

```
Authorization  = "Authorization" ":" credentials
```

HTTP access authentication is described in Section 11 of the protocol. If a request is authenticated and a realm specified, the same credentials *should* be valid for all other requests within this realm.

When a shared cache (see Section 13.7) receives a request containing an `Authorization` field, it *must not* return the corresponding response as a reply to any other request, unless one of the following specific exceptions holds:

- If the response includes the *proxy-revalidate* `Cache-Control` directive, the cache *may* use that response in replying to a subsequent request, but a proxy cache *must* first revalidate it with the origin server, using the request-headers from the new request to allow time for the origin server to authenticate the new request.

- If the response includes the *must-revalidate* `Cache-Control` directive, the cache *may* use that response in replying to a subsequent request, but all caches *must* first revalidate it with the origin server, using the request-headers from the new request to allow time for the origin server to authenticate the new request.

- If the response includes the *public* `Cache-Control` directive, it may be returned in reply to any subsequent request.

14.9 Cache-Control

The `Cache-Control` general-header field is used to specify directives that *must* be obeyed by all caching mechanisms along the request/response chain. The directives specify behavior intended to prevent caches from adversely interfering with the request or response. These directives typically override the default caching algorithms. Cache directives are unidirectional in that the presence of a directive in a request does not imply that the same directive should be given in the response.

Note that HTTP/1.0 caches may not implement `Cache-Control` and may only implement `Pragma: no-cache` (see Section 14.32).

Cache directives must be passed through by a proxy or gateway application, regardless of their significance to that application, since the directives may be applicable to all recipients along the request/response chain. It is not possible to specify a cache-directive for a specific cache.

```
Cache-Control   = "Cache-Control" ":" 1#cache-directive

cache-directive = cache-request-directive | cache-response-directive

cache-request-directive =
                 "no-cache" [ "=" <"> 1#field-name <"> ]
               | "no-store"
               | "max-age" "=" delta-seconds
               | "max-stale" [ "=" delta-seconds ]
               | "min-fresh" "=" delta-seconds
               | "only-if-cached"
               | cache-extension

cache-response-directive =
                 "public"
               | "private" [ "=" <"> 1#field-name <"> ]
               | "no-cache" [ "=" <"> 1#field-name <"> ]
               | "no-store"
               | "no-transform"
               | "must-revalidate"
               | "proxy-revalidate"
               | "max-age" "=" delta-seconds
               | cache-extension

cache-extension = token [ "=" ( token | quoted-string ) ]
```

When a directive appears without any `1#field-name` parameter, the directive applies to the entire request or response. When such a directive appears with a `1#field-name` parameter, it applies only to the named field or fields, and not to the rest of the request or response. This mechanism supports extensibility;

implementations of future versions of the HTTP protocol may apply these directives to header fields not defined in HTTP/1.1.

The `Cache-Control` directives can be broken down into these general operative categories:

- Restrictions on what is cachable; these may only be imposed by the origin server.
- Restrictions on what may be stored by a cache; these may be imposed by either the origin server or the user agent.
- Modifications of the basic expiration mechanism; these may be imposed by either the origin server or the user agent.
- Controls over cache revalidation and reload; these may only be imposed by a user agent.
- Control over transformation of entities.
- Extensions to the caching system.

14.9.1 What is Cachable   By default, a response is cachable if the requirements of the request method, request header fields, and the response status indicate that it is cachable. Section 13.4 summarizes these defaults for cachability. The following `Cache-Control` response directives allow an origin server to override the default cachability of a response:

- *public*   Indicates that the response is cachable by any cache, even if it would normally be non-cachable or cachable only within a non-shared cache. (See also `Authorization`, Section 14.8, for additional details.)
- *private*   Indicates that all or part of the response message is intended for a single user and *must not* be cached by a shared cache. This allows an origin server to state that the specified parts of the response are intended for only one user and are not a valid response for requests by other users. A private (non-shared) cache may cache the response.

    Note: This usage of the word *private* only controls where the response may be cached, and cannot ensure the privacy of the message content.

- *no-cache* Indicates that all or part of the response message *must not* be cached anywhere. This allows an origin server to prevent caching even by caches that have been configured to return stale responses to client requests.

  Note: Most HTTP/1.0 caches will not recognize or obey this directive.

14.9.2 What may be stored by caches The purpose of the `no-store` directive is to prevent the inadvertent release or retention of sensitive information (for example, on backup tapes). The `no-store` directive applies to the entire message, and may be sent either in a response or in a request. If sent in a request, a cache *must not* store any part of either this request or any response to it. If sent in a response, a cache *must not* store any part of either this response or the request that elicited it. This directive applies to both non-shared and shared caches. *must not store* in this context means that the cache *must not* intentionally store the information in non-volatile storage, and *must* make a best-effort attempt to remove the information from volatile storage as promptly as feasible and possible after forwarding it.

Even when this directive is associated with a response, users may explicitly store such a response outside of the caching system (e.g., with a `Save As` dialog). History buffers may store such responses as part of their normal operation.

The purpose of this directive is to meet the stated requirements of certain users and service authors who are concerned about accidental releases of information via unanticipated accesses to cache data structures. While the use of this directive may improve privacy in some cases, we caution that it is *not* in any way a reliable or sufficient mechanism for ensuring privacy. In particular, malicious or compromised caches may not recognize or obey this directive; and communications networks may be vulnerable to eavesdropping.

14.9.3 Modifications of the Basic Expiration Mechanism The expiration time of an entity may be specified by the origin server using the `Expires` header (see Section 14.21). Alternatively, it may be specified using the `max-age` directive in a response.

If a response includes both an `Expires` header and a `max-age` directive, the `max-age` directive overrides the `Expires` header, even if the `Expires` header is more restrictive. This rule allows an origin server to provide, for a given response, a longer expiration time to an HTTP/1.1 (or later) cache than to an HTTP/1.0 cache. This may be useful if certain HTTP/1.0 caches improperly calculate ages or expiration times, perhaps due to desynchronized clocks.

Note: most older caches, not compliant with this specification, do not implement any `Cache-Control` directives. An origin server wishing to use a `Cache-Control` directive that restricts, but does not prevent, caching by an HTTP/1.1-compliant cache may exploit the requirement that the `max-age` directive overrides the `Expires` header, and the fact that non-HTTP/1.1-compliant caches do not observe the `max-age` directive.

Other directives allow a user agent to modify the basic expiration mechanism. These directives may be specified on a request:

- *max-age*   Indicates that the client is willing to accept a response whose age is no greater than the specified time in seconds. Unless `max-stale` directive is also included, the client is not willing to accept a stale response.

- *min-fresh*   Indicates that the client is willing to accept a response whose freshness lifetime is no less than its current age plus the specified time in seconds. That is, the client wants a response that will still be fresh for at least the specified number of seconds.

- *max-stale*   Indicates that the client is willing to accept a response that has exceeded its expiration time. If `max-stale` is assigned a value, then the client is willing to accept a response that has exceeded its expiration time by no more than the specified number of seconds. If no value is assigned to `max-stale`, then the client is willing to accept a stale response of any age

If a cache returns a stale response, either because of a `max-stale` directive on a request, or because the cache is configured to override the expiration time of a response, the cache *must* attach a `Warning` header to the stale response, using `Warning 10 (Response is stale)`.

14.9.4 Cache Revalidation and Reload Controls   Sometimes a user agent may want or need to insist that a cache revalidate its cache entry with the origin server (and not just with the next cache along the path to the origin server), or to reload its cache entry from the origin server. `End-to-end` revalidation may be necessary if either the cache or the origin server has overestimated the expiration time of the cached response. End-to-end reload may be necessary if the cache entry has become corrupted for some reason.

End-to-end revalidation may be requested either when the client does not have its own local cached copy, in which case we call it *unspecified end-to-end revalidation,* or when the client does have a local cached copy, in which case we call it *specific end-to-end revalidation.*

The client can specify these three kinds of action using Cache-Control request directives:

- *End-to-end reload* The request includes a *no-cache* Cache-Control directive or, for compatibility with HTTP/1.0 clients, Pragma: no-cache. No field names may be included with the no-cache directive in a request. The server *must not* use a cached copy when responding to such a request.

- *Specific end-to-end revalidation* The request includes a max-age=0 Cache-Control directive, which forces each cache along the path to the origin server to revalidate its own entry, if any, with the next cache or server. The initial request includes a cache-validating conditional with the client's current validator.

- *Unspecified end-to-end revalidation* The request includes max-age=0 Cache-Control directive, which forces each cache along the path to the origin server to revalidate its own entry, if any, with the next cache or server. The initial request does not include a cache-validating conditional; the first cache along the path (if any) that holds a cache entry for this resource includes a cache-validating conditional with its current validator.

When an intermediate cache is forced, by means of a max-age=0 directive, to revalidate its own cache entry, and the client has supplied its own validator in the request, the supplied validator may differ from the validator currently stored with the cache entry. In this case, the cache may use either validator in making its own request without affecting semantic transparency.

However, the choice of validator may affect performance. The best approach is for the intermediate cache to use its own validator when making its request. If the server replies with 304 (Not Modified), then the cache should return its now validated copy to the client with a 200 (OK) response. If the server replies with a new entity and cache validator, however, the intermediate cache should compare the returned validator with the one provided in the client's request, using the strong comparison function. If the client's validator is equal to the origin server's, then the intermediate cache simply returns 304 (Not Modified). Otherwise, it returns the new entity with a 200 (OK) response.

If a request includes the no-cache directive, it should not include min-fresh, max-stale, or max-age.

In some cases, such as times of extremely poor network connectivity, a client may want a cache to return only those responses that it currently has stored, and not to reload or revalidate with the origin server. To do this, the client may include the only-if-cached directive in a request. If it receives this directive, a cache *should* either respond using a cached entry that is consistent with the other constraints of the request, or respond with a 504 (Gateway Timeout) status. However, if a group of caches is being operated as a unified system with good internal connectivity, such a request *may* be forwarded within that workable group of caches.

Because a cache may be configured to ignore a server's specified expiration time, and because a client request may include a max-stale directive (which has a similar effect), the protocol also includes a mechanism for the origin server to require revalidation of a cache entry on any subsequent use. When the must-revalidate directive is present in a response received by a cache, that cache *must not* use the entry after it becomes stale to respond to a subsequent request without first revalidating it with the origin server. (i.e., the cache must do an end-to-end revalidation every time, if, based solely on the origin server's Expires or max-age value, the cached response is stale.)

The must-revalidate directive is necessary to support reliable operation for certain protocol features. In all circumstances an HTTP/1.1 cache *must* obey the must-revalidate directive; in particular, if the cache cannot reach the origin server for any reason, it *must* generate a 504 (Gateway Timeout) response.

Servers should send the must-revalidate directive if and only if failure to revalidate a request on the entity could result in incorrect operation, such as a silently unexecuted financial transaction. Recipients *must not* take any automated action that violates this directive, and *must not* automatically provide an unvalidated copy of the entity if revalidation fails.

Although this is not recommended, user agents operating under severe connectivity constraints may violate this directive but, if so, *must* explicitly warn the user that an unvalidated response has been provided. The warning *must* be provided on each unvalidated access, and *should* require explicit user confirmation.

The `proxy-revalidate` directive has the same meaning as the `must-revalidate` directive, except that it does not apply to non-shared user agent caches. It can be used on a response to an authenticated request to permit the user's cache to store and later return the response without needing to revalidate it (since it has already been authenticated once by that user), while still requiring proxies that service many users to revalidate each time (in order to make sure that each user has been authenticated). Note that such authenticated responses also need the public cache-control directive in order to allow them to be cached at all.

14.9.5 No-Transform Directive   Implementors of intermediate caches (proxies) have found it useful to convert the media type of certain entity bodies. A proxy might, for example, convert between image formats in order to save cache space or to reduce the amount of traffic on a slow link. HTTP has to date been silent on these transformations.

Serious operational problems have already occurred, however, when these transformations have been applied to entity bodies intended for certain kinds of applications. For example, applications for medical imaging, scientific data analysis and those using `end-to-end` authentication, all depend on receiving an entity body that is bit for bit identical to the original entity-body.

Therefore, if a response includes the `no-transform` directive, an intermediate cache or proxy *must not* change those headers that are listed in Section 13.5.2 as being subject to the `no-transform` directive. This implies that the cache or proxy must not change any aspect of the entity-body that is specified by these specific headers.

14.9.6 Cache-Control Extensions   The `Cache-Control` header field can be extended through the use of one or more cache-extension tokens, each with an optional assigned value. Informational extensions (those which do not require a change in cache behavior) may be added without changing the semantics of other directives. Behavioral extensions are designed to work by acting as modifiers to the existing base of cache directives. Both the new directive and the standard directive are supplied, such that applications which do not understand the new directive will default to the behavior specified by the standard directive, and those that understand the new directive will recognize it as modifying the requirements associated with the standard directive. In this way, extensions to the `Cache-Control` directives can be made without requiring changes to the base protocol.

This extension mechanism depends on an HTTP cache obeying all of the `cache-control` directives defined for its native HTTP-version, obeying certain extensions, and ignoring all directives that it does not understand.

For example, consider a hypothetical new response directive called *community* which acts as a modifier to the *private* directive. We define this new directive to mean that, in addition to any non-shared cache, any cache which is shared only by members of the community named within its value may cache the response. An origin server wishing to allow the UCI community to use an otherwise private response in their shared cache(s) may do so by including:

```
Cache-Control: private, community="UCI"
```

A cache seeing this header field will act correctly even if the cache does not understand the *community* cache-extension, since it will also see and understand the *private* directive and thus default to the safe behavior.

Unrecognized cache-directives *must* be ignored; it is assumed that any cache-directive likely to be unrecognized by an HTTP/1.1 cache will be combined with standard directives (or the response's default cachability) such that the cache behavior will remain minimally correct even if the cache does not understand the extension(s).

14.10 Connection

The `Connection` general-header field allows the sender to specify options that are desired for that particular connection and *must not* be communicated by proxies over further connections.

The `Connection` header has the following grammar:

```
Connection-header = "Connection" ":" 1#(connection-token)
connection-token  = token
```

HTTP/1.1 proxies *must* parse the `Connection` header field before a message is forwarded and, for each connection-token in this field, remove any header field(s) from the message with the same name as the connection-token. Connection options are signaled by the presence of a connection-token in the `Connection` header field, not by any corresponding additional header field(s), since the additional header field may not be sent if there are no parameters associated with that connection option.

HTTP/1.1 defines the `close` connection option for the sender to signal that the connection will be closed after completion of the response. For example:

```
Connection: close
```

in either the request or the response header fields indicates that the connection should not be considered *persistent* (Section 8.1) after the current request/response is complete.

HTTP/1.1 applications that do not support persistent connections *must* include the `close` connection option in every message.

14.11 *Content-Base*

The `Content-Base` entity-header field may be used to specify the base URI for resolving relative URLs within the entity. This header field is described as `Base` in RFC 1808, which is expected to be revised.

```
Content-Base      = "Content-Base" ":" absoluteURI
```

If no `Content-Base` field is present, the base URI of an entity is defined either by its `Content-Location` (if that `Content-Location` URI is an absolute URI) or the URI used to initiate the request, in that order of precedence. Note, however, that the base URI of the contents within the entity-body may be redefined within that entity-body.

14.12 Content-Encoding

The `Content-Encoding` entity-header field is used as a modifier to the media-type. When present, its value indicates what additional content codings have been applied to the entity-body, and thus what decoding mechanisms *must* be applied in order to obtain the media-type referenced by the `Content-Type` header field. `Content-Encoding` is primarily used to allow a document to be compressed without losing the identity of its underlying media type.

```
Content-Encoding  = "Content-Encoding" ":" 1#content-coding
```

Content codings are defined in Section 3.5. An example of its use is:

```
Content-Encoding: gzip
```

The `Content-Encoding` is a characteristic of the entity identified by the `Request-URI`. Typically, the entity-body is stored with this encoding and is only decoded before rendering or analogous usage.

If multiple encodings have been applied to an entity, the content codings *must* be listed in the order in which they were applied.

Additional information about the encoding parameters *may* be provided by other entity-header fields not defined by this specification.

14.13 Content-Language

The `Content-Language` entity-header field describes the natural language(s) of the intended audience for the enclosed entity. Note that this may not be equivalent to all the languages used within the entity-body.

```
Content-Language  = "Content-Language" ":" 1#language-tag
```

Language tags are defined in Section 3.10. The primary purpose of `Content-Language` is to allow a user to identify and differentiate entities according to the user's own preferred language. Thus, if the body content is intended only for a Danish-literate audience, the appropriate field is:

```
Content-Language: da
```

If no `Content-Language` is specified, the default is that the content is intended for all language audiences. This may mean that the sender does not consider it to be specific to any natural language, or that the sender does not know for which language it is intended.

Multiple languages *may* be listed for content that is intended for multiple audiences. For example, a rendition of the *Treaty of Waitangi*, presented simultaneously in the original Maori and English versions, would call for:

```
Content-Language: mi, en
```

However, just because multiple languages are present within an entity does not mean that it is intended for multiple linguistic audiences. An example would be a beginner's language primer, such as *A First Lesson in Latin*, which is clearly intended to be used by an English-literate audience. In this case, the `Content-Language` should only include `en`.

Content-Language may be applied to any media type–it is not limited to textual documents.

14.14 Content-Length

The `Content-Length` entity-header field indicates the size of the message-body, in decimal number of octets, sent to the recipient or, in the case of the HEAD method, the size of the entity-body that would have been sent had the request been a GET.

```
Content-Length   = "Content-Length" ":" 1*DIGIT
```

An example is:

```
Content-Length: 3495
```

Applications *should* use this field to indicate the size of the message-body to be transferred, regardless of the media type of the entity. It must be possible for the recipient to reliably determine the end of HTTP/1.1 requests containing an entity-body, e.g., because the request has a valid `Content-Length` field, uses `Transfer-Encoding: chunked` or a multipart body.

Any `Content-Length` greater than or equal to 0 is a valid value. Section 4.4 describes how to determine the length of a message-body if a `Content-Length` is not given.

Note: The meaning of this field is significantly different from the corresponding definition in MIME, where it is an optional field used within the *message/external-body* content-type. In HTTP, it *should* be sent whenever the message's length can be determined prior to being transferred.

14.15 Content-Location

The `Content-Location` entity-header field may be used to supply the resource location for the entity enclosed in the message. In the case where a resource has multiple entities associated with it, and those entities actually have separate locations by which they might be individually accessed, the server should provide a `Content-Location` for the particular variant which is returned. In addition, a server *should* provide a `Content-Location` for the resource corresponding to the response entity.

```
Content-Location = "Content-Location" ":"
                    ( absoluteURI | relativeURI )
```

If no `Content-Base` header field is present, then the value of `Content-Location` also defines the base URL for the entity (see Section 14.11).

The `Content-Location` value is not a replacement for the original requested URI; it is only a statement of the location of the resource corresponding to this particular entity at the time of the request. Future requests *may* use the `Content-Location` URI if the desire is to positively identify the source of that particular entity.

A cache cannot assume that an entity with a `Content-Location` different from the URI used to retrieve it can be used to respond to later requests on that `Content-Location` URI. However, the `Content-Location` can be used to differentiate between multiple entities retrieved from a single requested resource, as described in Section 13.6.

If the `Content-Location` is a relative URI, the URI is interpreted relative to any `Content-Base` URI provided in the response. If no `Content-Base` is provided, the relative URI is interpreted relative to the `Request-URI`.

14.16 Content-MD5

The `Content-MD5` entity-header field, as defined in RFC 1864 [23], is an MD5 digest of the entity-body for the purpose of providing an end-to-end message integrity check (MIC) of the entity-body. (Note: an MIC is good for detecting accidental modification of the entity-body in transit, but is not proof against malicious attacks.)

```
Content-MD5    = "Content-MD5" ":" md5-digest
md5-digest     = <base64 of 128 bit MD5 digest as per RFC 1864>
```

The `Content-MD5` header field may be generated by an origin server to function as an integrity check of the entity-body. Only origin servers may generate the `Content-MD5` header field; proxies and gateways *must not* generate it, as this would defeat its value as an end-to-end integrity check. Any recipient of the entity-body, including gateways and proxies, *may* check that the digest value in this header field matches that of the entity-body as received.

The MD5 digest is computed based on the content of the entity-body, including any `Content-Encoding` that has been applied, but not including any `Transfer-Encoding` that may have been applied to the message-body. If the message is received with a `Transfer-Encoding`, that encoding must be removed prior to checking the `Content-MD5` value against the received entity.

This has the result that the digest is computed on the octets of the entity-body exactly as, and in the order that, they would be sent if no `Transfer-Encoding` were being applied.

HTTP extends RFC 1864 to permit the digest to be computed for MIME composite media-types (e.g., `multipart/*` and `message/rfc822`), but this certainly does not change how the digest is computed as defined in the preceding paragraph.

Note: There are several consequences of this. The entity-body for composite types may contain many body parts, each with its own MIME and HTTP headers (including `Content-MD5`, `Content-Transfer-Encoding`, and `Content-Encoding` headers). If a body-part has a `Content-Transfer-Encoding` or `Content-Encoding` header, it is assumed that the content of the body part has had the encoding applied, and the body part is included in the `Content-MD5` digest as is–i.e., after the application. The `Transfer-Encoding` header field is not allowed within body parts.

Note: while the definition of `Content-MD5` is exactly the same for HTTP as in RFC 1864 for MIME entity-bodies, there are several ways in which the application of `Content-MD5` to HTTP entity-bodies differs from its application to MIME entity-bodies. One is that HTTP, unlike MIME, does not use `Content-Transfer-Encoding`, and does use `Transfer-Encoding` and `Content-Encoding`. Another is that HTTP more frequently uses binary content types than MIME, so it is worth noting that, in such cases, the byte order used to compute the digest is the transmission byte order defined for the type. Lastly, HTTP allows transmission of text types with any of several line break conventions and not just the canonical form using CRLF. Conversion of all line breaks to CRLF should not be done before computing or checking the digest: the line break convention used in the text actually transmitted should be left unaltered when computing the digest.

14.17 Content-Range

The `Content-Range` entity-header is sent with a partial entity-body to specify where in the full entity-body the partial body should be inserted. It also indicates the total size of the full entity-body. When a server returns a partial response to a client, it must describe both the extent of the range covered by the response, and the length of the entire entity-body.

```
Content-Range          = "Content-Range" ":" content-range-spec
content-range-spec     = byte-content-range-spec
byte-content-range-spec = bytes-unit SP first-byte-pos "-"
                         last-byte-pos "/" entity-length

entity-length          = 1*DIGIT
```

Unlike byte-ranges-specifier values, a `byte-content-range-spec` may only specify one range, and must contain absolute byte positions for both the first and last byte of the range.

A `byte-content-range-spec` whose `last-byte-pos` value is less than its `first-byte-pos` value, or whose `entity-length` value is less than or equal to its `last-byte-pos` value, is invalid. The recipient of an invalid `byte-content-range-spec` *must* definitely ignore it, together with any content transferred along with it.

Examples of `byte-content-range-spec` values, assuming that the entity contains a total of 1234 bytes:

- The first 500 bytes:
  bytes 0–499/1234

- The second 500 bytes:
  bytes 500–999/1234

- All except for the first 500 bytes:
  bytes 500–1233/1234

- The last 500 bytes:
  bytes 734–1233/1234

When an HTTP message includes the content of a single range (for example, a response to a request for a single range, or to a request for a set of ranges that overlap without any holes), this content is transmitted with a `Content-Range` header, and a `Content-Length` header showing the number of bytes actually transferred. For example:

```
HTTP/1.1 206 Partial content
Date: Wed, 15 Nov 1995 06:25:24 GMT
Last-modified: Wed, 15 Nov 1995 04:58:08 GMT
Content-Range: bytes 21010-47021/47022
Content-Length: 26012
Content-Type: image/gif
```

When an HTTP message includes the content of multiple ranges (for example, a response to a request for multiple non-overlapping ranges), these are transmitted as a multipart MIME message. The multipart MIME content-type used for this purpose is defined in this specification to be *multipart/byteranges*. See appendix 19.2 for its definition.

A client that cannot decode a MIME multipart/byteranges message should not ask for multiple byte ranges in a single request.

When a client requests multiple byte ranges in one request, the server *should* return them in the order that they appeared in the request.

If the server ignores a `byte-range-spec` because it is invalid, the server should treat the request as if the invalid `Range` header field did not exist. (Normally, this means return a `200` response containing the full entity). The reason is that the only time a client will make such an invalid request is when the entity is smaller than the entity retrieved by a prior request.

14.18 Content-Type

The `Content-Type` entity-header field indicates the media type of the entity-body sent to the recipient or, in the case of the `HEAD` method, the media type that would have been sent had the request been a `GET`.

```
Content-Type  = "Content-Type" ":" media-type
```

Media types are defined in Section 3.7. An example of the field is

```
Content-Type: text/html; charset=ISO-8859-4
```

Further discussion of methods for identifying the media type of an entity is provided in Section 7.2.1.

14.19 Date

The `Date` general-header field represents the date and time at which the message was originated, having the same semantics as `orig-date` in RFC 822. The field value is an HTTP-date, as described in Section 3.3.1.

```
Date  = "Date" ":" HTTP-date
```

An example is:

```
Date: Tue, 15 Nov 1994 08:12:31 GMT
```

If a message is received via direct connection with the user agent (in the case of requests) or the origin server (in the case of responses), then the date can be assumed to be the current date at the receiving end. However, since the date–as it is believed by the origin–is important for evaluating cached responses, origin servers *must* include a `Date` header field in all responses. Clients *should* only send a `Date` header field in messages that include an entity-body, as in the case of the `PUT` and `POST` requests, and even then it is optional. A received message which does not have a `Date` header field *should* be assigned one by the recipient if the message will be cached by that recipient or gatewayed via a protocol which requires a `Date`.

In theory, the date *should* represent the moment just before the entity is generated. In practice, the date can be generated at any time during the message origination without affecting its semantic value.

The format of the `Date` is an absolute date and time as defined by HTTP-date in Section 3.3; it *must* be sent in RFC1123-date format.

14.20 ETag

The `ETag` entity-header field defines the entity tag for the associated entity. The headers used with entity tags are described in Sections 14.20, 14.25, 14.26 and 14.43. The entity tag may be used for comparison with other entities from the same resource (see Section 13.3.2).

```
ETag = "ETag" ":" entity-tag
```

Examples of the header:

```
ETag: "xyzzy"
ETag: W/"xyzzy"
ETag: ""
```

14.21 Expires

The `Expires` entity-header field gives the date/time after which the response should be considered stale. A stale cache entry may not normally be returned by a cache (either a proxy cache or an user agent cache) unless it is first validated with the origin server (or with an intermediate cache that has a fresh copy of the entity). See Section 13.2 for further discussion of the expiration model.

The presence of an `Expires` field does not imply that the original resource will change or cease to exist at, before, or after that time.

The format is an absolute date and time as defined by HTTP-date in Section 3.3; it *must* be in RFC1123-date format:

```
Expires = "Expires" ":" HTTP-date
```

An example of its use is:

```
Expires: Thu, 01 Dec 1994 16:00:00 GMT
```

Note: if a response includes a `Cache-Control` field with the `max-age` directive, that directive overrides the `Expires` field.

HTTP/1.1 clients and caches *must* treat other invalid date formats, especially including the value 0, as in the past (i.e., already expired).

To mark a response as already expired, an origin server should use an `Expires` date that is equal to the `Date` header value. (See the rules for expiration calculations in Section 13.2.4.)

To mark a response as never expires, an origin server should use an `Expires` date approximately one year from the time the response is sent. HTTP/1.1 servers should definitely not send `Expires` dates more than one year in the future.

The presence of an `Expires` header field with a date value of some time in the future on an response that otherwise would by default be non-cachable indicates that the response is cachable, unless indicated otherwise by a `Cache-Control` header field (Section 14.9).

14.22 From

The `From` request-header field, if given, *should* contain an Internet email address for the human user who controls the requesting user agent. The address *should* be machine-usable, as defined by mailbox in RFC 822 (and as updated by RFC 1123):

```
From   = "From" ":" mailbox
```

An example is:

```
From: webmaster@w3.org
```

This header field *may* be used for logging purposes and as a means for identifying the source of invalid or unwanted requests. It *should not* be used as an insecure form of access protection. The interpretation of this field is that the request is being performed on behalf of the person given, who accepts responsibility for the method performed. In particular, robot agents *should* include this header so that the person responsible for running the robot can be contacted if problems occur on the receiving end.

The Internet email address in this field *may* be separate from the Internet host which issued the request. For example, when a request is passed through a proxy the original issuer's address *should* be used.

Note: The client *should* not send the From header field without the user's approval, as it may conflict with the user's privacy interests or their site's security policy. It is strongly recommended that the user be able to disable, enable, and modify the value of this field at any time prior to a request.

14.23 Host

The Host request-header field specifies the Internet host and port number of the resource being requested, as obtained from the original URL given by the user or referring resource (generally an HTTP URL, as described in Section 3.2.2). The Host field value *must* represent the network location of the origin server or gateway given by the original URL. This allows the origin server or gateway to differentiate between internally-ambiguous URLs, such as the root "/" URL of a server for multiple host names on a single IP address.

```
Host = "Host" ":" host [ ":" port ]    ; Section 3.2.2
```

A host without any trailing port information implies the default port for the service requested (i.e., "80" for an HTTP URL). For example, a request on the origin server for <http://www.w3.org/pub/WWW/> *must* include:

```
GET /pub/WWW/ HTTP/1.1
Host: www.w3.org
```

A client *must* include a `Host` header field in all HTTP/1.1 request messages on the Internet (i.e., on any message corresponding to a request for a URL which includes an Internet host address for the service being requested). If the `Host` field is not already present, an HTTP/1.1 proxy *must* add a `Host` field to the request message prior to forwarding it on the Internet. All Internet-based HTTP/1.1 servers *must* respond with a `400` status code to any HTTP/1.1 request message which lacks a `Host` header field.

See Sections 5.2 and 19.5.1 for other requirements relating to `Host`.

14.24 If-Modified-Since

The `If-Modified-Since` request-header field is used with the `GET` method to make it conditional: if the requested variant has not been modified since the time specified in this field, an entity will not be returned from the server; instead, a `304` (`Not Modified`) response will be returned without any message-body.

```
If-Modified-Since = "If-Modified-Since" ":" HTTP-date
```

An example of the field is:

```
If-Modified-Since: Sat, 29 Oct 1994 19:43:31 GMT
```

A `GET` method with an `If-Modified-Since` header and no `Range` header requests that the identified entity be transferred only if it has been modified since the date given by the `If-Modified-Since` header. The algorithm for determining this includes the following cases:

- If the request would normally result in anything other than a `200` (`OK`) status, or if the passed `If-Modified-Since` date is invalid, the response is exactly the same as for a normal `GET`. A date which is later than the server's current time is invalid.

- If the variant has been modified since the `If-Modified-Since` date, the response is exactly the same as for a normal `GET`.

- If the variant has not been modified since a valid If-Modified-Since date, the server *must* return a 304 (Not Modified) response.

The purpose of this feature is to allow efficient updates of cached information with a minimum amount of transaction overhead.

Note that the Range request-header field modifies the meaning of If-Modified-Since; see Section 14.36 for full details.

Note that If-Modified-Since times are interpreted by the server, whose clock may not be synchronized with the client.

Note that if a client uses an arbitrary date in the If-Modified-Since header instead of a date taken from the Last-Modified header for the same request, the client should be aware of the fact that this date is interpreted in the server's understanding of time. The client should consider unsynchronized clocks and rounding problems due to the different encodings of time between the client and server. This includes the possibility of race conditions if the document has changed between the time it was first requested and the If-Modified-Since date of a subsequent request, and the possibility of clock-skew-related problems if the If-Modified-Since date is derived from the client's clock without correction to the server's clock. Corrections for different time bases between client and server are at best approximate, due to network transmittal latency.

14.25 If-Match

The If-Match request-header field is used with a method to make it conditional. A client that has one or more entities previously obtained from the resource can verify that one of those entities is current by including a list of their associated entity tags in the If-Match header field. The purpose of this feature is to allow efficient updates of cached information with a minimum amount of transaction overhead. It is also used, on updating requests, to prevent inadvertent modification of the wrong version of a resource. As a special case, the value "*" matches any current entity of the resource.

```
If-Match = "If-Match" ":" ( "*" | 1#entity-tag )
```

If any of the entity tags match the entity tag of the entity that would have been returned in the response to a similar GET request (without the If-Match header) on that resource, or if "*" is given and any current entity exists for that resource, then the server *may* perform the requested method as if the If-Match header field did not exist.

A server *must* use the strong comparison function (see Section 3.11) to compare the entity tags in If-Match.

If none of the entity tags match, or if "*" is given and no current entity exists, the server *must not* perform the requested method, and *must* return a 412 (Precondition Failed) response. This behavior is most useful when the client wants to prevent an updating method, such as PUT, from modifying a resource that has changed since the client last retrieved it.

If the request would, without the If-Match header field, result in anything other than a 2xx status, then the If-Match header *must* be ignored.

The meaning of If-Match: * is that the method *should* be performed if the representation selected by the origin server (or by a cache, possibly using the Vary mechanism, see Section 14.43) exists, and *must not* be performed if the representation does not exist.

A request intended to update a resource (e.g., a PUT) *may* include an If-Match header field to signal that the request method *must not* be applied if the entity corresponding to the If-Match value (a single entity tag) is no longer a representation of that resource. This allows the users to indicate that they do not wish the request to be successful if the resource has been changed without their knowledge.

Examples are as follows:

```
If-Match: "xyzzy"
If-Match: "xyzzy", "r2d2xxxx", "c3piozzzz"
If-Match: *
```

14.26 If-None-Match

The If-None-Match request-header field is used with a method to make it conditional. A client that has one or more entities previously obtained from the resource can verify that none of those entities is current by including a list of their associated entity tags in the `If-None-Match` header field. The purpose of this feature is to allow efficient updates of cached information with a minimum amount of transaction overhead. It is also used, on updating requests, to prevent inadvertent modification of a resource which was not known to exist.

As a special case, the value "`*`" matches any current entity of the resource.

```
If-None-Match = "If-None-Match" ":" ( "*" | 1#entity-tag )
```

If any of the entity tags match the entity tag of the entity that would have been returned in the response to a similar GET request (without the `If-None-Match` header) on that resource, or if "`*`" is given and any current entity exists for that resource, then the server *must not* perform the requested method. Instead, if the request method was GET or HEAD, the server *should* respond with a 304 (Not Modified) response, including the cache-related entity-header fields (particularly ETag) of one of the entities that matched. For all other request methods, the server *must* respond with a status of 412 (Precondition Failed).

See Section 13.3.3 for rules on how to determine if two entity tags match. The weak comparison function can only be used with GET or HEAD requests.

If none of the entity tags match, or if "`*`" is given and no current entity exists, then the server *may* perform the requested method as if the `If-None-Match` header field did not exist.

If the request would, without the `If-None-Match` header field, result in anything other than a 2xx status, then the `If-None-Match` header *must*, as a consequence, be ignored.

The meaning of `If-None-Match: *` is that the method *must not* be performed if the representation selected by the origin server (or by a cache, possibly using the `Vary` mechanism, see Section 14.43) exists, and *should* be performed if the representation does not exist. This feature may be useful in preventing races between PUT operations.

Examples:

```
If-None-Match: "xyzzy"
If-None-Match: W/"xyzzy"
If-None-Match: "xyzzy", "r2d2xxxx", "c3piozzzz"
If-None-Match: W/"xyzzy", W/"r2d2xxxx", W/"c3piozzzz"
If-None-Match: *
```

14.27 If-Range

If a client has a partial copy of an entity in its cache, and wishes to have an up-to-date copy of the entire entity in its cache, it could use the Range request-header with a conditional GET (using either or both of If-Unmodified-Since and If-Match.) However, if the condition fails because the entity has been modified, the client would then have to make a second request to obtain the entire current entity-body.

The If-Range header allows a client to *short-circuit* the second request. Informally, its meaning is "if the entity is unchanged, send me the part(s) that I am missing; otherwise, send me the entire new entity."

```
If-Range = "If-Range" ":" ( entity-tag | HTTP-date )
```

If the client has no entity tag for an entity, but does have a Last-Modified date, it may use that date in an If-Range header. (The server can distinguish between a valid HTTP-date and any form of entity-tag by examining no more than two characters.) The If-Range header should only be used together with a Range header, and must be ignored if the request does not include a Range header, or if the server does not support the sub-range operation.

If the entity tag given in the If-Range header matches the current entity tag for the entity, then the server should provide the specified sub-range of the entity using a 206 (Partial Content) response. If the entity tag does not match, then the server should return the entire entity using a 200 (OK) response.

14.28 If-Unmodified-Since

The If-Unmodified-Since request-header field is used with a method to make it conditional. If the requested resource has not been modified since the time specified in this field, the server should perform the requested operation as if the If-Unmodified-Since header were not present.

If the requested variant has been modified since the specified time, the server *must not* perform the requested operation, and perfunctorily *must* return a 412 (Precondition Failed).

```
If-Unmodified-Since = "If-Unmodified-Since" ":" HTTP-date
```

An example of the field is:

```
If-Unmodified-Since: Sat, 29 Oct 1994 19:43:31 GMT
```

If the request normally (i.e., without the `If-Unmodified-Since` header) would result in anything other than a 2xx status, the `If-Unmodified-Since` header should be ignored.

If the specified date is invalid, the header is ignored.

14.29 Last-Modified

The `Last-Modified` entity-header field indicates the date and time at which the origin server believes the variant was last modified.

```
Last-Modified  = "Last-Modified" ":" HTTP-date
```

An example of its use is:

```
Last-Modified: Tue, 15 Nov 1994 12:45:26 GMT
```

The exact meaning of this header field depends on the implementation of the origin server and the nature of the original resource. For files, it may be just the file system last-modified time. For entities with dynamically included parts, it may be the most recent of the set of last-modify times for its component parts. For database gateways, it may be the last-update time stamp of the record. For virtual objects, it may be the last time the internal state changed.

An origin server *must not* send a `Last-Modified` date which is later than the server's time of message origination. In such cases, where the resource's last modification would indicate some time in the future, the server *must* replace that date with the message origination date.

An origin server should obtain the `Last-Modified` value of the entity as close as possible to the time that it generates the `Date` value of its response. This allows a recipient to make an accurate assessment of the entity's modification time, especially if the entity changes near the time that the response is generated.

HTTP/1.1 servers *should* send `Last-Modified` whenever feasible.

14.30 Location

The `Location` response-header field is used to redirect the recipient to a location other than the `Request-URI` for completion of the request or identification of a new resource. For `201` (`Created`) responses, the `Location` is that of the new resource which was created by the request. For 3xx responses, the location *should* indicate the server's preferred URI for automatic redirection to the resource. The field value consists of a single absolute URI.

```
Location        = "Location" ":" absoluteURI
```

An example is:

```
Location: http://www.w3.org/pub/WWW/People.html
```

Note: The `Content-Location` header field (Section 14.15) differs from `Location` in that the `Content-Location` identifies the original location of the entity enclosed in the request. It is therefore possible for a response to contain header fields for both `Location` and `Content-Location`. Also see Section 13.10 for cache requirements of some methods.

14.31 Max-Forwards

The `Max-Forwards` request-header field may be used with the `TRACE` method (Section 14.31) to limit the number of proxies or gateways that can forward the request to the next inbound server. This can be useful when the client is attempting to trace a request chain which appears to be failing or looping in mid-chain.

```
Max-Forwards   = "Max-Forwards" ":" 1*DIGIT
```

The `Max-Forwards` value is a decimal integer indicating the remaining number of times this request message may be forwarded.

Each proxy or gateway recipient of a `TRACE` request containing a `Max-Forwards` header field *should* check and update its value prior to forwarding the request. If the received value is 0, the recipient *should not* forward the request; instead, it *should* respond as the final recipient with a `200` (`OK`) response containing the received request message as the response entity-body (as described in Section 9.8). If the received `Max-Forwards` value is greater than 0, then the forwarded message *should* contain an updated `Max-Forwards` field with a value decremented by 1.

The `Max-Forwards` header field *should* be ignored for all other methods defined by this specification and for any extension methods for which it is not explicitly referred to as part of that method definition.

14.32 Pragma

The `Pragma` general-header field is used to include implementation-specific directives that may apply to any recipient along the request/response chain. All pragma directives specify optional behavior from the viewpoint of the protocol; however, some systems *may* require that behavior be consistent with the directives.

```
Pragma            = "Pragma" ":" 1#pragma-directive

pragma-directive  = "no-cache" | extension-pragma
extension-pragma  = token [ "=" ( token | quoted-string ) ]
```

When the `no-cache` directive is present in a request message, an application *should* forward the request toward the origin server even if it has a cached copy of what is being requested. This pragma directive has the same semantics as the `no-cache` cache-directive (see Section 14.9) and is defined here for backwards compatibility with HTTP/1.0. Clients *should* include both header fields when a `no-cache` request is sent to a server not known to be HTTP/1.1 compliant.

`Pragma` directives *must* be passed through by a proxy or gateway application, regardless of their significance to that application, since the directives may be applicable to all recipients along the request/response chain. It is not possible to specify a pragma for a specific recipient; however, any pragma directive not relevant to a recipient *should* be ignored by that recipient.

HTTP/1.1 clients *should not* send the `Pragma` request-header. HTTP/1.1 caches *should* treat `Pragma: no-cache` as if the client had sent `Cache-Control: no-cache`. No new `Pragma` directives will be defined in HTTP.

14.33 Proxy-Authenticate

The `Proxy-Authenticate` response-header field *must* be included as part of a 407 (`Proxy Ahentication Required`) response. The field value consists of a challenge that indicates the authentication scheme and parameters applicable to the proxy for this `Request-URI`.

```
Proxy-Authenticate  = "Proxy-Authenticate" ":" challenge
```

The HTTP access authentication process is described in Section 11. Unlike WWW-Authenticate, the `Proxy-Authenticate` header field applies only to the current connection and *should not* be passed on to downstream clients. However, an intermediate proxy may need to obtain its own credentials by requesting them from the downstream client, which in some circumstances will appear as if the proxy is forwarding the `Proxy-Authenticate` header field.

14.34 Proxy-Authorization

The `Proxy-Authorization` request-header field allows the client to identify itself (or its user) to a proxy which requires authentication. The `Proxy-Authorization` field value consists of credentials containing the authentication information of the user agent for the proxy and/or realm of the resource being requested.

```
Proxy-Authorization    = "Proxy-Authorization" ":" credentials
```

The HTTP access authentication process is described in Section 11. Unlike `Authorization`, the `Proxy-Authorization` header field applies only to the next outbound proxy that demanded authentication using the `Proxy-Authenticate` field. When multiple proxies are used in a chain, the `Proxy-Authorization` header field is consumed by the first outbound proxy that was expecting to receive credentials. A proxy *may* relay the credentials from the client request to the next proxy if that is the mechanism by which the proxies cooperatively authenticate a given request.

14.35 Public

The `Public` response-header field lists the set of methods supported by the server. The purpose of this field is strictly to inform the recipient of the capabilities of the server regarding unusual methods. The methods listed may or may not be applicable to the `Request-URI`; the `Allow` header field (Section 14.7) *may* be used to indicate methods allowed for a particular URI.

```
Public          = "Public" ":" 1#method
```

Example of use:

```
Public: OPTIONS, MGET, MHEAD, GET, HEAD
```

This header field applies only to the server directly connected to the client (i.e., the nearest neighbor in a chain of connections). If the response passes through a proxy, the proxy *must* either remove the `Public` header field or replace it with one applicable to its own capabilities.

14.36 Range

Byte Ranges   Since all HTTP entities are represented in HTTP messages as sequences of bytes, the concept of a byte-range is meaningful for any HTTP entity. (However, not all clients and servers necessarily need to support byte-range operations.)

Byte-range specifications in HTTP apply to the sequence of bytes in the entity-body (not necessarily the same as the message-body).

A byte-range operation may specify a single range of bytes, or a set of ranges within a single entity.

```
ranges-specifier = byte-ranges-specifier

byte-ranges-specifier = bytes-unit "=" byte-range-set

byte-range-set  = 1#( byte-range-spec | suffix-byte-range-spec )

byte-range-spec = first-byte-pos "-" [last-byte-pos]
```

```
first-byte-pos  = 1*DIGIT

last-byte-pos   = 1*DIGIT
```

The `first-byte-pos` value in a `byte-range-spec` gives the `byte-offset` of the first byte in a range. Further, the `last-byte-pos` value gives the `byte-offset` of the last byte in the range; that is, the byte positions specified are inclusive. Byte offsets start at zero.

If the `last-byte-pos` value is present, it must be greater than or equal to the `first-byte-pos` in that `byte-range-spec`, or the `byte-range-spec` is invalid. The recipient of an invalid `byte-range-spec` must ignore it.

If the `last-byte-pos` value is absent, or if the value is greater than or equal to the current length of the entity-body, `last-byte-pos` is taken to be equal to one less than the current length of the entity-body in bytes.

By its choice of `last-byte-pos`, a client can limit the number of bytes retrieved without knowing the size of the entity.

```
suffix-byte-range-spec = "-" suffix-length

suffix-length = 1*DIGIT
```

A `suffix-byte-range-spec` is used to specify the suffix of the entity-body, of a length given by the `suffix-length` value. (That is, this form specifies the last N bytes of an entity-body.) If the entity is shorter than the specified suffix-length, the entire entity-body is used.

Examples of `byte-ranges-specifier` values (assuming an entity-body of length 10,000):

- The first 500 bytes (byte offsets 0–499, inclusive):
    bytes=0–499
- The second 500 bytes (byte offsets 500–999, inclusive):
    bytes=500–999
- The final 500 bytes (byte offsets 9500–9999, inclusive):
    bytes=–500
    or
    bytes=9500-

- The first and last bytes only (bytes 0 and 9999):
  bytes=0-0,-1
- Several legal but not canonical specifications of the second 500 bytes (byte offsets 500–999, inclusive):
  bytes=500-600,601-999
  bytes=500-700,601-999

Range Retrieval Requests HTTP retrieval requests using conditional or unconditional GET methods may request one or more subranges of the entity, instead of the entire entity, using the Range request header, which applies to the entity returned as the result of the request:

```
Range = "Range" ":" ranges-specifier
```

A server *may* ignore the Range header. However, HTTP/1.1 origin servers and intermediate caches *should* support byte ranges when possible, since range supports efficient recovery from partially failed transfers, and supports efficient partial retrieval of large entities.

If the server supports the Range header and the specified range or ranges are appropriate for the entity:

- The presence of a Range header in an unconditional GET modifies what is returned if the GET is otherwise successful. In other words, the response carries a status code of 206 (Partial Content) instead of 200 (OK).

- The presence of a Range header in a conditional GET (a request using one or both of If-Modified-Since and If-None-Match, or one or both of If-Unmodified-Since and If-Match) modifies what is returned if the GET is otherwise successful and the condition is true. It does not affect the 304 (Not Modified) response returned if the conditional is false.

In some cases, it may be more appropriate to use the If-Range header (see Section 14.27) in addition to the Range header.

If a proxy that supports ranges receives a Range request, forwards the request to an inbound server, and receives an entire entity in reply, it *should* only return the requested range to its client. It *should* store the entire received response in its cache, if that is consistent with its cache allocation policies.

14.37 *Referer*

The `Referer` request-header field allows the client to specify, for the server's benefit, the address (URI) of the resource from which the `Request-URI` was obtained (the *referer*, although the header field is misspelled.) The `Referer` request-header allows a server to generate lists of back-links to resources for interest, logging, optimized caching, etc. It also allows obsolete or mistyped links to be traced for maintenance. The `Referer` field *must not* be sent if the `Request-URI` was obtained from a source that does not have its own URI, such as input from the user keyboard.

```
Referer          = "Referer" ":" ( absoluteURI | relativeURI )
```

Example:

```
Referer: http://www.w3.org/hypertext/DataSources/Overview.html
```

If the field value is a partial URI, it *should* be interpreted relative to the `Request-URI`. The URI *must not* include a fragment.

Note: Because the source of a link may be private information or may reveal an otherwise private information source, it is strongly recommended that the user be able to select whether or not the `Referer` field is sent. For example, a browser client could have a toggle switch for browsing openly/anonymously, which would respectively enable/disable the routine sending of `Referer` and `From` information.

14.38 *Retry-After*

The `Retry-After` response-header field can be used with a `503` (`Service Unavailable`) response to indicate how long the service is expected to be unavailable to the requesting client. The value of this field can be either an HTTP-date or an integer number of seconds (in decimal) after the time of the response.

```
Retry-After  = "Retry-After" ":" ( HTTP-date | delta-seconds )
```

Two examples of its use are:

```
Retry-After: Fri, 31 Dec 1999 23:59:59 GMT
Retry-After: 120
```

In the latter example, the delay is 2 minutes.

14.39 Server

The `Server` response-header field contains information about the software used by the origin server to handle the request. The field can contain multiple product tokens (Section 3.8) and comments identifying the server and any significant subproducts. The product tokens are listed in order of their significance for identifying the application.

```
Server          = "Server" ":" 1*( product | comment )
```

Example:

```
Server: CERN/3.0 libwww/2.17
```

If the response is being forwarded through a proxy, the proxy application *must not* modify the `Server` response-header. Instead, it *should* include a `Via` field (as described in Section 14.44).

Note: Revealing the specific software version of the server may allow the server machine to become more vulnerable to attacks against software that is known to contain security holes. Server implementors are encouraged to make this field a configurable option.

14.40 Transfer-Encoding

The `Transfer-Encoding` general-header field indicates what (if any) type of transformation has been applied to the message body in order to safely transfer it between the sender and the recipient. This differs from the `Content-Encoding` in that the transfer coding is a property of the message, not of the entity.

```
Transfer-Encoding      = "Transfer-Encoding" ":" 1#transfer-coding
```

Transfer codings are defined in Section 3.6. An example is:

```
Transfer-Encoding: chunked
```

Many older HTTP/1.0 applications do not understand the `Transfer-Encoding` header.

14.41 Upgrade

The `Upgrade` general header allows the client to specify what additional communication protocols it supports and would like to use if the server finds it appropriate to switch protocols. The server *must* use the `Upgrade` header field within a `101 (Switching Protocols)` response to indicate which protocol(s) are being switched.

```
Upgrade        = "Upgrade" ":" 1#product
```

For example:

```
Upgrade: HTTP/2.0, SHTTP/1.3, IRC/6.9, RTA/x11
```

The `Upgrade` header field is intended to provide a simple mechanism for transition from HTTP/1.1 to some other, incompatible protocol. It does so by allowing the client to advertise its desire to use another protocol, such as a later version of HTTP with a higher major version number, even though the current request has been made using HTTP/1.1. This eases the difficult transition between incompatible protocols by allowing the client to initiate a request in the more commonly supported protocol while indicating to the server that it would like to use a *better* protocol if available (where *better* is determined by the server, possibly according to the nature of the method and/or resource being requested).

The `Upgrade` header field only applies to switching application-layer protocols upon the existing transport-layer connection. `Upgrade` cannot be used to insist on a protocol change; its acceptance and use by the server is optional. The capabilities and nature of the application-layer communication after the protocol change is entirely dependent upon the new protocol chosen, although the first action after changing the protocol *must* be a response to the initial HTTP request containing the `Upgrade` header field.

The Upgrade header field only applies to the immediate connection. Therefore, the upgrade keyword *must* be supplied within a Connection header field (Section 14.10) whenever Upgrade is present in an HTTP/1.1 message.

The Upgrade header field cannot be used to indicate a switch to a protocol on a different connection. For that purpose, it is more appropriate to use a 301, 302, 303, or 305 redirection response.

This specification only defines the protocol name HTTP for use by the family of Hypertext Transfer Protocols, as defined by the HTTP version rules of Section 3.1 and future updates to this specification. Any token can be used as a protocol name; however, it will only be useful if both the client and server associate the name with the same protocol.

14.42 User-Agent

The User-Agent request-header field contains information about the user agent originating the request. This is for statistical purposes, the tracing of protocol violations, and automated recognition of user agents for the sake of tailoring responses to avoid particular user agent limitations. User agents *should* include this field with requests. The field can contain multiple product tokens (Section 3.8) and comments identifying the agent and any subproducts which form a significant part of the user agent. By convention, the product tokens are listed in order of their significance for identifying the application.

```
User-Agent     = "User-Agent" ":" 1*( product | comment )
```

Example:

```
User-Agent: CERN-LineMode/2.15 libwww/2.17b3
```

14.43 Vary

The Vary response-header field is used by a server to signal that the response entity was selected from the available representations of the response using server-driven negotiation (Section 12). Field-names listed in Vary headers are those of request-headers. The Vary field value indicates either that the given set of header fields encompass the dimensions over which the representation might vary, or that the dimensions of variance are unspecified ("*") and thus may vary over any aspect of future requests.

```
Vary  = "Vary" ":" ( "*" | 1#field-name )
```

An HTTP/1.1 server *must* include an appropriate Vary header field with any cachable response that is subject to server-driven negotiation. Doing so allows a cache to properly interpret future requests on that resource and informs the user agent about the presence of negotiation on that resource. A server *should* include an appropriate Vary header field with a non-cachable response that is subject to server-driven negotiation, since this might provide the user agent with useful information about the dimensions over which the response might vary.

The set of header fields named by the Vary field value is known as the *selecting* request-headers.

When the cache receives a subsequent request whose Request-URI specifies one or more cache entries including a Vary header, the cache *must not* use such a cache entry to construct a response to the new request unless all of the headers named in the cached Vary header are present in the new request, and all of the stored selecting request-headers from the previous request match the corresponding headers in the new request.

The selecting request-headers from two requests are defined to match if and only if the selecting request-headers in the first request can be transformed to the selecting request-headers in the second request by adding or removing linear white space (LWS) at places where this is allowed by the corresponding BNF, and/or combining multiple message-header fields with the same field name following the rules about message headers in Section 4.2.

A Vary field value of "*" signals that unspecified parameters, possibly other than the contents of request- header fields (i.e., the network address of the client), play a role in the selection of the response representation. Subsequent requests on that resource can only be properly interpreted by the origin server, and thus a cache *must* forward a (possibly conditional) request even when it has a fresh response cached for the resource. See Section 13.6 for use of the Vary header by caches.

A `Vary` field value consisting of a list of field-names signals that the representation selected for the response is based on a selection algorithm which considers *only* the listed request-header field values in selecting the most appropriate representation. A cache *may* assume that the same selection will be made for future requests with the same values for the listed field names, for the duration of time in which the response is fresh.

The field-names given are not limited to the set of standard request-header fields defined by this specification. Field names are case insensitive.

14.44 Via

The `Via` general-header field *must* be used by gateways and proxies to indicate the intermediate protocols and recipients between the user agent and the server on requests, and between the origin server and the client on responses. It is analogous to the `Received` field of RFC 822 and is intended to be used for tracking message forwards, avoiding request loops, and identifying the protocol capabilities of all senders along the request/response chain.

```
Via =   "Via" ":" 1#( received-protocol received-by [ comment ] )

received-protocol = [ protocol-name "/" ] protocol-version
protocol-name     = token
protocol-version  = token
received-by       = ( host [ ":" port ] ) | pseudonym
pseudonym         = token
```

The `received-protocol` indicates the protocol version of the message received by the server or client along each segment of the request/response chain. The `received-protocol` version is appended to the `Via` field value when the message is forwarded so that information about the protocol capabilities of upstream applications remains visible to all recipients.

The protocol-name is optional if and only if it would be HTTP. The received-by field is normally the host and optional port number of a recipient server or client that subsequently forwarded the message. However, if the real host is considered to be sensitive information, it *may* be replaced by a pseudonym. If the port is not given, it *may* be assumed to be the default port of the received-protocol.

Multiple `Via` field values represent each proxy or gateway that has forwarded the message. Each recipient *must* append its information such that the end result is ordered according to the sequence of forwarding applications.

Comments *may* be used in the `Via` header field to identify the software of the recipient proxy or gateway, analogous to the `User-Agent` and `Server` header fields. However, all comments in the `Via` field are optional and *may* be removed by any recipient prior to forwarding the message.

For example, a request message could be sent from an HTTP/1.0 user agent to an internal proxy code-named "fred," which uses HTTP/1.1 to forward the request to a public proxy at `nowhere.com`, which completes the request by forwarding it to the origin server at `www.ics.uci.edu`. The request received by `www.ics.uci.edu` would then have the following `Via` header field:

```
Via: 1.0 fred, 1.1 nowhere.com (Apache/1.1)
```

Proxies and gateways used as a portal through a network firewall *should not*, by default, forward the names and ports of hosts within the firewall region. This information *should* only be propagated if explicitly enabled. If not enabled, the received-by host of any host behind the firewall *should* be replaced by an appropriate pseudonym for that host.

For organizations that have strong privacy requirements for hiding internal structures, a proxy *may* combine an ordered subsequence of `Via` header field entries with identical received-protocol values into a single such entry. In this instance, example:

```
Via: 1.0 ricky, 1.1 ethel, 1.1 fred, 1.0 lucy
```

could be collapsed to:

```
Via: 1.0 ricky, 1.1 mertz, 1.0 lucy
```

Applications *should not* combine multiple entries unless they are all under the same organizational control and the hosts have already been replaced by pseudonyms. Applications *must not* combine entries which have different received-protocol values.

14.45 *Warning*

The Warning response-header field is used to carry additional information about the status of a response which may not be reflected by the response status code. This information is typically, though not exclusively, used to warn about a possible lack of semantic transparency from caching operations.

Warning headers are sent with responses using:

```
Warning    = "Warning" ":" 1#warning-value

warning-value = warn-code SP warn-agent SP warn-text
warn-code  = 2DIGIT
warn-agent = ( host [ ":" port ] ) | pseudonym
                  ; the name or pseudonym of the server adding
                  ; the Warning header, for use in debugging
warn-text  = quoted-string
```

A response may carry more than one Warning header.

The warn-text should be in a natural language and character set that is most likely to be intelligible to the human user receiving the response. This decision may be based on any available knowledge, such as the location of the cache or user, the Accept-Language field in a request, the Content-Language field in a response, etc. The default language is English and the specific default character set is ISO-8859-1.

If a character set other than ISO-8859-1 is used, it *must* be encoded in the warn-text using the method described in RFC 1522 [14].

Any server or cache may add Warning headers to a response. New Warning headers should be added after any existing Warning headers. A cache *must not* delete any Warning header that it received with a response. However, if a cache successfully validates a cache entry, it *should* remove any Warning headers previously attached to that entry except as specified for specific Warning codes. It *must* then add any Warning headers received in the validating response. In other words, Warning headers are those that would be attached to the most recent relevant response.

When multiple Warning headers are attached to a response, the user agent *should* display as many of them as possible, in the order that they appear in the response. If it is not possible to display all of the warnings, the user agent should follow these heuristics:

- Warnings that appear early in the response take priority over those appearing later in the response.
- Warnings in the user's preferred character set take priority over warnings in other character sets but with identical warn-codes and warn-agents.

Systems that generate multiple `Warning` headers should order them with this user agent behavior in mind.

This is a list of the currently-defined `warn-codes`, each with a recommended `warn-text` in English, and a description of its meaning.

- *10: Response is stale*   *Must* be included whenever the returned response is stale. A cache may add this warning to any response, but may never remove it until the response is known to be fresh.
- *11: Revalidation failed*   *Must* be included if a cache returns a stale response because an attempt to revalidate the response failed, due to an inability to reach the server. A cache may add this warning to any response, but may never remove it until the response is successfully revalidated.
- *12: Disconnected operation*   *Should* be included if the cache is intentionally disconnected from the rest of the network for a period of time.
- 13: Heuristic expiration   *Must* be included if the cache heuristically chose a freshness lifetime greater than 24 hours and the age of the response is greater than 24 hours.
- *14: Transformation applied*   *Must* be added by an intermediate cache or proxy if it applies any transformation changing the content-coding (as specified in the `Content-Encoding` header) or media-type (as specified in the `Content-Type` header) of the response, unless this `Warning` code already appears in the response *must not* be deleted from a response even after its revalidation.
- *99: Miscellaneous warning*   The warning text may include arbitrary information to be presented to a human user, or logged. A system receiving this warning *must not* take any automated action.

The warning text may include arbitrary information to be presented to a human user, or logged. A system receiving this warning *must not* take any automated action.

14.46 WWW-Authenticate

The `WWW-Authenticate` response-header field *must* be included in `401` (`Unauthorized`) response messages. The field value consists of at least one challenge that indicates the authentication scheme(s) and parameters applicable to the `Request-URI`.

```
WWW-Authenticate  = "WWW-Authenticate" ":" 1#challenge
```

The HTTP access authentication process is described in Section 11. User agents *must* take special care in parsing the `WWW-Authenticate` field value if it contains more than one challenge, or if more than one `WWW-Authenticate` header field is provided, since the contents of a challenge may itself contain a comma-separated list of authentication parameters.

Glossary

ANSI	American National Standards Institute
API	Application Programming Interface
ARPANET	Advanced Research Projects Agency Network
ASCII	American Standard Code for Information Interchange
BNF	Backus-Naur Form
BSD	Berkeley Software Distribution
CGI	Common Gateway Interface
CPU	Central Processing Unit
DARPA	Defense Advanced Research Projects Agency
DLL	Dynamic Link Library
email	Electronic mail
FTP	File Transfer Protocol
FTPD	File Transfer Procotol Daemon
GMT	Greenwich Mean Time
GZIP	GNU Zip (As found in RFC1952)
HTML	Hypertext Markup Language
IANA	Internet Assigned Numbers Authority
IESG	Internet Engineering Steering Group
IETF	Internet Engineering Task Force
IP	Internet Protocol

JPEG	Joint Photographic Experts Group
LAN	Local Area Network
MIME	Multipurpose Internet Mail Extensions
NT	Windows NT (New Technology)
POP3	Post Office Protocol Version 3
RFC	Request For Comments
SMTP	Simple Mail Transfer Protocol
TCP	Transmission Control Protocol
TCP/IP	Transmission Control Protocol/Internet Protocol
URI	Uniform Resource Indentifier
URL	Uniform Resource Locator
US ASCII	American Standard Code for Information Interchange
WAN	Wide Area Network

Bibliography

1 Fielding, R., et al., RFC 2068, HyperText Transfer Protocol, HTTP/1.1. January 3, 1997, (162 pages). `ftp://ds.internic.net/rfc/rfc2068.txt`.

2 Franks, J., et al. RFC 2069, HyperText Transfer Protocol, HTTP. Digest Access Authentication, January 3, 1997, (18 pages). `ftp://ds.internic.net/rfc/rfc2069.txt`.

index

Bold numerals indicate important entries.

V

validate **101**
validator **31**
value **48**, 320
"vanity" servers **16**
variant **31**
Vary 3, **114**, 127, 320, 363
Via **90**, 320, 365
virtual domains **16**
Visual Age C++ **185**

W

W3Conn() **185**, 203, 216, 220, 224
warn-agent **114**, 320, 367
warn-code **114**, 320, 367
Warning 95, 99, **114**, 320, 367
warning-value **114**, 320, 367
warn-text **114**, 320, 367

weak **51**, 101, 320
weak comparison **102**
Web robots **15**
Web surfing **3**
weekday **38**, 320
Windows **287**, 299–307, 308
  CGI **305**
  CreateProcess() **304**
  ExecCgi() **299**
  95 **9**
  NT 4, 134, 136, 146, 177, 182
  SECURITY_ATTRIBUTES **305**
winsock **146**
wkday **38**, 320
write() **147**, 238, 285
WSACleanup() **147**, 183
WSAStartup() **182**
WWW-Authenticate 113, **115**, 118, 320, 369

CD contents

The accompanying CD contains quite a bit of information to aid in your understanding of HTTP. Book code as well as source code from W3C and Apache are included. The CD is browsable by any Web browser directly or by running one of the included HTTP servers.

The contents include:

- Complete book in HTML format
- Complete source code from the book
- Complete index of RFCs and STDs
- W3C library code and Jigsaw server
- Apache HTTP server distribution
- A trial version of IBM® VisualAge™ for C++ for Windows™ Version 3.5
- Other trial applications of interest